GOD'S HIDDEN TREASURES

GOD'S HIDDEN TREASURES

THE PARABLES OF JESUS

WILLIAM H. WETMORE

© 2002 by William H. Wetmore. All rights reserved.

Printed in the United States of America.

Packaged by WinePress Publishing, PO Box 428, Enumclaw, WA 98022. The views expressed or implied in this work do not necessarily reflect those of WinePress Publishing. The author is ultimately responsible for the design, content, and editorial accuracy of this work.

No part of this publication may be reproduced, stored in a retrieval system or transmitted in any way by any means, electronic, mechanical, photocopy, recording or otherwise, without the prior permission of the copyright holder except as provided by USA copyright law.

Unless otherwise noted, all Scriptures marked RSVB are taken from the Revised Standard Version of the Bible. Copyright © 1946, 1952, 1971 by the Division of Christian Education of the National Council of the Churches of Christ in the U.S.A. Used by permission.

Scriptures marked NIV are taken from the Holy Bible, New International Version, Copyright © 1973, 1978, 1984 by the International Bible Society. Used by permission of Zondervan Publishing House. The "NIV" and "New International Version" trademarks are registered in the United States Patent and Trademark Office by International Bible Society.

ISBN 1-57921-456-8
Library of Congress Catalog Card Number: 2002101500

In the Old Testament, God spoke through Asaph: "I (God) will open my mouth in a parable; I will utter **dark sayings** from of old" (Psa. 78:2).

Approximately 1,000 years later, Matthew records the same message (Matt. 13:34–35).

"All this Jesus said to the crowds in parables; indeed he said nothing to them without a parable. This was to fulfill what was spoken by the prophet: 'I will open my mouth in parables, I will utter what has been **hidden** since the foundation of the world'"

Dedication

This book is dedicated to our children, Ben and Cathy,
In joy and with thanksgiving
for their faithful witness and service to Jesus Christ.

The Purpose of the Parables:
That the King of glory may reign in our lives

The earth is the Lord's, and everything in it,
the world and all who live in it;
for he founded it upon the seas
and established it upon the waters.

Who may ascend the hill of the Lord?
Who may stand in his holy place?
He who has clean hands and a pure heart,
Who does not lift up his soul to an idol
Or swear by what is false.

He will receive blessings from the Lord
And vindication from God his Savior.
Such is the generation of those who seek him,
who seek your face, O God of Jacob.

Lift up your heads, O you gates,
Be lifted up, you ancient doors,
That the King of glory may come in.
Who is this King of glory?
The Lord strong and mighty,
The Lord mighty in battle.

Lift up your heads, O you gates,
Lift them up, you ancient doors,
That the King of glory may come in.
Who is he, this King of glory?
The Lord Almighty—
He is the King of glory.
(Psa. 24 NIV)

Contents

Preface xi
Part I—An Overall Perspective of the Parables
1. The Parables: Their Uniqueness, Simplicity, and Importance.... 15
2. The Reasons that Jesus Taught in Parables 21
3. Jesus Christ, The Author of the Parables 29
4. The Characteristics and Nature of Parables 35

Part II—The Biblical Themes and Commentaries on the Parables
5. The Biblical Themes of the Parables 43
6. Theme 1—The Parables of the Character of God 53
7. Theme 2—The Parables of the Kingdom of Heaven 77
8. Theme 3—The Parables of the Alternatives in Life 105
9. Theme 4—The Parables of the Christian Character 115
10. Theme 5—The Parables of Repentance 173
11. Theme 6—The Parables of the Responsibility for
    Evangelism 185
12. Theme 7—The Parables of our Role as Christian Stewards 195
13. Theme 8—The Parables of the Power of Prayer 215
14. Theme 9—The Parables of the Preparation for the Final
    Judgment 231
15. Theme 10—The Parables of the Final Judgment 263

Part III—Epilogue
16. The Biblical Themes and God's Revelations 281

Preface

The parables of Jesus Christ have been extensively studied over the centuries, and rightfully so. The numerous commentaries have all contributed significantly to the great understanding and the application of their truths. They have produced dramatic life-changing experiences and set before the world the wisdom and messages in these important teachings of Jesus Christ. Previous books on this subject have examined the parables on an individual basis. However, this book examines the parables from the perspective that the *parables present great messages about the major Biblical themes (e.g. the Kingdom of Heaven)*. Therefore, rather than focusing on the message of each parable, I was more interested in combining those parables under ten major themes. In this way, I "*looked through*" the parables to uncover insights into the great messages of God to His people. It is my hope that this approach will be equally interesting to others and that new light and new understanding will arise. Further, the parables *contain God's Revelations: His commands, promises, truths and warnings*. These also require examination. In addition, the parables of Jesus Christ represent continuity with the great teachings of the Old Testament, as well as develop new themes in the New Testament. In doing so, the parables are directly and closely related to all of the great truths of

God's Hidden Treasures

the Bible and so this connection between the parables of Jesus and other great truths are important to understand. There have been a tremendous number of excellent commentaries written on the parables, and I trust that this study will add something to that ageless dialogue. In one way, I believe that this book offers a different approach and potentially new insights that are revealing, informative and helpful.

I have recently finished a teaching on *The Parables of Jesus*, and I began to examine the parables in the light of my other teaching series, particularly on the *Foundations of Faith* and the *General Teachings of Jesus*. As expected, the life of Jesus is closely related to His teaching. For that reason, this book will discuss His earthly ministry, as a vital foundation for the study of the parables. Because of that, the examination of the parables will be deferred until this necessary introductory material is completed.

This book is addressed primarily to the lay people, for I am summarizing many of the essential truths that offer a major foundation for living the Christian life. The parables are major signposts that will guide and direct our lives.

I particularly want to thank my wife, Jane, whose constant support, encouragement and review of the text has been most helpful. In addition, I want to thank many good friends, Dr. David Helms, Pastor, First Baptist Church, Southern Pines, N.C., Dr. Donald Hardman, Pastor, Christ Fellowship Church, Dr. Kenneth Cross, Sandhills PCA and William Korver, Pastor of Community Evangelical Church, for their fellowship, wisdom and encouragement.

With full confidence in the power of the Holy Spirit, who is always our teacher, I present these thoughts on the parables of Jesus Christ and the great themes that they illuminate. These same teachings, these same messages continue to have deep and important eternal meaning in the lives of people of every age.

To God be the glory
William Wetmore

God's Hidden Treasures

The Parables of Jesus are presented in three parts

Part I—An Overall Perspective of the Parables

Part II—The Biblical Themes and Commentaries on the Parables

Part III—Epilogue
Reflections on Biblical Themes
Reflections on God's Revelations

Part I—An Overall Perspective of the Parables

Chapter 1—The Parables: Their Uniqueness, Simplicity, and Importance

Chapter 2—The Reasons That Jesus Taught in Parables

Chapter 3—Jesus Christ, the "Author" of the Parables

Chapter 4—The Characteristics and Nature of Parables

Part 1
An Overall Perspective of the Parables

CHAPTER ONE

The Parables: Their Uniqueness, Simplicity, and Importance

"I will open my mouth in parables, I will utter dark sayings from of old,—" (Psa. 78:2)

"Jesus spoke all these things to the crowd in parables; he did not say anything to them without using a parable." (Matt. 13:34)

"He (Jesus) said, 'the knowledge of the secrets of the kingdom of God has been given to you, but to others I speak in parables . . .'" (Lk. 8:10)

The parables are the greatest "stories" ever told because they are *"told"* by Jesus Christ, God Incarnate. Every Christian, over the years, has become familiar with their great messages; numerous sermons have been preached; many books have been written, and they warrant the tremendous attention that they have received, for they are priceless and timeless treasures that constantly benefit from serious examination. Christians continue to enjoy these wonderful stories for they contain eternal commands, promises, truths and warnings.

These parables are more than *"great stories"*, because they tell us volumes about the sovereignty and will of God, the purpose for

God's Hidden Treasures

His creation, the lives that He calls us to lead, the Final Judgment and the eternal destiny for every person.

So why this book? What is its uniqueness and significance? There are two specific reasons.

First, the parables are related to Ten Biblical Themes (e.g. the Kingdom of Heaven) and, in combination, Jesus tells us much about these great themes of Scripture.

Second, the parables contain 104 important messages (commands, promises, truths, and warnings). The parables provide the world with important summaries of these messages.

Let me amplify. *The first reason is that the combination of parables, relating to major Scriptural themes, provide more insight into a given theme, such as the Kingdom of Heaven, and a far more significant picture is presented than is available from the study of a single parable on that subject.* However, if we examine all the parables dealing with that theme (e.g. the Kingdom of Heaven), then the result is a composite picture with considerably more understanding regarding the totality of what Jesus is teaching. In other words, it is important to *look beyond—to look through them—*and discover the great theological truths that the *combination of parables* presents. The individual parables contain a unique value in themselves, but they become far more significant when combined and viewed against the major themes of Scripture. That is the uniqueness of the parables that this book presents. Chapter 5 (page 43) lists the 10 themes that are discussed in the parables. The 34 parables listed in chapter 5 are organized as they relate to these major themes: *The Character of God, the Kingdom of Heaven, The Alternatives in Life, The Christian Character, The Need for Repentance, Our Responsibility in Evangelism, Our Role as Christian Stewards, The Quality and Power of Prayer, The Preparation for the Final Judgment, and The Final Judgment.*

The second reason for the uniqueness of this book is that it examines the manner in which God reveals Himself in the parables, through commands, promises, truths, and commands; which are essential for salvation.

Now the parables themselves are *unique* because they present messages with simplicity: they are vitally important because they

Chapter One

present summaries of some of the great truths of God. They are *unique*, because they present vital information regarding Christ's earthly life, His teachings, His ministry and His mission. This *uniqueness* is further demonstrated in the degree to which the parables present Old and New Testament themes and truths.

There is certain *simplicity* about the parables because, in most cases, the messages they present are clear and precise; the parables are meant for everybody. They contain messages for believers and non-believers. As such they provide guidance and instruction for believers in living the Christian life. Further, they contain specific truths and warnings for non-believers who have, for the moment, rejected Jesus Christ as Savior and Lord. In fact, there are many parables that are addressed particularly to non-believers, e.g. The Wicked Tenants, The Ten Virgins, The Sheep and the Goats, The Wheat and the Tares.

The purpose of the parables is that everyone will obey the commands, accept the promises, recognize the truths, and respond to the warnings. The parables are written so that lives would be changed, that none should perish, and that all that would be saved. God takes no delight in the death of a sinner. Christ calls on everyone to repent, be restored and reconciled to God the Father. In one measure, the *"born again"* will find the truths of the parables to have a special divine character.

In addition, there is an unmistakable *importance* to the parables because they provide great truths about God and ourselves, truths that are essential in following Jesus Christ as Savior and Lord. It is with this broad perspective in mind that this book addresses the parables with the understanding that there are *seven interrelated characteristics* in the parables of Jesus that are important to understand.

First, there is a distinct relationship between the parables of Jesus and many of the great themes of the Old Testament. For example, forgiveness, restoration, and the Final Judgment are important themes in the Old Testament; this is equally true in these parables.

God's Hidden Treasures

Second, the parables become more meaningful when examined in relation to the events in the *earthly life and death* of Jesus. Jesus' earthly ministry can be related to several important events, e.g. 1. To the command at the beginning of His earthly ministry, *"Repent for the Kingdom of God is at hand";* 2. To His reasons for coming into the world; to seek and to save the lost; and 3. To the reasons for His death which was to fulfill all Scripture and to die for the sins of the world. Understanding these events adds new meaning to the parables. In addition, His kingdom and His Second Coming are two of the great themes of His parables.

Third, in His earthly ministry, Jesus first used *signs*, which constituted His *indirect claims* to divinity. When they were misunderstood or ignored, He made *direct claims, e.g., I am the Good Shepherd, who lays down His life for the sheep.*

Fourth, when these claims were rejected, Jesus began to teach in *parables*, to warn the unbelievers and to convey spiritual truths to His disciples. The Jews' rejection of Jesus set the stage for His teaching in parables.

Fifth, Jesus knew that only the *"born again, those born of the Spirit"* would understand the divine message of the parables. However, Jesus continued to teach in parables as a warning to those who had rejected Him.

Sixth, The parables are best understood when viewed and treated in their *totality*; for they represent a progressive statement of great Biblical themes. The parables present a *"window"* through which we can grasp the great truths and great themes of Scripture. For that reason, *totality and interrelationship* of the parables is important.

Seventh, the parables of Jesus represent His *final means of teaching* about God, about Himself, about the kingdom of heaven, the character of the Christian life, the end of the age, and the Judgment to come. The parables were to encourage but also to warn that there will be a Day when each person will be held accountable for what we have done or not done, as God has commanded.

Therefore, these seven statements constitute the major characteristics of this commentary—and add further depth to the themes

Chapter One

discussed in the parables. The parables are part of the message from God and about God. Every word of God and every message from God have a divine purpose; it is to be understood and applied in the life of a believer and non-believers. God's Son and God's word has power and authority; the parables need to be read and understood in that context. With this perspective, the parables are presented as follows:
- The *reasons* that Jesus taught in parables
- The *Author* of the Parables, Jesus Christ.
- *The nature of parables* and their uniqueness in conveying great truths
- The *ten major themes* of the parables
- The 34 parables that relate to the *major themes* of Scripture.
- A *detailed discussion* of the parables in relationship to the ten themes
- A *summary of the Biblical Themes and God's Revelations.*

CHAPTER TWO

The Reasons that Jesus Taught in Parables

"The stone the builders rejected has become the capstone; the LORD has done this, and it is marvelous in our eyes." (Psalm 118:22; Matt. 21:42)

"Jesus answered him, 'Truly, truly, I say to you, unless one is born anew (from above), he cannot see the kingdom of God' . . . 'How can a man be born when he is old?' . . . Jesus answered, 'Truly, truly, I say to you, unless one is born of water and the Spirit, he cannot enter the kingdom of God.'" (Jn. 3:3, 5)

"They are darkened in their understanding and separated from the life of God because of the ignorance that is in them due to the hardening of their hearts." (Eph. 4:18)

We begin by addressing the reasons that Jesus Christ taught in parables, for His reasons are vital in order to understand the character and purpose of the parables.

It is important to recognize the parables were used in the Old Testament and by the rabbinical teachers of Jesus' day. As such, parables were a method of teaching that paralleled life by taking ordinary events and identifying them with the lives of the hearers. However, Jesus did something that was distinctive in His parables, and that distinctiveness will unfold as our discussion proceeds.

God's Hidden Treasures

His parables have a divine and eternal character. The parables have messages for everyone, believer and non-believer. For the believer, the parables offer hope, guidance and instruction; for the non-believer, the parables contain great truths and severe warnings. However in the midst of the parables, Jesus presents divine truths that only the *"born again"* will fully understand and apply.

The key to Jesus speaking in parables is given in Matt. 13:10–17, and Matt 13:34–35. In Matt. 13:10–17, Jesus told His disciples that you have been given the secrets of the kingdom. *"Then the disciples came and said to him (Jesus), "Why do you speak to them in parables?" And he answered them, "<u>To you</u> it has been given to know <u>the secrets of the kingdom of heaven</u>, but to them it has not been given. For to him who has will more be given, and he will have abundance; but from him who has not, even what he has will be taken away. This is why I speak to them in parables, because seeing they do not see, and hearing they do not hear, nor do they understand. With them indeed is fulfilled the prophecy of Isaiah which says: 'You shall indeed hear but never understand, and you shall indeed see but never perceive. For this people's heart has grown dull, and their ears are heavy of hearing, and their eyes they have closed, lest they should perceive with their eyes, and hear with their ears, and understand with their heart, and turn for me to heal them.' But blessed are your eyes, for they see, and your ears, for they hear. Truly, I say to you, many prophets and righteous men longed to see what you see, and did not see it, and to hear what you hear, and did not hear it."*

In Matt. 13:34–35, Matthew records, *"All this Jesus said to the crowds in parables; indeed he said nothing to them without a parable. This was to fulfill what was spoken by the prophet: 'I will open my mouth in parables, I will utter what has been <u>hidden since the foundation of the world</u>.'"*

Jesus taught in parables to teach the world, both believers and non-believers, the secrets of the kingdom and truths that have been hidden since the foundation of the world.

The reasons that Jesus taught in parables are closely related both to the character of the Jews and the character of God.

A. Regarding the Character of the Jews, Jesus taught in parables:

Chapter Two

First, because the Jews had rejected His indirect claims (signs) and His direct claims to deity;

Second, because the Jews had "hardened their hearts";

Third, because the Jews did not understand, nor accept the truth, that a person must be "born again" ("Born of the Spirit") to "see" and "enter" the Kingdom of God. To His disciples, Jesus presented in the parables both the secrets of the kingdom and the warning to those who continued to reject the Word of God.

B. Regarding the Character of God, Jesus taught in parables:

First, Jesus did so in fulfillment of the Scriptures;

Second, because this was His final approach to the hardened hearts of the Jews;

Third, because God "is forbearing towards you, not wishing that any should perish, but that all should reach repentance";

Fourth, because God's steadfast love endures forever (Psa. 136:1)

These seven reasons deserve further explanation.

A. Regarding the Character of the Jews;

- *First, because the Jews had rejected His indirect and direct claims to deity;*

Jesus had made both indirect and direct claims to deity, and the Jews had rejected or ignored those claims. In His *indirect claims (signs)*, Jesus had changed water into wine (e.g. at the Wedding Feast in Canaan), had healed many people, had given sight to the blind, had raised Lazarus from the dead, and the signs were misunderstood. John recorded that Jesus did many other signs, all pointing to His Presence among His people. In Jn. 20:30, the apostle wrote, "*Now Jesus did many other signs in the presence of the disciples, which are not written in this book; but these are written that you may believe that <u>Jesus is the Christ</u>, the Son of God, and that believing you may have <u>life in his name</u>.*" The signs were given for two reasons: that Jesus is the Christ; and that those who "*believe in Him*" (trusted in Him) would have eternal life. Since His indirect claims were ignored, misrepresented or misunderstood, Jesus made direct claims. He told them that He was the Good Shepherd, that

God's Hidden Treasures

He was the Bread of Life, that He was the Truth, the Way, and the Life, that He was the Life and the Resurrection. Equally so, these direct claims were rejected or ignored. In fact, after the raising of Lazarus, the High Priest, Caiaphas, said, *"It is expedient that one should die for the people and that the whole nation should not perish."* (Jn. 11:50) His arrest and death were already being planned. The Jews rejected His righteous claims to deity.

- *Second, because the Jews had "hardened their hearts";*

Now this second reason, this "hardening of hearts" is unfortunately consistent with the history of the Jews in both the Old and New Testaments. In general, a hardened heart is one that is *"not easily moved."* However, the hardening of men's hearts by God is not only a way of punishment, but it is its own punishment for sin. As Paul wrote (Rom. 9:18), *"So then he has mercy upon whomever he will, and he hardens the hearts of whomever he will."* In Romans 11:7, Paul wrote regarding the election of the people of Israel and the remnant, chosen by grace, *"What then? Israel failed to obtain what it sought. The elect obtained it, but the rest were hardened."* Paul continued (Rom. 11:25), *"Lest you be wise in your own conceits, I want you to understand this mystery, brethren; a hardening has come upon Israel, until the full number of the Gentiles has come in, and so all Israel will be saved."* Then Paul quoted from Jeremiah 31:33 and Isaiah 27:9 in which Paul explained that a Deliver will come from Zion and take away their sins. The apostle John also wrote (Jn. 12:40) of the hardening of the hearts of Israel, quoting from Isaiah 6:10, *"He has blinded their eyes and hardened their hearts, lest they should see with their eyes and perceive with their hearts, and so turn to me to heal them."* When hearts are hardened against the word of God and the Person of God, then the truths of God can never be received nor understood.

- *Third, because the Jews did not understand that a person must be "born again."*

Jesus spoke in parables, knowing that only those who had been *"born again"* would fully accept His message. In many regards, these parables were His last means of explaining to the world His character and His mission. The apostle John wrote, *"But to all who*

Chapter Two

received him, who believed in his name, he gave power to become the children of God, who were born, not of blood nor of the will of the flesh nor of the will of man, but of God." (Jn. 1:12). Those who are *"born of God"* have received the second birth. So Jesus began to teach in parables, because only those who had been *"born again"* would accept His teachings.

However, Jesus continually reached out to all, both believers and non-believers. It is God's perfect patience that none should perish. So Jesus emphasized the consequences of failing to trust in Him, as God Incarnate. Therefore, the parables contain many details of the failure to be good tenants in God's Vineyard as well as the Final Judgment in which believers and non-believers will be judges. Believers will be judged for their works as evidence of faith; non-believers will be judged for the sin and rejection of the Son of God.

Since being *born again* is one of the keys to understanding many of the parables, then this term needs to be understood. The second birth is a spiritual birth that John recorded in the words of Jesus to Nicodemus (Jn. 3:3, 5) *". . . truly, truly, I say to you, unless one is born anew (from above), he cannot <u>see</u> the kingdom of God . . . truly, truly, I say to you, unless one is born of water and the Spirit, he cannot <u>enter</u> the kingdom of God."* So how is a person *"born again"*? The new birth, called "regeneration", means the "re-creating" of a fallen, sinful human being, by the gracious sovereign initiative of Almighty God. It restores a relationship with God in Christ and produces a radical and complete transformation in the *soul*. Regeneration (the new birth) changes us from sinful, lawless, God-less, self-seeking people into people of trust and loving faithfulness to God. *"If any one is in Christ, he is a new creation." (2 Cor. 5:17).* This new birth is the work of the Holy Spirit. It is a mysterious exercise of divine sovereignty. Charles Wesley got it right. In his great hymn, Hark, the Herald Angels Sing, Wesley wrote in the third stanza, *"Hark, the heaven born Prince of Peace; Hail the Son of Righteousness. Light and life to all He brings, Risen with healing in his wings; Mild he lays his glory by, born no more that men may die. Born to raise the sons of earth; **born to give them second birth . . .**"*

God's Hidden Treasures

The Bible begins with the book of Genesis, which relates to the first birth. In like manner, regeneration is the second birth; it is the work of the cross for the forgiveness of sins. The meaning of the *"new birth"* is common throughout the Bible. Every appeal to undergo a radical transformation of life from the self-centered to the God-centered is, in effect, an appeal to be *"born again."* Anytime that there is a dramatic change in a person's life in which they turn from an old life of sin and wickedness to a new life by accepting Jesus Christ as Lord and Savior, following the commandments of God, then a *"new birth"* has occurred. Therefore, the new birth is not restricted to the New Testament, for there are many Old Testament experiences (Isa. 1:16; Jer. 31:33; Psa. 51:5–11; Zech. 13:1) that must be regarded as a *"new birth."* Two classic Old Testament examples are that of Moses at the burning bush and Isaiah in the Temple (Isa. 6:1–8). There is no more dramatic evidence of the new birth than that of Paul (Acts 9:10ff). He is the supreme witness to the second birth.

B. Regarding the Character of God, Jesus taught in parables;
- *First, Jesus did so in fulfillment of the Scriptures:*

In Psalm 78:2, God said that He would *"open my mouth in a parable; I will utter dark sayings from of old."* With Jesus Christ coming to earth, the Son of God spoke in parable, to fulfill what God spoke through the prophet Isaiah (Isa. spoke, 6:9–10). Using this Old Testament text, Jesus repeats, in Matthew 13:34–35, the message that God gave to Isaiah. Christ fulfilled the Scriptures in the parables;

- *Second, because this was His final approach to the hardened hearts of the Jews;*

His teaching on His divinity, first by His indirect claims (signs) and then by His direct claims (the great "I am" passages of John), were ignored or rejected by the Jews. However, Jesus continued to teach His disciples eternal truths and to seek the lost sheep of Israel by continual appeal and warnings regarding their rejection of Him and the Final Judgment that all must face.

Chapter Two

- *Third, because God "is forbearing towards you, not wishing that any should perish, but that all should reach repentance";*

God does not delight in the death of a sinner; He continues to seek the lost; He rejoices when a sinner comes home. Jesus continued to warn the Jews of the consequences of their continued rejection of the Living Word of God.

- *Fourth, because God's steadfast love endures forever (Psa. 136:1).*

God cannot change; His promises are eternal. However, His wrath is stored up for the day of Judgment when all will answer for our conduct in this life. God's love endures forever; His patience has a limit. (See the Parable of the Barren Fig Tree)

So the seven reasons (3 regarding Jews; 4 regarding God) that Jesus spoke in parables are: *first, because the Jews had rejected His indirect claims (signs) and His direct claims to deity; second, they had "hardened their hearts"; third, they did not understand that a person must be "born again" ("Born of the Spirit") to "see" and "enter" the Kingdom of God; fourth, Jesus did so in fulfillment of the Scriptures; fifth, because this was His final approach to the hardened hearts of the Jews; sixth, because God "is forbearing towards you, not wishing that any should perish, but that all should reach repentance"; seventh, because God's steadfast love for His creation endures forever (Psa. 136:1)*

With this introduction, we now move to the necessary understanding of the Person of Jesus Christ, the divine "Author" of these parables. Who is this Person who revealed such great truths and spoke with such power and authority?

CHAPTER THREE

Jesus Christ, The Author of the Parables

"He (God) humbled you . . . to teach you that man does not live on bread alone but on every word that comes from the mouth of the Lord." (Deut. 8:3)

"Your word is a lamp to my feet and a light for my path." (Psa. 119:105)

"As the rain and the snow come down from heaven, and return not thither but water the earth . . . so shall my word be that goes forth from my mouth: it will not return to me empty, but it shall accomplish that which I purpose and prosper in the thing for which I sent it." (Isa. 55:11)

"For the word of God is living and active, sharper than any two-edged sword . . . discerning the thoughts and intentions of the heart." (Heb. 4:12)

With an understanding of the reasons that Jesus taught in parables, we begin by addressing the question of the *authority* of the parables, which hinges on the authority of Jesus Christ. Jesus Christ, God Incarnate, is presenting these parables as the Word of the sovereign God. Therefore we can confidently state that the parables have authority in our lives because they are essential truths of the Bible, which is the *Written Word of God*, proclaimed by Jesus Christ, the *Living Word of God*.

For Christians the questions are: Do the parables have authority in my life? How seriously must I view the parables? Under what conditions do the parables apply to me? Are parables just interesting stories and are they relevant in my life? These and other questions must be faced and the answers must be clear. The parables must be taken seriously; they apply to every person; they have great relevancy in our lives. They have authority.

To understand this authority more fully, it is essential to know Jesus Christ, who came into the world to reveal God's purpose and God's will. This *"Written Word,"* the Bible, is God's Word, *"my word that comes forth from my mouth."* (Isa. 55:11). The apostle Paul wrote, *". . . you have been acquainted with the sacred writings, which are able to instruct you for salvation through faith in Christ Jesus. All scripture is inspired by God and profitable for teaching, for correction, for reproof and training in righteousness, that the man of God would be complete, equipped for every good work."* (2 Tim. 3:15–17). *Inspired* means God-breathed. Paul was convinced that *"the scriptures are able to instruct us for salvation."* He was also convinced that the scriptures are *"profitable for teaching, for correction, for reproof and for training in righteousness."* He was likewise convinced that the purpose of the scriptures was to make us *"complete, equipped for every good work."* The breath of God brought forth His Word, the scriptures. The apostle Peter wrote (2 Pet. 1:20), *"First of all, you must understand this, that no prophecy of scripture is a matter of one's own interpretation, because no prophecy ever came by the impulse of man, but men moved by the Holy Spirit spoke from God."* Because Jesus Christ is the *"Author"* of the parables, then these parables take on an eternal and undeniable authority and importance.

Therefore, since all Scripture is from God; since it is to instruct us for salvation, and since it is to make us complete, equipped for every good work, then there is every reason that we must take seriously the teaching of Jesus Christ in the parables. So we recognize fully the power and authority of the parables. We do so because Jesus Christ, God Incarnate, is the *"Author"* of the parables.

Chapter Three

However, we must state that Jesus is far more than the *"Author"* of these parables. The Son of God must be seen primarily as the *"Author"* of our salvation. In Heb. 5:9, Jesus is identified as the *"source of eternal salvation to all who obey him."* Other texts translate Heb. 5:9 as He *"became the author of eternal salvation."* He is the first in the company of the faithful, far exceeding in faithfulness the Old Testament saints mentioned in the 11th chapter of Hebrews. In that regard, He is the perfect example of faith. To understand the parables, it is vital to *"believe and receive"* (Jn. 1:12) Jesus Christ as Savior and Lord and the Author of our salvation. Only then will we comprehend the majesty and truths of the parables, knowing that they represent the words of God Himself. With that brief introduction, let us examine more fully the Person of Jesus Christ, for such understanding will give even greater depth and significance to the parables.

There are many statements in Scripture that define Jesus Christ. *He is fully God.* As Paul stated in Colossians 1:15f, *"He is the image of the invisible God; the first born of all creation; for in him all things were created, in heaven and on earth, visible and invisible . . . all things were created through him and for him. He is before all things, and in him all things hold together . . . For in him all the fullness of God was pleased to dwell."* *He is fully human.* He is physically born, growing, and learning, subject to hunger and finally led to the cross and to burial. Although there is this emphasis on His true humanity, we must remember that He is sinless and totally different from other men. *He is the Son of God.* This is the name given to him by the heavenly voice at His baptism (Lk. 1:35), at His transfiguration (Mk. 1:11), by Peter (Matt. 16:16), by the demons (Mk. 5:7), and the centurion (Mk. 15:39). *He is the Son of Man.* Jesus used this title more than any other. He seemed to be thinking of Dan. 7:13, in which the "Son of man" is a heavenly figure. *He is fully the Messiah.* Jesus of Nazareth is the One anointed with the Spirit and with power (Acts 10:38) to be the true Messiah or Christ (Jn. 1:41; Rom. 9:5). *He is The Suffering Servant.* Jesus' self-identification with mankind is brought out in the great passages, particularly Isaiah, of the Suffering Servant (49:1–6; 52:13–15; 53:1–12; Matt. 12:18). *He is Lord.* Though Paul often uses the title, the *"Son*

God's Hidden Treasures

of God", he most frequently refers to Jesus as Lord. His Lordship extends over the course of history (Col. 2:15) and must be the ruling concern in the life of the church (Eph. 6:7: I Cor. 7:10, 25). *He is the Living Word.* The statement *"the Word became flesh"* (Jn. 1:14) relates Jesus both to the Wisdom of God and to the Law of God. In the New Testament, it becomes clear that the Word is not merely a message proclaimed, but it is the Person of Jesus Christ. *He is the Head of the Body, the church.* (Col. 1:16). *He is the beginning, the first-born from the dead, that in everything he might be pre-eminent. He is the Friend of tax collectors and sinners.* (Matt. 11:19); *He is the Rock of our Salvation* (I Cor. 10:1–4; Exo. 17:6); *He is the Living Water* (Jn. 4:11); *He is the Bread of Life* (Jn. 6:35); *He is the Light of the World* (Jn. 8:12; 9:5); *He is the Door of the Sheep* (Jn. 10:7); *He is the Good Shepherd, Who lays down His life for the sheep* (Jn. 10:11); *He is the Resurrection and the Life* (Jn. 11:25); *He is the Way, the Truth and the Life* (Jn. 14:6); *He is the True Vine* (Jn. 15:1, 5); *He is the Alpha and the Omega* (Rev. 1:8); *He is the First and the Last* (Rev. 1:17).

These are the major *claims* that the Bible makes about Jesus Christ. For such claims to have meaning, His *character* must support His claims. This He surely did. He was *holy*; i.e. He was set apart from mankind, even though He has come to share human nature with us; He knew that He was *without sin*, although He became sin for our sake; He *associated Himself with us* in baptism, in crucifixion, and in persecution; As the Savior of the world, He *willingly and deliberately laid down His life.* He said that no one takes my life from me; I lay it down of my own free will and I will take it up again, referring to His resurrection; He knew that He was both *Savior and Lord*, in fulfillment of the Old Testament; He knew that He was *eternal*, before Abraham; He knew that *He and the Father were One* (Jn. 17); He lived in unbroken communion with the Father; He knew that He *did nothing except that which the Father commanded Him;* He knew that He had been *sent by the Father* to do the will of the Father; He knew He was both *Lord and Master*; He knew that He *must die to ratify the new covenant* for the forgiveness of sins as foretold in Jeremiah 31; He knew that *He*

Chapter Three

would return to the Father (Jn. 16:28); He knew that *He would come again;* He knew that *He would send another Comforter*, the Holy Spirit. God's richest blessing for all mankind came at Christ's expense; that is grace.

This is who He is; this is what the Scriptures say about Him, and this is what He claimed for Himself.

So the parables have authority because Jesus Christ is their *"Author"*, and He has all authority in heaven and on earth (Matt. 28:18). Therefore the parables of this Author must be accepted completely and obeyed as the eternal truths of God. The parables tell us much about specific aspects of His Presence among us, His earthly life, about His Second Coming and His judgment on all of creation.

Having dealt with the reasons that Jesus taught in parables and Jesus Christ the *"Author"* of the parables, it is important now to understand the characteristics and the nature of parables, these eternal great truths that Jesus taught with such power and wisdom.

CHAPTER FOUR

The Characteristics and Nature of Parables

"I will open my mouth in a parable; I will utter dark sayings from of old." (Psa. 78:2)

"I spoke to the prophets; it was I who multiplied visions, and through the prophets gave parables." (Hos. 12:10)

"As they heard these things, he proceeded to tell a parable, because he was near to Jerusalem, and because they supposed that the kingdom of God was to appear immediately." (Lk. 19:11)

With this introduction to the *Author* of the parables, it is well to discuss the *definition* of a parable, *its content* and its *characteristics*. Parables are an important means of teaching throughout the Bible, for parables represent God's method of presenting eternal commandments, promises, truths and warnings. To non-believers, parables are interesting stories with little significant meaning in their lives. However, believers, the *born again*, find great insight and know that the truths of the parables must be reflected in their lives. They find in the parables the deep significance that God is presenting to them. In spite of that difference, it is still important for both believers and non-believers to understand the character and nature of parables.

So what is a parable? Well, the *definition* I find most appropriate is: *"a parable is the means of drawing committed Christians to the presence and purpose of God in their midst and the critical nature of their situation."* (Baker's Dictionary of Theology) However, others define it as *"an earthly saying with a heavenly meaning."* (Harper's Bible Dictionary) Further, the New English Bible and the Jerusalem Bible treat parables as *"a story with a meaning or moral concerning mysteries from the past."* Again it is important to understand that a parable will only have meaning to a *committed Christian*. Anyone else will never understand the treasure that Jesus is presenting.

The *content* of the parables is generally drawn from the religious, social, political and domestic life of that time. For that reason, a parable is generally designed to present to the hearer a real, familiar life situation in which a judgment or decision can be made about a single major point. This judgment by the individual leads to an understanding of the main message that the parable contains. Parables generally emphasize a teaching about any one of three subjects: *first, God* (e.g. His will and purpose, His justice, His forgiveness and redemption), *second, Mankind* (e.g. our sinful condition, the alternatives that all people face in life, our responsibility to evangelize, our need to be good stewards, etc.), and *third*, the *Final Judgment* of God on Mankind.

- Basic Concept of a Parable

The basic *characteristic* of parables in both the Old and New Testament is that it is considered a *"dark saying"* (Hos. 12:10), implying that the message of the parable will not be understood by the superficial listener. Therefore Jesus speaks in parables so that His disciples, *"those within"*, can know the mystery and understand the truth that the parable presents. His purpose is to reveal to His disciples all the mysteries (Lk. 18:16–18). For the *"born again"*, the mystery is grasped and the kingdom is *"seen"*, not by the power of human reason but by the power of the Holy Spirit (Jn. 3:3–6). For that reason, a parable may be seen as *blinding the understanding of the non-committed*, especially if men go no further than understanding a general truth or a moral lesson rather than

Chapter Four

understanding that this word is meant *to convert the heart*. In this way, they may *"see"* and not *"perceive"* (Mk. 4:12). They may *"see"* its consequences, but *"perceiving"* is to understand the significance of the event for our lives and its meaning for our eternal relationship to God.

- *Old Testament Scriptures regarding Parables*

Parables are evident throughout the Old Testament, beginning in Deuteronomy and continuing through many Old Testament passages; therefore the Old Testament parables and themes set the stage for many of the parables of Jesus. In examining the parables, it becomes clear that both the Old and New Testament parables are God's response to rebellious and hardened hearts of those who fail to honor God. In all situations, God *"spoke"* through the prophets to the people, that they would *not "hear"* nor *"see"* the messages that were essential for their salvation. Several Old Testament passages set the tone for Jesus speaking in parables;

1. *Deuteronomy 29:4*—Moses speaks to the Israelites—*"But to this day, the Lord has not given you a mind to understand, or eyes to see, or ears to hear . . ."*

2. *Isaiah 6:9–11*—*"And he (a seraphim) said 'Go and say to this people: Hear and hear, but do not understand; see and see, but do not perceive.' Make the hearts of this people fat, and their ears heavy, and shut their eyes; let them see with their eyes, and hear with their ears, and understand with their hearts, and turn and be healed."*

3. *Isaiah 42:19–20*—God spoke, through Isaiah, against idolatry—*"who say to molten images, 'you are our gods.'"* And God said—*"Hear, you deaf; and look, you blind, that you may see! Who is blind but my servant, and deaf as my messenger whom I send? Who is as blind as my dedicated one, or blind as the servant of the Lord?"*

4. *Jeremiah 5:21*—God speaks out, through Jeremiah, against idolatry—*"serving foreign gods in your land"*—God said—*"Declare this to the house of Jacob, and proclaim it to Judah: Hear this, O foolish and senseless people, who have eyes, but see not, who have ears, but hear not."*

5. *Ezekiel 12:2–3*—God spoke to His servant, Ezekiel—*"Son of man, you dwell in the midst of a rebellious people, who have eyes to*

see, but see not, who have ears to hear, but hear not; for they are a rebellious house."

This is exactly the tone that we see in the parables of Jesus. In His generation, Jesus also found a people who did not see nor perceive the truths that He was presenting. The people *"heard"* but did not hear; they could "see" but they could not perceive. This is one of the great sorrows that God's truths are lost on those who have ears but do not hear, who have eyes, but cannot see the things of God.

- *Examples of Old Testament Parables*

Because the Old Testament is rich in parables, it is well to identify a few examples, which emphasize that parables are the manner of God's teaching throughout all of the Scriptures to convey great truth regarding Himself, human morality and the Final Judgment. Some Old Testament examples are: the parables regarding Jotham and Abimalech, in which the message and a truth are presented by considering the relationship between different types of trees (Judges 9:7–15); the story, regarding Absalom, Joab, and a "wise woman" from Tekoa (2 Sam. 14:1–24). There are other Old Testament parables, such as 2 Kings 14:9 (Joash); Isaiah 5:1–6, dealing with judgment on the fruitful life. The Book of Ezekiel is particularly rich in the use of parables, e.g. 17:2–10, dealing with two eagles and a vine; 24:3–14, dealing with the "cooking pot"; 37:1–14, that well-known passage dealing with the dry bones. In some of these parables, there is an allegorical context.

One of the most famous of the Old Testament parables is the rebuke of David by Nathan (2 Sam. 12:1–14). The events involve David's lustful love affair with Bathsheba, followed by David's deliberate attempt to have Bathsheba's husband, Uriah, killed in battle. As the parable goes, *"the Lord sent Nathan to David."* Nathan, the prophet, told David a story about two men, one very rich and the other very poor. The rich man had *"very many flocks"* and the poor man had only *"one little ewe lamb."* This little ewe lamb has become like one of the family—for *"it grew up with him and with his family."* Now a traveler came to visit the rich man, who was unwilling to take one of his own flocks to prepare for the wayfarer,

Chapter Four

but *"he took the poor man's lamb and prepared it for the man."* David was angry against the rich man, and he said to Nathan—*"the man who has done this deserves to die; he shall restore the lamb fourfold, because he did this thing, and because he had no pity."* And Nathan said to David—*"You are the man."* Nathan continued—*"Thus says the Lord, the God of Israel, I anointed you king over Israel, I delivered you . . . I gave you the house of Israel and the house of Judah . . . I would add to you as much more. Why have you despised the word of the Lord, to do what is evil in his sight?"* A repentant David said to Nathan—*"I have sinned against the Lord."* An awareness of two great sins led to repentance, and David's repentance led to God's forgiveness—and David's salvation.

So a parable conveys an important truth from God that reveals His Presence and His purpose and informs the hearer of a need for a change which will lead to a closer relationship with God. These important truths have authority, because they bear the very stamp of God.

With this introduction, *Part II* classifies the 34 parables according to *Ten Biblical Themes,* and then examines the individual parables, in detail.

Part II—Biblical Themes and Commentaries on the Parables

Chapter 5: The Biblical Themes of the Parables
Chapter 6: The Parables of the Character of God
Chapter 7: The Parables of the Kingdom of Heaven
Chapter 8: The Parables of the Alternatives in Life
Chapter 9: The Parables of the Christian Character
Chapter 10: The Parables of Repentance
Chapter 11: The Parables of the Responsibility for Evangelism
Chapter 12: The Parables of our Role as Christian Stewards
Chapter 13: The Parables of the Power of Prayer
*Chapter 14: The Parables of the Preparation for the Final
         Judgment*
Chapter 15: The Parables of the Final Judgment

Part 2
Biblical Themes and Commentaries on the Parables

CHAPTER FIVE

The Biblical Themes of the Parables

"I (God) spoke to the prophets; it was I who multiplied visions, and through the prophets gave parables." (Hos. 12:10)

". . . he (Jesus) did not speak to them (the Jews) without a parable, but privately to his own disciples, he explained everything." (Mk. 4:34)

The parables present closely interrelated eternal truths. In that regard, they constitute a method of teaching and a series of messages that Jesus is presenting to the world in general and to the *"born again"* in particular. Others will read and enjoy these timeless stories, but their true significance will never truly penetrate their hearts and accomplish the life-changing results.

Now, to understand the parables, Jesus is presenting major truths about many significant subjects, e.g. the kingdom of heaven. Each parable by itself presents only a portion of the total message regarding that theme. Therefore, each parable on a given theme provides vital information, necessary for a composite picture of the theme that Jesus is presenting. For that reason, I believe that all the parables, relating to a given theme, should be examined and the combined messages from all of the parables is necessary so that the full significance of each subject (e.g. the kingdom of heaven) will be evident.

This book approaches the parables by determining the major biblical themes that they present and then combines all the parables relating to a given theme, so that the totality of the message on each theme is set before the reader. In addition to the **Biblical Themes**, the parables also present **God's Revelations** contained in important commands, promises, truths and warnings. These Revelations are a rich storehouse of knowledge essential for the Christian life.

It is interesting that the major Biblical themes are found throughout the parables. This should not be surprising. Certainly one of the great overriding themes of Scripture is related to the Grace and Judgment of God. Further, there is the theme of *repentance and forgiveness* for those who seek the face of God. In addition, there is the theme of *sin, death and judgment* and it will be evident throughout many of the parables. Sin is the act or thought that separates mankind from God. Death is the result of sin and can be viewed both physically and spiritually. We may be alive physically, but we can be dead spiritually; for as long as rebellion and idolatry rule in our hearts, we are separated from God and "dead in sin."

The author of Hebrews wrote (9:27), *"And just as it is appointed for men to die once, and after that comes judgment . . ."* We will all die physically, and then we shall face the judgment. The parables speak at length about our preparedness for the Second Coming of Christ and our need to be prepared for the Final Judgment. For that reason alone, the parables set before us great truths that will help and direct us in the preparation for the Judgment that is certain to come. Further, there are the great examples of the alternatives that people face in this life and the consequences of those decisions. In addition, there is the truth that there are consequences to sin and that there is accountability for every act of every person. We shall see these and other truths in this examination of the time-honored parables.

Chapter Five

For these reasons, it is important to *"look through"* the parables and seek the great truths that Jesus is presenting. In other words, the parables are the *"window"* through which **Biblical Themes** are set before the world. The parables present interrelated messages, and they present a series of great messages of hope, warnings and promises.

Christian literature recognizes several lists of the Parables of Jesus. In all cases, there is minimal disagreement. However, there are respectful differences on the exact number of parables. For example, many consider that Luke 15 has three parables, one on the lost sheep, one on the lost coin, and a third, called the Prodigal Son. However, these three stories are closely interconnected and are essential elements of one parable. In Luke 15, Jesus is telling one parable with three stories; the first two stories set the stage for the third. It is interesting to note that various other studies will list as many as 40 parables while others might show as few as 30. Now many parables have received time-honored status (e.g. The Good Samaritan, The Prodigal Son, The Parable of the Talents, The Parable of the Sheep and the Goats). However, many others (e.g. The Parable of the Ten Virgins, The Parable of the Shrewd Manager, The Parable of the Friend at Midnight, and the Barren Fig Tree) are less well-known, but they deserve our attention and exposition.

Thirty-four (34) parables are correlated to the ten Biblical Themes. This sequence is generally consistent with most commentaries on this subject. In addition, the Biblical text is given for only one of the accounts; not all versions of the same parable are presented.

1. *The Parable of the House on the Rock (1-1) page 60*
2. *The Parable of the Two Debtors (4-1) page 118*
3. *The Parable of the New Wine and Old Wineskins (4-2) page 123*
4. *The Parable of the Sower (6-1) page 187*
5. *The Parable of the Wheat and the Tares (3-1) page 107*
6. *The Parable of the Mustard Seed (2-1) page 81*
7. *The Parable of Leaven (2-2) page 83*

God's Hidden Treasures

8. The Parable of the Treasure hidden in the Field (2-3) page 85
9. The Parable of the Pearl of Great Value (2-4) page 89
10. The Parable of the Net Thrown into the Sea (2-5) page 91
11. The Parable of the Training for the Kingdom (2-6) page 94
12. The Parable of the Ungrateful and Wicked Servant (1-2) page 64
13. The Parable of the Good Samaritan (4-3) page 128
14. The Parable of the Friend at Midnight (8-1) page 219
15. The Parable of the Poor, Rich Fool (4-4) page 135
16. The Parable of the Faithful and Wise Manager (7-1) page 198
17. The Parable of Christ's Return; the Unexpected Hour (9-1) page 238
18. The Parable of the Barren Fig Tree (4-5) page 142
19. The Parable of Humility (4-6) page 146
20. The Parable of the Great Banquet (4-7) page 150
21. The Parable of the Lost and Found (5-1) page 175
22. The Parable of the Shrewd Manager (7-2) page 203
23. The Parable of the Rich Man and Lazarus (9-2) page 246
24. The Parable of the Unworthy Servant (4-8) page 155
25. The Parable of Persistent Prayer (8-2) page 223
26. The Parable of our Perspective in Prayer (8-2) page 227
27. The Parable of the Workers in the Vineyard (2-7) page 97
28. The Parable of the Response to Authority (4-9) page 160
29. The Parable of God-given Talents (4-10) page 163
30. The Parable of the Wicked Tenants (1-3) page 68
31. The Parable of the King's Wedding Feast (10-1) page 270
32. The Parable of the Lessons from the Fig Tree (9-3) page 252
33. The Parable of the Ten Virgins (9-4) page 255
34. The Parable of the Final Judgment (10-2) page 275

From this list of 34, it is possible to arrange the parables, not according to chronological order, but according to the **Biblical Theme** that they present. In this way, it is possible to understand

Chapter Five

not only the parable, but to *"look through"* the parables and sense a summary series of truths that the parables contain. Again, the parables tell us much about the Person of Jesus Christ; we should always look for such evidence as we read and reread these marvelous truths.

Finally, it is possible to identify many of *God's Revelations* (commands, promises, truths and warnings) that are contained in the parables. These will be summarized at the end of the each chapter, as well as fully summarized in Chapter 17.

An examination of the parables discloses ten themes. The parables begin with the Character of God and progress through the messages of the Final Judgment. The order is significant and revealing; the truths are to be accumulated and digested so that this life is purposeful and a witness, as well as a preparation for the next. In examining the major themes of the parables, they fall essentially into three major categories: *God, Mankind, and God's Judgment on Mankind*:

I. God
Theme 1—The Character of God
Theme 2—The Kingdom of Heaven

II. Mankind
Theme 3—The Alternatives in Life
Theme 4—The Christian Character
Theme 5—Repentance
Theme 6—Our Responsibility for Evangelism
Theme 7—Our Roles as Christian Stewards
Theme 8—The Quality and Power of Prayer

III. God's Judgment on Mankind
Theme 9—The Preparation for the Judgment
Theme 10—The Final Judgment

As expected, all ten **Biblical Themes** are equally and critically important. However, in some of the parables, the themes do not receive equal attention, for some will be the *primary* message while there will be *secondary* messages of great significance. In examining these themes, it is interesting to note that they are consistent with the major themes that Jesus discloses in His ministry, particularly those related to the Sermon on the Mount. In that discourse, there is the wisdom of the Beatitudes in which there is an expression of the character of individuals which are pleasing to God and the conditions of God's approval; there are the summary messages about being the *"light of the world and the salt of the earth"*; there is that great definition of love, which include, not excludes, our enemy; there is the measure of righteousness which is of the heart; there is finally the definition of ambition, which is to seek *first* the kingdom of heaven and His righteousness. These expressions of Christian character, Christian love, Christian righteousness, and Christian goals—all are reflected in the parables.

One other point is that both the Old and New Testaments present the truth that people will be held accountable for their actions or lack of actions, for all God's *punishment* of sin is to remind us that God is Sovereign, *"they will know that I am the Lord."* (Eze. 24:27); that we would *repent*, turn from *"idolatry"* and be *restored* to Him. Where sin abounds, then there will be punishment; but, if we repent, then God will forgive us, and we will be restored to Him. This important message is disclosed throughout the parables. Further, the parables present eternal truths about the nature of God, our relationship to Him, and the eternity that He has revealed for all who love Him, obey Him and serve Him.

As mentioned previously, the parables generally stress one theme; however, that should not be taken literally; there are many parables in which there are several major themes. In considering the *primary* and related *secondary* themes, this aspect of the parables will be shown in approximately half of the parables, listed on pages 49–52. This is remarkable. For that reason, it is appropriate to include these other truths; therefore they will be identified, with the expectation that multiple themes will add greatly to the message of the parable. One example of multiple themes is that associated with the *Parable of the Lost and Found (the lost sheep, the lost coin, and the two lost sons: Luke 15)*. Scripture supports this as one parable. In that parable, Jesus speaks of the *Kingdom of Heaven* (the great joy when the "lost" are found); the *Character of God*, a God who forgives graciously; the *Alternatives in Life* in which there is a choice between the things of this world and the things of God,

Chapter Five

the *Christian Character* in which sinners are called to repentance and to return to the Father, and finally a message of *Repentance*, which is the main theme of this parable. Because of this, there is every reason to expect that Jesus may present multiple themes in a single parable and that does not detract or diminish the *primary* message that the parables present. With this introduction, let us now examine the parables in relation to the themes.

I. God

Theme 1—The Character of God (primary)

1–1. The Parable of the House on the Rock:
Matt. 7:24–27 (page 60)
1–2. The Parable of the Ungrateful and Wicked Servant:
Matt. 18:23–35 (page 64)
1–3. The Parable of the Wicked Tenants:
Matt. 21:33–46 (page 68)

The Character of God (secondary)

1–4. The Parable of the Two Debtors
1–5. The Parable of the Sower
1–6. The Parable of the Friend at Midnight
1–7. The Parable of the Barren Fig Tree
1–8. The Parable of the Lost and Found
1–9. The Parable of the Workers in the Vineyard

Theme 2—The Kingdom of Heaven (primary)

2–1. The Parable of the Mustard Seed: Matt. 13:31 (page 81)
2–2. The Parable of Leaven: Mk. 13:33 (page 83)
2–3. The Parable of the Treasure Hidden in a Field: Matt. 13:44 (page 85)
2–4. The Parable of the Pearl of Great Value: Matt. 13:45–46 (page 89)
2–5. The Parable of the Net Thrown into the Sea: Matt. 13:47–50 (page 91)
2–6. The Parable of the Training for the Kingdom: Matt. 13:52–54 (page 94)
2–7. The Parable of the Workers in the Vineyard: Matt. 20:1–16 (page 97)

God's Hidden Treasures

The Kingdom of Heaven (secondary)
2–8. The Parable of the Sower
2–9. The Parable of the Wheat and the Tares
2–10. The Parable of the Good Samaritan
2–11. The Parable of the Approaching Hour
2–12. The Parable of the Lost and the Found
2–13. The Parable of the Response to Authority
2–14. The Parable of God-given Talents
2–15. The Parable of the Wicked Tenants
2–16. The Parable of the King's Wedding Feast
2–17. The Parable of the Ten Virgins

II. Mankind
Theme 3—The Alternatives in Life (primary)
3–1. The Parable of the Wheat and the Tares: Matt. 13:24–30 (page 107)

The Alternatives in Life (secondary)
3–2. The Parable of the House on the Rock
3–3. The Parable of the Two Debtors
3–4. The Parable of the Sower
3–5. The Parable of the Good Samaritan
3–6. The Parable of the Poor, Rich Fool
3–7. The Parable of the Lost and Found
3–8. The Parable of the Rich Man and Lazarus
3–9. The Parable of God-given Talents
3–10. The Parable of the Wicked Tenants
3–11. The Parable of the Ten Virgins

Theme 4—The Christian Character (primary)
4–1. The Parable of the Two Debtors: Lk. 7:36–50 (page 118)
4–2. The Parable of New Wine and Old Wineskins: Matt. 9:14–17 (page 123)
4–3. The Parable of the Good Samaritan: Lk. 10:25–37 (page 128)
4–4. The Parable of the Poor, Rich Fool: Lk. 12:15–21 (page 135)
4–5. The Parable of the Barren Fig Tree: Lk. 13:6–9 (page 142)
4–6. The Parable of Humility: Lk. 14:7–11 (page 146)
4–7. The Parable of the Great Banquet: Lk. 14:12–24 (page 150)

Chapter Five

4–8. The Parable of the Unworthy Servant: Lk. 17:7–10 (page 155)
4–9. The Parable of Response to Authority: Matt. 21:28–32 (page 160)
4–10. The Parable of God-given Talents: Matt. 25:14–30 (page 163)

The Christian Character (secondary)

4–11. The Parable of the House on the Rock
4–12. The Parable of the Unworthy Servant
4–13. The Parable of the Friend at Midnight
4–14. The Parable of the Approaching Hour (Wedding Feast)
4–15. The Parable of the Lost and Found
4–16. The Parable of Workers in the Vineyard
4–17. The Parable of the Wicked Tenants
4–18. The Parable of the Ten Virgins

Theme 5—The Neccessity of Repentance (primary)

5–1. The Parable of the Lost and Found: Lk. 15:1–31 (page 175)
 (the lost sheep; the lost coin, and the two lost sons)

Theme 6—Our Responsibility for Evangelism (primary)

6–1. The Parable of the Sower: Matt. 13:1–9; 18–23 (page 187)

Theme 7—Our Roles as Christian Stewards (primary)

7–1. The Parable of the Faithful and Wise Manager: Lk. 12:42–48 (page 198)
7–2. The Parable of the Shrewd Manager: Lk. 16:1–15 (page 203)

Theme 8—The Quality and Power of Prayer (primary)

8–1. The Parable of the Friend at Midnight: Lk. 11:5–13 (page 219)
8–2. The Parable of Persistent Prayer: Lk. 18:1–8 (page 223)
8–3. The Parable of Our Perspective in Prayer: Lk. 18:9–14 (page 227)

III. God's Judgment on Mankind
Theme 9—The Preparation for the Judgment (primary)

9–1. The Parable of Christ's Return; the Unexpected Hour: Lk. 12:32–40 (page 238)
9–2. The Parable of the Rich Man and Lazarus: Lk. 16:19–31 (page 246)

God's Hidden Treasures

9–3. The Parable of the Lessons from the Fig Tree: Matt. 24:32–35 (page 252)

9–4. The Parable of the Ten Virgins: Matt. 25:1–13 (page 255)

Theme 10—The Final Judgment (primary)

10–1. The Parable of the King's Wedding Feast: Matt. 22:1–13 (page 270)

10–2. The Parable of the Sheep and the Goats: Matt. 25:31-46 (page 275)

The Final Judgment (secondary)

10–3. The Parable of the Sower

10–4. The Parable of the Wheat and the Tares

The numbers beside each parable (e.g. 1–1) relates this parable to the first theme (The Character of God) and is the first parable in that category. In each case, the first number relates to the Biblical Theme; the second number relates to the listing of that parable within the category. In succeeding chapters, each theme will be examined.

CHAPTER SIX

Theme 1—The Parables of The Character of God

"The Lord our God is one Lord . . ." (Deut. 6:4)

"For thou, O Lord, art good and forgiving, abounding in steadfast love to all who call on thee." (Psa. 86:5)

"The Lord is the everlasting God . . ." (Isa. 40:28)

"God showed his love for us in that while we were yet sinners Christ died for us." (Rom. 5:8)

Before examining the parables, it is important to understand the attributes of God that are covered in the parables. For that reason, we shall first deal with this subject.

God's Characteristics

The *Character of God* is richly revealed in the parables, for they tell us much about His will and His purpose. His character is a subject of such magnitude that only selective dimensions can be discussed here. However, the parables direct our attention to several of His holy and important characteristics: e.g. His love (His grace and His mercy), His joy, His forgiveness, and His patience. God is revealed in His *Living Word*, Jesus Christ, and His *Written Word*, the Scriptures. However, God is also revealed in creation

God's Hidden Treasures

and in conscience (Romans chapter 1). Both the Living Word and the Written Word are inseparable and are authoritative; to accept one is to accept the other. In addition, these two Words contain all truth and all light. God has two distinct characteristics, one transferable and the other non-transferable. His non-transferable character is His omnipotence, omniscience, and omnipresence. His transferable character is His love, patience, joy, holiness, righteousness, justice, etc. These characteristics, are transferable to us, as we reflect His image in His world. Above all, *God is love*; but He is also a God of righteousness and He cannot abide man's sinful nature. He is a God of holy justice and His wrath is evidence of His righteous anger against all sin and against those who rebel against Him. His justice is firm to those who reject, ignore and fail to accept His Son. It is God's will that, *"at the name of Jesus, every knee shall bow and every tongue confess him Lord, to the glory of God the Father."* (Phil. 2:10). God calls us to know His character and to be in His image. Although Jesus came into the world to redeem the world, He also came to *"reveal"* the Father. Jesus said that, if you have seen me, you have seen the Father. Because the Father and the Son are One, the fullness of God is revealed in the Son of God. (Col. 1:15–18). Of His infinite attributes, five important characteristics that are uniquely revealed in the parables are *His grace (love), His mercy (love)*, His *wrath,* His *joy,* His *forgiveness, His patience and His judgment*. Since the parables emphasize these characteristics, further discussion is warrant. This does not detract from His other characteristics, particularly His holiness, His justice, His righteousness and His hope.

> *His Love (grace and mercy)*
> "For God so loved the world that he gave his only Son, that whoever believes in him would not perish but have eternal life." (Jn. 3:16)

This is the greatest measure of His love, that He gave His Son to redeem the world. On that basis, we should never doubt or question the love of God. God is a God of love (I Jn. 4:8), expressed in both His grace and His mercy. His grace is giving us the love we do

Chapter Six

not deserve; His mercy is not giving us His wrath, which we do deserve. The Bible is the message of God's love, revealed through His Son and through His Word. We would not know love, if we did not know God. The apostle Paul summarized his perspective on love in I Corinthians 13, which is probably the greatest expression of love ever written. In addition to Paul, the apostle John is one of the great ambassadors of the gospel of love. The message of God's love is evident in many of the parables, particularly in the Parable of the Lost and Found (grace) and the Parable of the Good Samaritan (mercy).

His Wrath

"He who believes in the Son has eternal life; he who does not obey the Son shall not see life, but the wrath of God rests upon him." (Jn. 3:36)

"Since, therefore, we are now justified by his blood, much more shall we be saved by him from the wrath of God." (Rom. 5:9)

God's wrath is the result of God's holy and just opposition to sin. God's love is inherent in His Person; His wrath is demonstrated in opposition to the wickedness of mankind. Sin is a rebellion against His grace; it is the rejection of His mercy. Paul wrote (Rom. 1:18–2:11)—*"For the wrath of God is revealed from heaven against all ungodliness and wickedness of men, who by their wickedness suppress the truth."* Paul goes on to describe the nature of that evil and to state three times—*"God gave them up . . ."* (1:24, 26, 28). Man's sin sets the stage for God's wrath.

The Bible portrays God's wrath, not as an emotion but as His holy and just determined opposition to evil. Therefore, the wrath of God is God's punishment of sin in this life and in the next. These inflictions include death, exile, hardening of hearts, and the cutting off of the people of God because of idolatry or unbelief. Such evil, justifying God's wrath, will lead to everlasting punishment in hell of fire where the flame is never quenched. The day of wrath is God's final judgment against sin; it is His irrevocable condemnation of rebellious and hardhearted sinners. The Old Testament describes God as *"slow to anger and plenteous in mercy."* Only if we understand the magnitude of God's wrath can we begin to

God's Hidden Treasures

appreciate the glory of His grace. Although God's wrath is just and holy, He does present a way of escape and a way of salvation. He calls us to repent, to return unto Him, to receive His forgiveness and renewal and to be restored to fellowship with Him. In the New Testament, the call is to faith, to repentance, to baptism in the name of the Lord Jesus who saves us from the wrath to come (1 Thess. 1:9–10). We are justified by His blood and reconciled by his death; we shall be saved from the wrath of God by His life (Rom. 5:9–10).

God's wrath is expressed in many of the parables, particularly the Parables of the Wheat and the Tares (5), The Wicked Tenants (30) and The King's Wedding Feast (31) (See pages 45 and 46).

His Joy

". . . for the joy of the Lord is your strength." (Neh. 8:10)
". . . there will be more joy in heaven over one sinner who repents, than over ninety-nine righteous persons who need no repentance." (Lk. 15:7)

His joy is the ultimate joy, and God wants His people to be joyful, full of His joy, not filled with the secular "joy" of this world. J. B. Payne (<u>Theology of the Older Testament)</u> and W. Morrice (<u>Joy in the New Testament</u>) describes joy as a delight of the mind arising from the consideration of a present or assured possession of a future good. As such, Dr. Payne identifies three types of joy; *natural joy, moral joy, and spiritual joy*. *Natural joy* is the evidence that the accomplishment of noble and high desires brings great satisfaction. *Moral joy* generally results from good works and honorable actions. The third is *spiritual joy*, which Paul lists as one of the *"fruits of the Spirit"* (Gal 5:22). Spiritual joy is that joy that is present in the midst of trials, when faithfulness to God and the standards of God are upheld. James wrote (James 1:2–4), *"Count it all joy, my brethren, when you meet various trials, for you know that the testing of your faith produces steadfastness. And let steadfastness have its full effect, that you may be perfect and complete, not lacking in anything."* James writes that Christians should rejoice at being tested, for testing produces steadfastness, and that should make us *"perfect and complete."* But there is a fourth evidence of joy, which I call *divine*

Chapter Six

joy. This is the joy of God and of heaven when a sinner repents. Paul also encourages all Christians to have *"joy in the faith"* (Phil 1:25).

Jesus gives His disciples then, and the world today, the most profound teaching on joy. In the Beatitudes, Jesus lists the characteristics of a life committed to God and in which the natural result is joy. Jesus concludes with these words," *Rejoice and be glad."* (Matt. 5:12) Paul wrote in the same vein, *"Rejoice always . . ."* (I Thess. 5:16). This theme of joy is presented in many of the parables. In Matt. 13:44, the Parable of the Treasure Hidden in a Field, Jesus spoke of *"a man found . . . then in his joy he goes and sells all that he has and buys the field."* In the Parable of the Lost and Found (Luke 15), Jesus, in each of the three stories, reveals the *joy in heaven* when a sinner repents. In addition, the Parable of the Talents emphasized the reward of faithfulness, *"enter into the joy of your master."* (Matt 25:21). Jesus encouraged His followers by His words and actions, and He explained the reason, *"that my joy may be in you, and that your joy may be full."* (Jn. 16:11) The joy of Christ is permanent; *"no one will take your joy from you."* His joy was to do the will of the Father who sent Him. Joy was one of the principal characteristics of the early church; they were with *"glad and generous hearts, praising God and having favor with all people"* (Acts 2:46). Joy is the character of God and of the Christian church.

His Forgiveness
"Repent and be baptized every one of you in the name of Jesus Christ for the forgiveness of sin; and you will receive the gift of the Holy Spirit." (Acts 2:38)

Forgiveness is one of the great acts of God, who promises to forgive our sins, if we confess them, repent and return to Him. As God is the God of forgiveness, that is also to be one of our characteristics. We are to forgive others—to the same degree that we have been forgiven. Forgiveness is pardoning another in spite of mistakes, sins and errors. How many times are Christians to forgive one another, *"seventy times seventy"* or endlessly. The Bible treats this subject of forgiveness with clarity, confidence and certainty.

God's Hidden Treasures

> "... for I will forgive their iniquities and I will remember their sins no more." (Jer. 31:34)
>
> "... for this is the blood of the new covenant which is poured out for many for the forgiveness of sins." (Matt. 28:28)
>
> "And Peter said to them, 'Repent and be baptized every one of you in the name of Jesus Christ for the forgiveness of sins; and you will receive the gift of the Holy Spirit.'" (Acts 2:38)

These texts tell us much about forgiveness. *First,* if God should remember our iniquities, who could stand before Him? No one. However, God is the God of grace and mercy. *Second,* God has promised to forgive and to *"remember them no more"* when we repent. Christianity is the only religion, the only relationship, that promises forgiveness. As a theological term, forgiveness is God's pardon of the sins of human beings. However, we are not only forgiven; we are restored and reconciled to fellowship with the Father. The initiative for forgiveness comes from God (John 3:16; Col. 2:13), in the same way that the initiative in love lies with God. In addition, only God has the authority and the ability to forgive sins (Matt. 1:21), and this forgiveness is an essential part of the gospel message (Acts 2:38). God's forgiveness of us demands that we forgive others, because grace brings responsibility and obligation (Matt. 18:23–35). When we repent, God forgives us of our sins against Him. We cannot forgive those who have sinned against God, but we must forgive the sins of another who has sinned against us. A forgiving spirit is the essential character of a true follower of Jesus Christ (Matt. 5:43–48). His forgiveness is shown in many parables, e.g. the Parable of the Two Debtors (Lk. 7:36–50).

His Patience and Forbearance

> "And I (Paul) am the foremost of sinners; but I received mercy for this reason, that in me, as the foremost, Jesus Christ might display his perfect patience for an example to those who were to believe in him for eternal life." (I Tim. 1:15b–16)
>
> "The Lord... is forbearing towards you, not wishing that any should perish, but that all should reach repentance." (2 Pet. 3:9)

One of the great attributes of God is His unfailing patience with even the greatest of sinners. God was patient with Paul, be-

Chapter Six

cause God knew that Paul was to be His instrument to *"suffer for the sake of my (Jesus') name",* by taking the gospel to the Gentile world. In the same manner, God is patient with all His people; not wishing that any would perish, but that all would come to salvation through faith In Jesus Christ. One of the prime examples of God's patience in the parables is that of the Barren Fig Tree (Lk. 13:6–9). God is patient and forbearing so that we would repent, which would lead to good works and bearing fruit for the kingdom of God. Bearing fruit is the evidence of repentance and fellowship with God.

His Judgment

Judgment represents a process in which a verdict is reached and justice and righteousness is achieved. It is an essential part of every society; it clearly is essential to Christianity. Therefore, Abraham asked, *"Shall not the Judge of all the earth do right?"* (Gen. 18:25). Indeed, God is the God of righteous judgment, and *"all his ways are justice"* (Deut 32:4). *"Righteousness and justice are the foundation of his throne." (Psa. 97:2).* As God is just and righteous, He demands it of His people. That there will be a final judgment is regarded as an eternal truth (Rom. 3:5–6). The resurrection of the dead and eternal judgment are two of the primary teachings about Christ (Heb. 6:1–2); all face the judgment (Heb. 12:23). It is as inescapable as death (Heb. 9:27). Even the family of God is included and indeed judgment begins with them, 1 Pet. 4:17, *"For the time has come for judgment to begin with the household of God . . ."* Christ will save believers, but their work will be judged on that day. *"Then shall all the trees of the wood sing for you before the Lord, for he comes, for he comes to judge the earth. He will judge the world with righteousness, and the people with his truth."* All people, of every race, every nation and every creed, will answer to God.

The New Testament reinforces the Old Testament thoughts about judgment. However, there is a striking new dimension, namely, that judgment is connected with the cross of Christ. As He approached the time of His death, Jesus said, *"Now is the judgment of this world, now shall the ruler of this world be cast out."* (Jn. 12:31).

God's Hidden Treasures

God's present judgment of people is forcefully defined in Romans 1, when Paul spoke three times *"God gave them up . . ."* (1:24, 26, 28). God cannot stand evil, and this is expressed in His judgments here and now. An interesting aspect of present judgment is brought out in the words of Jesus: *"This is the verdict. Light has come into the world, but men loved darkness instead of light because their deeds were evil"* (John 3:19). The love of darkness is itself judgment. <u>The Evangelical Dictionary of Biblical Theology</u> is a particularly rich source on this subject, as well as the writings of H. Butterfield (<u>Christianity and History</u>) and Leon Morris (<u>The Biblical Doctrine of Judgment</u>). The judgment of God is expressed in the Parable of the Wheat and the Tares, the Parable of the Rich Man and Lazarus, the Parable of the Wicked Tenants and the Parable of The Sheep and Goats.

The Character of God (Primary)
1–1. The Parable of the House on the Rock
1–2. The Parable of the Ungrateful and Wicked Servant
1–3. The Parable of the Wicked Tenants

The Character of God (Secondary)
1–4. The Parable of the Two Debtors
1–5. The Parable of the Sower
1–6. The Parable of the Friend at Midnight
1–7. The Parable of the Barren Fig Tree
1–8. The Parable of the Lost and Found
1–9. The Parable of the Workers in the Vineyard

1–1. The Parable of the House on the Rock: Matt. 7:24–27
"Every one then who hears these words of mine and does them will be like a wise man who built his house upon the rock; and the rain fell, and the floods came, and the winds blew and beat upon that house, but it did not fall, because it had been founded on the rock. And every one

Chapter Six

who hears these words of mine and does not do them will be like a foolish man who built his house upon the sand; and the rain fell, and the floods came, and the winds blew and beat against that house, and it fell; and great was the fall of it."

Commentary

We begin by examining the context in which Jesus told this parable. Recall that He had been teaching what is called the Sermon on the Mount. Now He concludes with comparative statements regarding those who hear His words and do them in contrast to those who hear and reject His teachings. So Jesus places before the crowd, and before the world today, the question of the foundation on which we build our *"house."* There are three texts, among many, that provide additional insight into this parable.

Isa. 28:16—"Behold, I am laying in Zion for a foundation a stone, a tested stone, a precious cornerstone, of a sure foundation:"

I Cor. 3:11—"For no other foundation can any one lay than that which is laid, which is Jesus Christ."

2 Tim. 2:19—"But God's firm foundation stands, bearing this seal: 'The Lord knows those who are his' and 'Let every one who names the name of the Lord depart from iniquity.'"

This parable emphasizes our *"hearing"*, which is a measure of our understanding and acceptance of what we hear. When we hear, the question is whether we do what we hear, or do we ignore the message. In this parable, the wise man hears and does the will of God; the foolish man hears, but does not do the will of God. This parable tells us much about God and much about ourselves. It tells us that God is the Rock; it tells us that we can be wise or foolish. In Scripture, foolish means to be morally corrupt.

In this parable, Jesus compares *two men, two foundations and two houses.*

First, there is the matter of the *two men*, and the choice they make in selecting the foundations upon which they build their house. They have a choice before them, either to build on the rock or on the sand. This parable tells us much about the two types of men, and it also tells us much about ourselves. Would we build so as to establish a sound and strong future? Would we make

God's Hidden Treasures

decisions that have a bearing on eternal life? Or would the cares of this world cause us to seek the easy road, the easy path, and thereby build on the sand. Do we commit to God or to the pleasures of this world?

Second, there is the matter of the *two foundations.* The first house is built upon the rock; no storm or flood or wind could damage the house, because *"it had been founded on the rock."* This is the house of the *wise man.* The second house is built upon the sand; when the storms came, the house will fall—*"and great will be the fall of it."* This, said Jesus, is the house of the *foolish man.* Consider the rock from these Old and New Testament Scriptures:

Deut. 32:4—"The <u>Rock</u>, his work is perfect; for all his ways are justice. A God of faithfulness and without iniquity."

I Sam. 2:2—"There is none holy like the Lord, there is none beside thee; there in no rock like our God."

2 Sam. 22:2—"The Lord is my <u>rock</u>, and my fortress, and my deliverer . . ."

Psa. 19:14—"Let the words of my mouth and the meditations of my heart be always acceptable in thy sight, O Lord, my <u>rock</u> and my redeemer."

Isa. 26:4—"Trust in the Lord for ever, for the Lord God is an everlasting <u>rock</u>."

I Cor. 10:4—"I want you to know, brethren, that our fathers were all under the cloud . . . and all ate the same supernatural food and all drank the same supernatural drink. For they drank from the supernatural Rock which followed them, and the <u>Rock</u> was Christ."

Throughout both the Old and New Testament, the Rock is God.

Third, there are two houses. The word *"house"* is used in Scripture in many different senses; let us examine just a few. The 23rd Psalm speaks of *"I shall dwell in the house of the Lord forever."* Here David is referring to the kingdom of heaven. The house is also spoken of in the sense of lineage or family, e.g. Joseph was of the house of David (Luke 1:27). In Jn. 14:2, the house of God is heaven—*"in my Father's house are many rooms . . ."* Paul speaks of the human body: *"For we know that if the earthly tent we live in is destroyed, we have a building from God, a house not made with hands,*

Chapter Six

eternal in the heavens." (2 Cor. 5:1–2). God does not dwell in temples or churches or any physical structure. In Acts 7:47–50, Paul wrote of the Temple built by Solomon and Paul wrote (quoting from Isa. 66:1–2), *"But it was Solomon who built a house for him. Yet the Most High does not dwell in houses made with hands; as the prophet (Isaiah) says 'Heaven is my throne, and earth is my footstool. What house will you build for me, says the Lord, or what is the place of my rest? Did not my hand make all these things?'"* A house in the highest sense denotes dwelling with God, the house of the Lord; it means that we have a lineage from Abraham and our house expresses righteousness, as Abraham was righteous; it means our house is eternal in the heavens.

That is the house that the wise man is to build. The house built on the Rock is a spiritual house and it will not fall because its foundation is the Rock; the house built on the sand will fall when the storms come. Therefore the quality of the house is determined by the quality of the foundation. To live a life that bears much fruit, we are to build our *"house"* upon the Person of Jesus Christ, God Incarnate. In our lives, we need to recognize the Rock, honor Him, serve Him and live a life worthy of Him.

Summary of Biblical Themes
Theme 1—The Character of God

God is the *"solid rock"* which should be the *"foundation"* of our lives. We need to honor and respect the teaching of Jesus, for He and the Word of God are the Rock on which our faith is based. We are to hear and to do. "Rock," means God's love, support and protection of His people.

This parable contains two secondary themes;
Theme 3—The Alternatives in Life

We can build on the *"rock"* or on the *"sand."* To build on the Rock, we have to make a conscious decision to spend time in God's Word and to live a life worthy of God. He is our "foundation."

God's Hidden Treasures

Theme 4—The Christian Character

The Christian *"hears"* the words of Jesus Christ and applies them in our lives. *"Hearing"* the words means accepting the truths and adopting them, so that the Word of God will dominate our lives. We must abide in Him and He in us. (Jn. 15:5)

Summary of God's Revelations

This parable has truths and warnings. The truths are; first, *the house built on the Rock will stand against all the storms; second, if you hear the Words of Jesus and do it, you are wise; it you hear and don't do it, you are foolish.* The warning is: do not *be foolish, by ignoring the truths that we hear.*

1–2. The Parable of the Ungrateful and Wicked Servant: Matt. 18:23–35

"Therefore the kingdom of heaven may be compared to a king who wished to settle accounts with his servants. When he began the reckoning, one was brought to him who owed him ten thousand talents; and as he could not pay, his lord ordered him to be sold, with his wife and children and all that he had, and payment to be made. So the servant fell on his knees, imploring him, 'Lord, have patience with me, and I will pay you everything.' And out of pity for him the lord of that servant released him and forgave him the debt. But that same servant, as he went out, came upon one of his fellow servants who owed him a hundred denarii; and seizing him by the throat he said, 'Pay what you owe.' So his fellow servant fell down and besought him, 'Have patience with me, and I will pay you.' He refused and went and put him in prison till he should pay the debt. When his fellow servants saw what had taken place, they were greatly distressed, and they went and reported to their lord all that had taken place. Then his lord summoned him and said to him, 'You wicked servant! I forgave you all that debt because you besought me; and should not you have had mercy on your

Chapter Six

fellow servant, as I had mercy on you?' And in anger his lord delivered him to the jailers, till he should pay all his debt. So also my heavenly Father will do to every one of you, if you do not forgive your brother from your heart."

Commentary

This parable emphasizes the *forgiving* character and the *patience* of God, as well as the punishment and penalty for ingratitude and wickedness. In this chapter, Jesus was teaching His disciples regarding *"who is the greatest in the kingdom of heaven"*; the answer is that it is every person who is like a little child, fully dependent on God, will be the greatest in the kingdom. The evidence of greatness is *humility,* which is not thinking badly of oneself; it is thinking first of others. From this discussion, Jesus moves to the question of sin and the degree to which forgiveness is to be granted. Peter asked, *"Lord, how often shall my brother sin against me, and I forgive him? As many as seven times? Jesus said to him—"I do not say to you seven times, but seventy times seven."* (Matt. 18;22) In other words, Jesus is saying that forgiveness is limitless and boundless to the degree that we are to forgive those who *"sin"* against us. That is what God does; that is what we are to do. The first key word is *forgiveness*, which is the measure of love. Christians are to forgive others as we have been forgiven (Matt. 6:12). The second key word is *patience*, which Paul identifies as one of the fruits of the Spirit (Gal. 5:22). God is patient with us; we must be patient with each other.

In the parable, Jesus speaks of the relationship between a king and his servants. One man owed the king 10,000 talents (about $10 million) which the servant could not repay. So the king ordered the man to be sold, with his family and all his possessions. The man begged the king for *"patience . . . and I will repay you everything."* Then the king *"out of pity for him, released the man and forgave him the debt."* It's interesting that the king could so quickly and so generously forgive such an enormous debt. But the king had compassion on him; that is what God does for us when we come *debt-laden and racked with pain.* Jesus tells us to come to him, when we are heavy laden and He will refresh us. (Matt. 11:28) Refresh is the same as comforting, renewing and supporting. Then

God's Hidden Treasures

this same *"forgiven"* man went to another servant who owed him 100 denarii (about $20) and demanded payment. When the second servant could not repay the debt and asked for *"patience, he put him in prison until he could repay the debt."* When the other servants saw what had happened, they went and reported the event to the king. The king called the first servant in, *"I showed mercy on you because you asked me; should you have not shown mercy on your fellow servants, as I had mercy on you?"* Therefore the king had the servant thrown into jail until he had repaid all his debt. Jesus concludes with this message. *"So also my heavenly Father will do to every one of you, if you do not forgive your brother from your heart."* There is a penalty for not forgiving others as we have been forgiven.

The subjects here are *gratitude, patience* and *forgiveness*. The servant is first ungrateful, then wicked; ungrateful because he saw forgiveness as a one-way street. Forgiveness was for him but not for others. He asked for and received forgiveness, but he could not extend it to others. We are to be grateful for the rich blessings that God has bestowed on us. We are to be patient, as God is patient. We are to recognize forgiveness as one of the preeminent virtues of God. God forgives the repentant, which is based on the recognition of, and confession of, sin.

There are three points regarding forgiveness. *First*, being in God's image, we are to forgive in the same manner as we have been forgiven. *The second point* is that our forgiveness of others has no limit, regardless of the number of times that the same offense has been committed. The *third point* is that we are to forgive *"from the heart."* Forgiveness is measured in the true depth of our forgiveness. True forgiveness does not remember; it does not hold a grudge. In Jeremiah 31:34, God said that He would forgive our iniquities (sins) and then He continues, *"I will remember their sins no more."* That is the attitude that we must have. If God forgives and remembers no more, we can do no less.

In the parable, notice how differently people act when they seek something from another, compared to when someone owes them. We are *"humble"* in seeking forgiveness; we are sometimes *"haughty"* when we demand anything from others. Notice the change in the demeanor of the master, who has forgiven and set a standard and then finds that his standard, given to some, is ignored when it is not in their best interest. We should have mercy on others just as God has mercy on us; we cannot expect mercy, if we cannot show mercy. And Jesus makes it clear; forgiving others is not just an outward sign, but it must be forgiveness *"from our heart."*

In the Sermon on the Mount, Jesus repeats this message that the laws must be written on our heart. He said that our righteousness must exceed that of the scribes and Pharisees, who were mostly concerned with an external conformity to the Law. Jesus said that is not enough. *"You must not do as they do."* (Matt. 6:8). Jesus said that righteousness is a matter of the heart. The first question for us is: are God's laws written on our hearts? The second question is: can we forgive in the same measure that we ask God to forgive us? The third question is: if we forgive, can we also forget. God forgives our sins, and He remembers them no more. (Jer. 33:33). We must do the same. God says that He desires mercy, not sacrifices (Hos. 6:6). Christianity is a community of forgiven people; we are also to be a community of grateful and patient people.

Summary of Biblical Themes
Theme 1—The Character of God

Forgiveness is one of the great promises and characteristics of God. Therefore, forgiveness is required of us. In addition, God is steadfast and patient in His love. That is what we are to show to those around us.

Three other themes, covered in this parable, are:
Theme 2—The Kingdom of Heaven

The kingdom of heaven welcomes those who forgive, are patient and grateful.
Theme 3—The Alternatives in Life

We can seek forgiveness for ourselves but refuse to forgive others, as we can forgive freely, continuously and without reservation.

God's Hidden Treasures

Theme 4—The Christian Character

In addition, Jesus tells the disciples, that two of the preeminent virtues of the Christian life are *gratitude* for all that God has given us, as well as the willingness and desire to *forgive others*. In addition to forgiveness and gratitude, the characteristic of patience must be fully understood and developed in our lives.

Summary of God's Revelations

There are four commands: to *forgive and show mercy; our actions must be from the heart; be grateful for God's forgiveness; express gratitude in our actions; be patient with each other.*

1–3. The Parable of the Wicked Tenants: Matt. 21:33–46

"Hear another parable. There was a householder who planted a vineyard, and set a hedge around it, and dug a wine press in it, and built a tower, and let it out to tenants, and went into another country. When the season of fruit drew near, he sent his servants to the tenants, to get his fruit; and the tenants took his servants and beat one, killed another, and stoned another. Again he sent other servants, more than the first; and they did the same to them. Afterward he sent his son to them, saying, 'They will respect my son.' But when the tenants saw the son, they said to themselves, 'This is the heir; come, let us kill him and have his inheritance.' And they took him and cast him out of the vineyard, and killed him. When therefore the owner of the vineyard comes, what will he do to those tenants? They said to him, 'He will put those wretches to a miserable death, and let out the vineyard to other tenants who will give him the fruits in their seasons.' Jesus said to them, 'have you never read in the scriptures: The very stone which the builders rejected has become the head of the corner; this was the Lord's doing, and it is marvelous in our eyes?' Therefore I tell you, the kingdom of God will be taken away from you and given to a nation produc-

Chapter Six

ing the fruits of it. And he who falls on this stone will be broken to pieces; but when it falls on anyone, it will crush him'."

Commentary

It is interesting that this parable follows so closely on the heels of the previous parable (1–2), dealing also with forgiveness, patience and gratitude. However, again we see the great *patience* of God, although we also see the greatest wickedness which is the rejection of His Son.

Again the context is important. Jesus is on that fateful journey to the cross, and this is the beginning of those final earthly days leading up to the crucifixion, the resurrection, and the ascension. The opposition of the Jewish authorities continued to increase, and Jesus knew that His *"time was about to be fulfilled."* He set his face for Jerusalem, knowing what lay ahead. There is the triumphant march into Jerusalem, only to be followed by that dark and fateful period. There are the events of the first *"Palm Sunday"*, when Jesus enters Jerusalem, how the crowds greeted him, *"Hosanna to the Son of David . . ."* Later Jesus drove the moneychangers out of the temple; He defined His Father's house as a house of prayer; He healed the blind and the lame and continues His teaching about faith, about prayer, *"And whatever you ask in prayer, you will receive, if you have faith."* (21:22). Such teachings only deepened both the fear and the anger of the chief priests and scribes. Then Matthew follows with the account of the fig tree with *no fruit* on it, and Jesus used that example to teach about the faith that will move mountains. Moving from that episode, Matthew reports that Jesus went into the temple where He was teaching and the chief priests and elders challenged Him and asked by what authority did He do these things. From these episodes of *unfruitfulness* and the challenges and questions of the Jewish authorities, Jesus tells this parable which deals with the unfruitfulness of those to whom God had entrusted His vineyard.

The parable has many facets: *the Character of God, our stewardship, honoring God, giving honor to the Son of God, Day of Judgment, when judgment will be pronounced on those who are responsible for the "management" of God's "Vineyard."*

God's Hidden Treasures

In this parable, Jesus is now leading up to the Day of Judgment. He sets before all people the impact of the Judgment on our past, present and future actions, both for the believers and non-believers. Non-believers will be judged on their denial and refusal to accept Jesus Christ as Savior and Lord; believers will be judged on what they have done with the talents and opportunities that God has given them.

The parable is simple in the most profound of terms. The householder *"rented"* (not gave) the vineyard to some tenants; notice that the householder always *owns* the vineyard; it is eternally His. When harvest time approached, the householder sent his servants to collect *"his fruit."* But the tenants *"seized the servants, beat one, killed another, and stoned a third."* Then he sent more servants, who were treated exactly the same. *Finally he sent his son*, believing that the tenants would respect him. Instead of respect and honor, the tenants took him, threw him out of the vineyard and *killed* him. Can you understand or imagine the patience of the householder who has seen such treatment of his servants and now the treatment of his son? The householder will come, bring them to a wretched end and rent the vineyard to other tenants who will give him his share of the crop at harvest time. *"Wretched"* are those who will be sent into *"exile"*, which is far from God. However, in this case, the *"exile"* is not one in Babylon, where God will one day bring them *"home."* Now the exile will be eternally removed from God. As Paul wrote in Romans 1:24, 26, 28, *"God gave them up . . ."* Evil people will be separated from God and lost in their own darkness. Being *"given up "* and removed far from God is their *"wretched end."*

Who do you suppose are the various servants that the *"Landlord"* sent and who were brutally mistreated by the tenants? Most likely, they were the prophets that God has sent, time and time again, to proclaim His messages and who were ignored and rejected by the Jews. Jesus concludes this parable with three thoughts:
1. *The stone the builders rejected has become the capstone; the Lord has done this and it is marvelous in our eyes.*

Chapter Six

2. *The kingdom of God will be taken from you and given to a people who will produce its fruit.*
3. *He who falls on the stone will be broken to pieces; but he on whom it falls will be crushed.*

First, Jesus Christ is the stone that the *builders* rejected, and He has become the head of the corner, the cornerstone, the most important stone in any structure. It is the stone upon which all other stones in the structure depend. It is interesting that the *"builders"* (the Jews) have rejected the most important stone of all. Paul takes up this same message in Col. 1:17, "He *is before all things and in him all things hold together."* Jesus quotes from Psa. 118:22–23; this is also a statement included in Isa. 28:16, *"Behold, I am laying in Zion for a foundation a stone, a tested stone, a precious cornerstone, of a sure foundation; he who believes will not be in haste."* This great message is taken up in many places in the New Testament (Lk. 9:22; Acts 4:11; Rom. 9:33; Eph. 2:20; I Pet. 2:7). Peter uses this same text and thought in his address to the Sanhedrin (Acts 4:11). The stone, which is the key to any *"structure"* is also the stone which is rejected.

Second, there is the warning that the kingdom of God will be taken from unworthy tenants and given to others who will produce the fruit of the kingdom. Jesus sends a warning, then and now, that the kingdom will be taken from any people who fail to produce good fruit, who reject God and His Son, and it will be given to a people who will be fruitful. The warning that Jesus gives is the same that John the Baptist gave to the Pharisees and Sadducees (Matt. 3:8), *"Bear fruit that befits repentance."* God will not stand idly by and patiently see constant rebellion, arrogance and rejection. This message is repeated in The Parable of the Wedding Feast in Matthew 22:1–14.

Third, there is a warning regarding the Day of Judgment, a warning against constant rejection of the *"stone"*; those who *"fall on the stone will be broken into pieces."* Continued rejection of the *"stone"* will mean ultimate destruction. Falling on the stone is one thing; but those on whom the stone falls will be crushed. *Crushed is the final and ultimate devastation.*

God's Hidden Treasures

Summary of Biblical Themes
Theme 1—The Character of God

God is patient with the *"tenants"* of His Vineyard, but He will not tolerate constant rejection and rebellion. He has sent forth His Word, through His prophets and through His Son, to warn the people of their sins, and to teach them the way to righteousness (Heb. 1:1). God will redeem His creation and give the kingdom to a people worthy of His love. God is just in His condemnation of sin; His punishment is certain, for there are consequences to constant and deliberate sin.

Five other themes are presented in this parable:

Theme 2—The Kingdom of Heaven

Only those who "receive and believe" the Son will enter the kingdom of heaven. Ignoring the *"landlord"* and believing that the vineyard is ours will lead to destruction; the stone will crush us.

Theme 3—The Alternatives in Life

Those who manage the Vineyard of God have two options; the first is to ignore the righteous claims of a holy God and believe that the vineyard is ours; the second is to accept the sovereign God as the righteous Owner of all Creation. We must accept the Word of God, given through His prophets and, in the last days, given through His Son.

Theme 4—The Christian Character

Christians recognize the Sovereignty of God, knowing that this world is His, and we are but stewards. When God sent His Word through His Son and through His Scripture, we are called to honor and obey that Word.

Theme 7-Our Role as Christian Stewards

Christian Stewardship is the recognition that God is the Landlord, and we are tenants in His world. We are to honor God's Son and God's possessions by producing good fruit so that God would be glorified. We work solely for Him and for His glory. God created everything; therefore, everything is God's by right; everything is ours as tenants and stewards.

Chapter Six

Theme 10—The Final Judgment

This parable describes the judgment that will fall on those who are unfaithful in the *"management of the Vineyard."* Jesus now sets before all people the impact of the Judgment on our actions. God is patient but He will not accept the rejection of His Son. The householder will *"put those wretches to a miserable death"* and rent the vineyard to more deserving and righteous tenants.

Summary of God's Revelations

God is revealed in His patience and determination that only the righteous shall inherit His kingdom. This parable deals with promises, truths and warnings. The promise is *the very stone that the builders have rejected has become the head of the corner.* The truth is *those who reject the Son will face a miserable death.* This truth is also a warning. Two other warnings are; first, *the kingdom of God will be taken away from those who rejected the Son and given to a nation producing the fruit of it;* second, *if anyone falls on this stone (Jesus Christ), it will break them to pieces; if the stone falls on anyone, it will crush them.*

There are six parables in which *The Character of God* is a *secondary* theme:
1-4. The Parable of the Two Debtors
1-5. The Parable of the Sower
1-6. The Parable of the Friend at Midnight
1-7. The Parable of the Barren Fig Tree
1-8. The Parable of the Lost and Found
1-9. The Parable of the Workers in the Vineyard

Summary of the Biblical Themes
Theme 1—The Character of God

In the Parable of the House on the Rock, God is the only <u>sure foundation</u>, the Rock, on which Christians are to build their lives.

In the Parable of the Ungrateful and Wicked Servant, God is *"<u>forgiving and patient</u>"* to all who come to Him humbly and repentant.

God's Hidden Treasures

In the Parable of the Wicked Tenants, God is a <u>just God</u> who will deal faithfully with those who disobey Him or fail to honor Him as the Sovereign God (Romans 1). He will give the *"kingdom"* to those who produce the *"fruit"* of it.

In the Parable of the Two Debtors, God <u>welcomes</u> those who worship and honor Him in spirit and in truth.

In the Parable of the Sower, a <u>patient God</u> sows His seeds, in the hope that it will bear much fruit in good soil. However, He also knows that only a few will accept the seed.

In the Parable of the Friend at Midnight, God <u>welcomes those who persist in prayer</u> and who seek first His kingdom and His righteousness.

In the Parable of the Barren Fig Tree, God shows the depth of <u>His patience</u>—not wishing that any should perish, but that all would bear good fruit.

In the Parable of the Lost and Found, God rejoices <u>when a sinner comes home</u>. Whenever, there is repentance, God is anxious to forgive.

In the Parable of the Workers in the Vineyard, God *invites* <u>all to work</u> in His vineyard—and the pay for everyone, regardless of the time spent, is equal. The payment is eternal life, for all who labor for God. He is <u>generous and impartial</u>.

God is the Rock, the sure foundation; He is the sovereign God who is forgiving and just to those who seek Him in a humble and contrite spirit; He is patient in dealing with His children and His creation; His judgment is just; He is patient as He measures our deeds; He welcomes the repentant sinners for this is a measure of His love; He calls us to a life of persistent prayer for this is the measure of our fellowship with Him; He rejoices when a sinner comes home for this is a measure of His joy; He extends to all an invitation to work in His vineyard; He seeks all to work for His glory and that none should perish, but that all should obtain eternal life; He is generous and impartial in His love for all who labor in His Vineyard; He is a God of just wrath to all those who reject His Son; He is the God of Judgment, Who will reward all for what we have done and not done in service and witness to Him; above

Chapter Six

all, He is sovereign in the course of history and in the fulfillment of redemption of His creation.

Summary of God's Revelations
Theme 1—The Character of God

God has revealed Himself by commands, promises, truths and warnings. The commands are: we must *hear and do the will of God, which is to be wise; don't be foolish, ignoring what you hear;* we must *forgive and show mercy; it must be from the heart; be grateful for God's forgiveness; express gratitude in action, be patient with each other.* The promise is: *the very stone that the builders have rejected has become the head of the corner.* The truths are: *the house built on the Rock will stand against all the storms; if you hear and do, you are wise; if you hear and don't do, you are foolish; those who reject the Son will face a miserable death.* This truth is also a warning. There are three warnings: *do not be foolish by ignoring the truths that we hear; those who reject the Son will receive a miserable death; the kingdom of God will be taken away from those who reject the Son and given to a nation producing the fruit of it; If anyone falls on this stone, it will break them to pieces; if the stone falls on anyone, it will crush them.*

CHAPTER SEVEN

Theme 2—The Parables of The Kingdom of Heaven

"*Thy kingdom is an everlasting kingdom . . .*" (Psa. 145:13)

"*But seek first His kingdom and his righteousness . . .*" (Matt. 6:33)

"*For the kingdom of God is not a matter of eating and drinking, but of righteousness, peace and joy in the Holy Spirit . . .*" (Rom. 14:17)

"*I tell you this, brethren; flesh and blood cannot inherit the kingdom of God.*" (I Cor. 15:50)

We turn now to the second of the ten themes that Jesus treats in the parables. Recalling that Jesus began His earthly ministry, stating, "*Repent, for the kingdom of heaven is at hand.*" (Matt. 4:17), it is therefore not surprising that both *repentance* and the *kingdom of heaven* are emphasized in the parables.

However, before looking at the parables, we should understand this kingdom to which Jesus directs our attention. To begin with, His kingdom is called by various terms, e.g. the kingdom of heaven, thy kingdom, His kingdom, the kingdom of my Father, and the kingdom of Jesus Christ. These all mean the same, but it is important to note that Jesus constantly refers to it as *the kingdom of heaven*. The gospel is the gospel of the kingdom, the word of the kingdom;

God's Hidden Treasures

in the same manner, the inhabitants of the kingdom are called the sons of the kingdom. The kingdom of heaven is that universal kingdom that is present wherever the sovereign God reigns and His righteousness, love, joy and peace are evident. It is universal in the plan of God that all nations shall flow to His holy hill and be His children in His kingdom. The kingdom denotes God's sovereignty and loving power that can never pass away. The kingdom of heaven has its King, the Sovereign God, who has eternally been the King of His people. Although the Israelites had God as their King, they were determined to have *"a king like the other nations"* (I Sam. 8:20). *I Sam. 12:12—"But when you saw that Nahash king of the Ammonites was moving against you, you said to me 'No, we want a king to rule over us'—even though the Lord your God was your king."*

Turning to the subject of the kingdom, there are 66 references to the kingdom of God and 32 references to the kingdom of heaven in the Bible, emphasizing the importance of this subject.

Psa. 145:10–11—"All you have made will praise you, O Lord; your saints will extol you. They will tell of the glory of your kingdom and speak of your might, . . ."

Dan. 7:14—"He was given authority, glory and sovereign power; all peoples, nations, and men of every language worshipped him. His dominion is an everlasting dominion, that will not pass away, and his kingdom is one that will never be destroyed."

Matt. 10:7—"As you go, preach the message: 'The kingdom of heaven is near.'"

In the parables, Jesus proclaims that the kingdom of heaven is present in His own Person and through His word (Matt. 13:3–9, 18–23). The kingdom is present because Jesus Christ, the King is present. Its growth is inevitable (Matt. 13:24–30), because God is sovereign and His will for His kingdom is certain to be fulfilled. It is present now, but not in its fullness, for the final manifestation of the kingdom will occur when Christ comes again in all His glory (Matt. 25:31–36). However, the presence of the kingdom in this world forever controls the course of human life and human history (Matt. 13:24–30, 33). When the Son has accomplished his

Chapter Seven

rule, then He will return the kingdom to the Father (I Cor. 15:23–28).

When Jesus said that his kingdom was not of this world, He meant that it was not derived from earthly authority but from God; it is not to be like a human or earthly kingdom. It is a kingdom that we must enter with childlike simplicity (Mk. 10:15), *"Truly I say to you, whoever does not receive the kingdom of God like a little child shall not enter it."* The kingdom is one that *we must seek* (Matt. 6:33), "but *seek first his kingdom and his righteousness and all these things will be given to you as well." (Matt. 6:33)*. In addition, it is a kingdom that is only for the *"born again"*, who alone can *"see"* and *"enter"* the kingdom (Jn. 3:3, 5), *"Unless one is born anew, he cannot see the kingdom of God . . . unless one is born of water and the Spirit, he cannot enter the kingdom of God."*

The *purpose of the kingdom* is the *redemption* of all mankind and delivering them from the powers of evil (I Cor. 15:23–28). Therefore, His kingdom is the redemptive rule of God in Christ, defeating Satan and the powers of evil and delivering mankind from corruption. It brings to mankind *"righteousness and peace and joy of the Holy Spirit"* (Rom. 14:17). By entering the kingdom, the righteous are delivered from the powers of darkness (Col. 1:13), *"For he has rescued us from the dominion of darkness and brought us into the kingdom of the Son he loves."* In addition, Jesus included in what we call the Lord's Prayer, that constant Christian desire, *"Thy kingdom come, thy will be done, on earth as it is in heaven."*

Now, there are seventeen parables that address this theme: seven (7) parables in which this message is *primary* and ten (10) that treat the theme as a *secondary* message. From these parables, a composite definition of God's kingdom begins to emerge.

The Kingdom of Heaven (primary)
2–1. The Parable of the Mustard Seed
2–2. The Parable of Leaven
2–3. The Parable of the Treasure Hidden in the Field
2–4. The Parable of the Pearl of Great Value
2–5. The Parable of the Net Thrown into the Sea
2–6. The Parable of the Training for the Kingdom

God's Hidden Treasures

    2–7. The Parable of the Workers in the Vineyard
            The Kingdom of Heaven (secondary)
    2–8. The Parable of the Sower
    2–9. The Parable of the Wheat and the Tares
    2–10. The Parable of the Good Samaritan
    2–11. The Parable of the Approaching Hour
    2–12. The Parable of the Lost and the Found
    2–13. The Parable of the Response to Authority
    2–14. The Parable of God-given Talents
    2–15. The Parable of the Wicked Tenants
    2–16. The Parable of the King's Wedding Feast
    2–17. The Parable of the Ten Virgins

The sheer number of parables illustrates the importance of this theme. In their totality, these seventeen parables provide a comprehensive view of the *kingdom of heaven*. In presenting these parables, Jesus asked, *"Have you understood all this?"* And the disciples answered *"yes."* Then Jesus told them, *"every scribe who has been trained for the kingdom of heaven is like a householder who brings out of his treasure what is new and what is old."* The question for the world today is the same that Jesus asked each of His disciples, *"Have you understood what I am telling you?"*

Since the majority of the parables dealing with this theme are from Matthew 13, it is important to examine this Gospel and understand the events that precede these parables. The sequence, leading up to Chapter 13, is: in Chapter 1, there is the genealogy of Jesus which lays the legal claim to the kingdom; Chapter 2 presents the birth of Jesus, the visit of the Wise Men, the flight to Egypt, and the return to Nazareth; Chapter 3 describes the baptism of Jesus; Chapter 4 outlines the Temptation in the Wilderness and the preparation for His earthly ministry; Chapter 5–7 includes the Beatitudes and the Sermon on the Mount; Chapter 8 describes the physical healing of the sick and the spiritual healing by the forgiveness of sin; Chapter 9 continues the healing episodes and the increasing opposition of the Pharisees; Chapter 10 begins with His calling the disciples and instructing them; Chapter 11 begins with these words, *"And when Jesus had finished instructing His twelve*

Chapter Seven

disciples, he went on from there to teach and preach in their cities."; Chapter 12 includes further teaching to the disciples and warnings to the rulers of Israel; as well as the request from the scribes and Pharisees for a sign—and Jesus tells them, *"An evil and adulterous generation seeks for a sign; but no sign shall be given to it except the sign of the prophet Jonah. For as Jonah was three days and three nights in the belly of the whale, so will the Son of man be three days and three nights in the heart of the earth. The men of Nineveh will arise at the judgment with this generation and condemn it; for they repented at the preaching of Jonah, and behold, something greater than Jonah is here."*

So this progression through the first 12 Chapters leads to the dramatic change that is about to occur in chapter 13. For Jesus has determined that the Jews are an *evil and adulterous* generation who will be condemned, even by the *"men of Nineveh who repented at the preaching of Jonah."* And Jesus said that One greater than Jonah in now in their midst. Since the Jews had rejected His signs and His direct claims to deity, then Jesus began to speak in parables. That is the context in which these series of parables on the kingdom of heaven take place. Also from this time on, Jesus spoke to His disciples and to the Jews, in general, primarily in parables.

2–1. The Parable of the Mustard Seed: Matt. 13:31

"Another parable he put before them, saying, 'The kingdom of heaven is like a grain of mustard seed which a man took and sowed in his field; it is the smallest of all seeds, but when it has grown it is the greatest of shrubs and becomes a tree, so that the birds of the air come and make nests in its branches."

Commentary

Jesus begins this parable by describing the kingdom of heaven *"like a grain of mustard seed"*; *"it is the smallest of all seeds . . . but it*

God's Hidden Treasures

is the greatest of shrubs and becomes a tree, so that the birds . . . come and make nests in its branches." The smallest to God is still monumental to us. It is difficult to appreciate or understand the sovereignty of God that takes the smallest and most insignificant and creates great wonders. There is nothing *"small"* in the mind of God; there is nothing *"small"* in His plans; there is nothing *"small"* about the people He calls to service. The mustard seed is almost insignificant; very few people would notice it. Yet, this *small* seed has invisible power; and the lesson is that it is not the *"size"* of a seed that counts; instead, it is the content and the certainty of what it will produce. The smallest can produce the greatest. Now consider the insignificant mustard seed. It can produce a tree that can reach a height of 12–15 ft; therefore, it is symbolic of the growth of anything from seemingly insignificant beginnings. In that regard, it is symbolic of the kingdom of heaven; it is symbolic of the seemingly powerless apostles of Jesus Christ; and it is most certainly an example of our faith. Jesus told the disciples, "*I tell you the truth, if you have faith as small as a mustard seed, you can say to this mountain 'move from here to there', and it will move. Nothing will be impossible for you."* (Matt. 17:20) The apostles would seem to be "powerless" in their world; they would not appear to have the strength or wisdom to overturn nations and principalities, but they did in the power of the Holy Spirit. The great events in Christianity are like mustard seeds; it doesn't appear possible that a small group of insignificant fishermen and tax collectors, the disciples of Jesus Christ, would be able to turn the world rightside up. What they did confounded the Jews and Gentiles, and all of civilization since that time. What they preached appeared to be foolishness, impractical, unreal, not to be trusted. The world wonders even today: what is all this teaching of loving your enemies, of praying for those who persecute you, of the idea that the meek shall inherit the earth, that you should hunger and thirst after righteousness, that you are blessed when you are persecuted for righteousness sake. Isn't that contrary to human nature! It is contrary to human nature, but it is not contrary to the divine nature of a child of God.

Chapter Seven

The apostle Paul must have appeared to be a *"mustard seed"*, for how could one man, in poor health, with great opposition, turn the world rightside up for Jesus Christ. Martin Luther must well have been a *"mustard seed"*, for how could one seemingly insignificant German monk stand so confidently before Charles V, Emperor of the Holy Roman Empire, and the Papal authorities and be faithful to the Word of God. And there have been countless *"mustard seeds"* for the Gospel of God who have given their lives for the kingdom of heaven. God is calling you and me to be such a *"mustard seed."* Never doubt the power of what God has given, even to the least of us. That is our constant prayer; *"Thy kingdom come, on earth as it is in heaven."* This mustard seed, this kingdom will flourish!

Summary of Biblical Themes
Theme 2—The Kingdom of Heaven

The kingdom appears insignificant and unimportant to most human beings, but God's *"seed"* will produce a great *"tree."* His kingdom and His sovereignty may be difficult to *"see"* and to *"understand."* Its coming is inevitable; it will be fully consummated at the Last Day in all its glory.

Summary of God's Revelations

His revelations include the two truths: first, *the kingdom presently appears small and hard to discern. However, it will become a great tree that all will see;* second, *in the same way that the kingdom appears small and insignificant, so does the King, Jesus Christ, who had been humiliated, rejected, and crucified by lawless men.*

2–2. The Parable of Leaven: Mk. 13:33

"He told them another parable. 'The kingdom of heaven is like leaven which a woman took and hid in three measures of flour, till it was all leavened.'"

God's Hidden Treasures

Commentary

Jesus presents another parable concerning the apparent insignificant. Like the mustard seed, leaven (or yeast) is small, but it can have a powerful influence in making bread, which is one of the necessary staples for life. As leaven is critical to the life-giving power of the bread, in the same way, the gospel and the kingdom are essential for *spiritual life.*

Leaven can be viewed from two perspectives. For example, In the New Testament (Matt. 16:12), Jesus uses the term *"leaven"* as applied to either good or evil. In the negative sense, leaven can be viewed as the presence of evil. In Matthew 16:12, Jesus spoke severely of the *leaven of the Pharisees, which is the teaching of the Pharisees,* beware of that leaven. Paul also wrote (I Cor. 5:6), *"Do you not know that a little leaven leavens the whole lump?"* What Paul is warning everyone against is that a little "evil", a *"little false teaching"* can spread corruption throughout the entire church. Luke used the phrase of leaven *"which is hypocrisy"* (Lk. 12:1), a *"poison"* to be avoided by disciples.

In this passage, Jesus used the term, *"leaven"*, to describe the catalytic, all-permeating power of the kingdom of God, transforming the whole world as leaven transforms a lump of dough. Leaven symbolizes the penetrating power of the gospel. Without the *"leaven"*, there is no *"good"* bread. Without the leaven, evil dominates the world. The leaven appears insignificant, but so might the gospel appear to the world. People wonder: "How can the gospel of Jesus Christ change the way the world thinks, acts and lives?" And the answer is, because the *"gospel is the power of God for salvation to every one who has faith." (Rom. 1:17)* Leaven, the gospel, in the hands of the Holy Spirit will change lives.

Finally, It is interesting that Jesus stated that the leaven was *"hidden in three measures of flour."* This is a significant, for *"three"* stands for what is solid, real, substantial, complete and entire. The dough is complete; it requires only the addition of the *leaven* for God's complete redemption to be fulfilled. The *leaven* that will produce that completeness is the cross and the gospel. Both parables (the mustard seed and the leaven) address the secular perception that the kingdom of God is insignificant. The Christian church

Chapter Seven

must ensure that this view does not prevail. The question is, when there is evil rampant in the world, where is the leaven? Where is the penetrating power of the gospel? Where is the church?

The bread is dependent on the leaven. In the same way, the world is dependent on the gospel. In the Final Judgment, all will be *"leaven"*, that is, there shall be no more evil in God's world; His kingdom will be complete, holy and purified; all evil will be cast into the pit of eternal punishment.

Summary of Biblical Themes
Theme 2—The Kingdom of Heaven

The kingdom is like *leaven*, which has a tremendous influence on all that encounter it. As leaven is to the bread, the kingdom provides purity in an otherwise evil world.

A secondary message is:
Theme 10—The Final Judgment

The important phrase here is *"until it was all leavened."* The kingdom will have holy and purified people; evil will not be present.

Summary of God's Revelations

This parable presents one truth: *The kingdom is like leaven, gradually bringing light and righteousness into a darkened world.*

**2–3. The Parable of the Treasure Hidden in a Field:
Matt. 13:34,44**

"All this Jesus said to the crowds in parables; indeed he said nothing to them without a parable. This was to fulfil what was spoken by the prophet: 'I will open my mouth in parables, I will utter what has been hidden since the foundation of the world.' . . . 'The kingdom of heaven is like treasure hidden in a field, which a man found and

God's Hidden Treasures

covered up; then in his joy he goes and sells all that he has and buys that field.'"

Commentary

In this parable, Jesus spoke of that which has been *"hidden since the foundation of the world"*; in the same light, Jesus speaks of the kingdom of heaven being like a *"treasure hidden in a field."* There is obviously a relationship between those phrases, "which is *hidden* since the foundation of the world" and "the kingdom of heaven." Their relationship is important to understand. Jesus talks about *"hidden things"*, a term which is used throughout the Old and New Testament.

Job 28:11, we read of bringing "hidden things to light."

Psalm 78:2, we read of "I will utter things hidden from of old . . ."

Daniel wrote concerning God—how "He revealed deep and hidden things."

Matthew 13:35, Jesus said that "I will utter things hidden . . ."

Romans 16:25, Paul wrote "of the mystery hidden for long ages past."

Colossians 2:3, Paul wrote of Jesus Christ, "in whom are hidden all the treasures . . ."

So what are these *"hidden things"*? Well, *"hidden"* relates to the will and activity of God in relation to man's ability to see and experience. *"Hidden"* refers to keeping something secret; to cover so that not a trace of anything can be seen; to put a veil over the object to disguise something. God can *"hide"* treasures from His people, until the fullness of time in which they can be revealed, e.g. the coming of the Messiah. Then what is *"hidden"* will be revealed; but that does not mean that all people will recognize the *"hidden."* For example, at the Incarnation, many in Judah must have seen the star, but the star was *"revealed"* only to a few shepherds *"abiding in their fields, keeping watch over their flocks by night"* and the angel chorus gave them the revelation. However, the true meaning of that star was obviously hidden from many who must have seen it. Again they saw, but did not perceive. In this sense, *"hidden"* could mean the message of redemption, the gospel that might be hidden. In many ways, hearts and minds are blinded and

Chapter Seven

even hardened to the purpose of God, and the message remains hidden until God determines to reveal it. So what are hidden are His will, His purpose, and the power and purpose of His redemption of all creation. It is revealing the way of salvation, not through the law or through works, but through grace and faith. What may be hidden may be the light of the gospel or the light of the glory of God or the means by which God would achieve the redemption of the righteous. The kingdom of God is hidden, as is the revelation by which God would redeem His creation. In the fullness of time, God reveals His will and His purpose to His people. That is the sense of *"hidden."*

In this parable, there is a *treasure, a field* and the treasure *is hidden in a field.*

What is a treasure? How do we identify the treasures in this world and in our lives? Treasures are to be sought, valued, protected, and, in many instances, a treasure may be worth dying for. Our priorities and our faith determine our treasures. Jesus speaks of the priorities in our lives, by *"laying up for ourselves treasures in heaven" (Matt. 19:21).* Jesus also made a clear distinction between the man who *"lays up treasures for himself and is poor towards the things of God."* (Lk. 12:21). Regarding treasure, consider the following passages:

Proverbs 2:4—*"if you seek it (the Word of God) like silver and search for it as for hidden treasure."*

Isa. 33:6—*". . . and he will be the stability of your times, abundance of salvation, wisdom and knowledge; the fear of the Lord is his treasure."* Here "fear" means reverence and awe.

Lk. 12:32-34—Listen to what Jesus said, regarding treasures—*"Fear not, little flock, for it is your Father's good pleasure to give you the kingdom . . . provide yourself . . . with a treasure in the heavens that does not fail, where no thief approaches and no moth destroys. For where your <u>treasure is, there will your heart be also</u>."*

2 Cor. 4:7—*"But we have this treasure in earthen vessels, to show that the transcendent power belongs to God and not to us."*

1 Tim. 6:17-19—*"Again do not be rich in the things of this world, the uncertain riches, but be rich in the things of God, who furnishes us with everything to enjoy."*

God's Hidden Treasures

In these passages, the Word of God is a treasure; the fear (the awe and reverence) of the Lord is a treasure; a heart open to God is a treasure; the gospel is a treasure; the things of God are treasures, for He supplies us with every treasure. He opens the window of heaven to pour out His treasures among His people. Those are but a few examples of treasures that God has for those who love Him.

So what is the *field*? The field is many things; it is the world where God sows His Word; it is also the hearts of God's people, who *"hid"* the Word in their hearts. The treasure is *"hidden"* in the world. Why is the treasure hidden in the field? Why doesn't God make the treasure so obvious and so apparent that everyone will *"see"* it and *"seek"* it? Well, He has, but the treasure, the gospel, still is a stumbling block to the Jews and foolishness to the Greek so what is open and obvious is not apparent and welcomed by all. God's message is not *"hidden"* to those who are His children; it is revealed to the *"born again"*; it is hidden to the non-believer. God has only the greatest love and desire for His people. Paul understood that, and so should we. *"We know that in everything God works for good with those who love him, who are called according to his purpose."* (Rom. 8:28). *Christians are to relinquish every physical possession in order to obtain this great spiritual treasure, the Kingdom of Heaven.*

Summary of Biblical Themes
Theme 2—The Kingdom of Heaven

The greatest treasures in life are not physical possessions, but they are love, joy, peace, eternal life, and fellowship with God. That is the character of the kingdom. When God and His righteousness are evident in our lives, then the kingdom is ours.

Chapter Seven

A secondary theme is:

Theme 4—The Christian Character

Christians are to discover this treasure, "sell" all our possessions and buy this treasure, hidden in the field. Once we have bought it, we must make it available to others that they would know the richness of the kingdom of God.

Summary of God's Revelations

This parable contains four truths: *the kingdom of heaven is priceless; every thing we "own" is like filthy rags compared to the kingdom; the only possession worth owning is the kingdom of heaven; there is joy in obtaining the kingdom.*

2–4. The Parable of the Pearl of Great Value: Matt. 13:45–46

"Again, the kingdom of heaven is like a merchant in search of fine pearls, who, on finding one pearl of great value, went and sold all that he had and bought it."

Commentary

It is interesting to see the continuous progression from the small and insignificant, but powerful, to the kingdom now defined as an object of great value. This parable further emphasizes the point of the previous one; that a treasure is found (this time a *"pearl"*) and the merchant sold *all* that he had and bought it. Jesus reiterates a message that He wants to be certain will be understood; we must be willing to give up everything for the kingdom of God. In many aspects, this parable has many similarities to the previous parable (2–3). This parable introduces a series of questions. *For example, who is the merchant? What is this "pearl of great value"? Why would this merchant sell all that he had and buy this particular pearl? What would he do with the pearl after he bought it?* Let us briefly examine these questions.

God's Hidden Treasures

Who is the merchant? Jesus said, *"the kingdom of heaven is like a merchant."* This is a mystery, that the kingdom is like a merchant. The kingdom does not find, and sell, and buy the pearl. The merchant does. So the only way this can be understood is in regard to the people of God to whom the kingdom is given. Therefore, the merchant is every Christian who *seeks first* the kingdom of God. The kingdom is like a merchant.

What is the *"pearl"* that we seek? Is that pearl the gospel? Would you "sell" everything you own to possess that pearl? Paul reminds us (Col. 3:2)—*"Set your mind on things that are above, not on things that are on earth."* The gospel reflects the values, the standards, the will and the mind of God.

What is the pearl of great value? Now, pearls were a measure of great wealth in New Testament times; the merchant in this parable was searching, apparently for the purest and largest pearl in the world. Such a pearl might well satisfy those who are consumed with a desire for wealth and material pleasure. If, however, the search is for that which would provide the greatest pleasure, enjoyment, and long lasting satisfaction, then the *"pearl"* might well be the *gospel message, the richness of salvation through faith alone in Christ alone*; perhaps that is what the *"merchant"* was seeking. Perhaps that is what every Christian merchant is seeking.

Why would this merchant sell all that he had and buy this particular pearl? It is quite likely that the merchant would *"sell"* all the "baggage" that interferes with our fellowship and relationship with God. The kingdom of heaven is for those who have divine priorities, who *"sell"* material possessions and *"buy"* this great treasure. Paul taught that we are weighed down by the possessions of this world.

What would he do with the pearl after he bought it? The pearl becomes the merchant's *possession*. The pearl may represent many things; Jesus does not restrict its definition. If the pearl is the kingdom of heaven, then its *owner* will enjoy eternal life. If the pearl is the gospel, then the *owner* would want to share this great treasure with others. If the pearl is Jesus Christ, then the merchant has found the greatest *treasure* to be imagined which he could enjoy personally as well as share with others. Whatever the pearl is, it is

Chapter Seven

his. When he shares his pearl, then his pearl becomes their pearl; his knowledge and commitment to the kingdom becomes their commitment to the same. His commitment to Jesus Christ can lead others to a like commitment. He would seek the lost, so that they would know the richness of the pearl, this gospel about the kingdom of God. Nothing in life is as highly prized as this pearl.

Summary of Biblical Themes
Theme 2—The Kingdom of Heaven

Pearls are among the most highly prized jewels; in the same way, the gospel is the most prized message; the kingdom of heaven is the most prized possessions. The gospel is a *"hidden"* pearl that is not fully appreciated in the modern world. People rarely search for the gospel; most are not prepared to give all their possessions for it. Yet it is the most precious and eternal possession that God has for His people.

Theme 4—The Christian Character

Jesus emphasized that the *"pearls"* that God has provided for His people are to be obtained at any cost. He is calling for a greater commitment, a greater sacrifice for the blessings that only God can provide. These pearls are fellowship with God, joy in that fellowship, love beyond understanding and peace that knows no bounds.

Summary of God's Revelations

God now reveals the tremendous value of the kingdom of heaven. The command is: sell everything we own and buy this pearl of great value; The truth is: there is no possession as valuable as the kingdom of heaven.

2–5. The Parable of the Net Thrown into the Sea: Matt. 13:47–50

"Again, the kingdom of heaven is like a net which was thrown into the sea and gathered fish of every kind; when it was full, men drew it

God's Hidden Treasures

ashore and sat down and sorted the good into vessels but threw away the bad. So it will be at the close of the age. The angels will come out and separate the evil from the righteous, and throw them into the furnace of fire; there men will weep and gnash their teeth."

Commentary

This parable is part of the great sequence of parables in Matthew chapter 13. Here Jesus uses the analogy of a *net, the sea, the fishermen*, and the net *"thrown"* into the sea. So what do these signify? The *"net"* is that which is used to *"catch"* the *"fish."* Jesus told Peter that He would make him a fisher of men. That is what Jesus wants to do with each of us. Now, fish are not naturally drawn to the net, and, if caught in the net, they will generally make every effort to escape. However, all the fish will be hauled into God's net.

Let us summarize what has been said in these parables of the kingdom. The kingdom is like a mustard seed, like leaven, like a treasure hidden in a field, like a merchant in search of fine pearls and now like a net thrown into the sea.

In this parable, the *"net"* is the kingdom; the net could also be the gospel that men will accept, reject, or ignore, and some will fight with all their might to escape the *"net."*

The *"sea"* is God's creation; it is His sovereign domain.

The *fishermen* are those to whom the gospel is entrusted and who *"throw"* the net of God into the sea, in an *evangelistic effort* to take the gospel of God to everyone.

The net is *"thrown"* into the sea because God takes a direct and active role in the redemption of His creation. In like manner, we are to be active in evangelism as well. In addition, God has equipped all whom He has called to take the gospel to the ends of the earth until all hear the good news of salvation through faith alone in Christ alone.

This parable gives insight into the universal character of the kingdom of heaven (Rom. 1:5) *"among all the nations"*. There will be every type of person in the *"net"*, but there will be a sorting out of the *"good"* and the *"bad"* fish. This parable states that the *"fish"* will be sorted *"at the close of the age."* *"The angels will come out and separate the evil from the righteous, and throw them into the furnace*

Chapter Seven

of fire" (Matt. 13:49). God's *"net"* will be thrown into the *"sea"* (His world), and the net will be full of every type of *"fish."* However, the *good* and the *evil* will co-exist until the end of the age. At the end of the age, there will be accountability, and the *good* will be welcomed into the kingdom while the *evil* will perish in outer darkness. The kingdom of God is a universal kingdom: it is God's perfect patience that none should perish, but that all should be saved. However, the *"net"* thrown by God and by the disciples of Jesus Christ will *"catch"* many people who will resist the gospel. Immediately following, Jesus is walking by the Sea of Galilee, and He sees Simon Peter and Andrew, his brother. Seeing that they were fishermen, Jesus told them to follow Him and *"I will make you fishers of men." (Matt. 4:19)*.

In many respects, this parable has many similarities to two other parables: The Parable of The Wheat and the Tares and the Parable of The Sheep and the Goats.

Summary of Biblical Themes
Theme 2—The Kingdom of Heaven

God takes an active role in bringing everyone into His kingdom. It is God's perfect patience that none should perish (2 Pet. 3:9). Therefore, He *"throws a net"* into the sea, bringing all *"the fish"* (good and evil) into His net.

There are three *secondary* themes:
Theme 4—The Christian Character

Christ calls us to be fishers of men; therefore we must seek the lost and be active in evangelism. As God throws a net into the sea, Christians are called to do the same. We *"fish"*; God will judge and sort the good from the bad.

Theme 6—Evangelism

Christians are to be *fishers of men*; like God, we are to be active, not passive, in seeking the lost. The church is to be an active fellowship, taking the gospel of God to a world in desperate need of redemption.

God's Hidden Treasures

Theme 10—The Final Judgment

At the Final Judgment, the fish will be brought into the net, and they will be separated, the evil from the righteous. The evil will be thrown into the furnace of fire and men will weep and gnash their teeth; the righteous will spend eternity with their Creator.

Summary of God's Revelations

This parable has a promise, a truth and a warning. The promise is: *all fish (good and bad) will be brought into the nets; the good will enter the kingdom.* The truth is: *God will judge everyone.* The warning is: *wicked and evil people will be cast into the furnace of fire.*

2–6. The Parable of the Training for the Kingdom: Matt. 13:52–54

"'Have you understood all this?' They said to him, 'Yes.' And he said to them, 'Therefore every scribe who has been trained for the kingdom of heaven is like a householder who brings out of his treasure what is new and what is old.' And when Jesus had finished these parables, he went away from there, and coming to his own . . ."

Commentary

Interspersed in these parables of the kingdom are a question and a statement. The question is *"Have you understood all this?"* The statement is that *"every scribe who has been trained for the kingdom of heaven is to bring out of his treasure that which is new and that which is old."* This is not a parable in the normal sense, but it is so closely connected as to command our attention. Let us examine the question and the statement.

The question is one that we should continually ask ourselves as we read each of these parables. Do we understand what we have just read? However, that is a question that applies not only to the parables, but to every word of Scripture. God does not want us to

Chapter Seven

be ignorant regarding His commands, His promises, His truths and His warnings. Understanding the Word of God is essential for living the Christian life. Paul notes the limits of human understanding by noting that the peace of God surpasses it (Phil 4:7). The pagans act as they do because they are *"darkened in their understanding"* (Eph 4:18). On the other hand, John affirms that understanding has been made possible by the revelation of Jesus (1 John 5:20).

Dr. Carl Schultz, (<u>Evangelical Dictionary of Biblical Theology</u>), provides considerable insight into the Biblical basis of understanding. Understanding is seen as a gift of God (Dan. 2:21) and it is to be prayed for (Psa. 119:34). In answer to the question, *"Where shall wisdom or understanding be found?"* the response is, *"God alone knows"* (Job 28:12,20,23). It also results from the study of the divine Law and Commandments (Ps 119:104). Hearing is no assurance of understanding (Dan 12:8). In the Bible, understanding is related to distinguish, or it is perceptive insight with the ability to judge. Understanding is associated with wisdom (Prov. 2:3). On the one hand, God is the most important object of understanding (Isa. 43:10; Jer. 9:24); although, He is beyond human understanding (Isa. 40:28). The meaning of the word, understand, is to gain insight into something. It can designate a positive quality as when the scribe concurred with Jesus about loving the Lord with *"all your understanding"* (Mark 12:33) and in Paul's prayer for the Colossians where he couples it with *"spiritual wisdom"* (Col. 1:9). It can be the means of understanding an important truth (2 Tim 2:7) or the Lord's will (Eph 5:17). There is also a negative quality to this word. Jesus used parables because of his audience's failure to understand (Matt 13:13).

In the Parable of the House on the Rock (page 60), Jesus speaks of the wise as those who hear His words and do them. That is the evidence of understanding. Christ invites us to come to Him for understanding. Jesus told us that we receive not, because we ask not. It is the will of Christ that all who read and hear the word should understand it. It is therefore good for us, when we have read or heard the word, to examine ourselves, or to be examined. In addition, Jesus told us that He has sent the Holy Spirit, who is

God's Hidden Treasures

our teacher and who will lead us into all truth. Our prayers to the Spirit of God will equip us with all understanding. The apostle John wrote 16:13), *"when the Spirit of truth comes, he will guide you into all the truth."* Then understanding will be complete.

Now we turn to the statement that the scribes are to bring out of his treasure that which is new and that which is old. In the context of this parable, the scribe does not fit the usual definition of a pharisaic teacher of the law, because Jesus refers to this *"scribe"* as one who is a *disciple of Jesus Christ*. This *"scribe"* has learned the truth of what Jesus has been teaching. He is a teacher of the *"law of Christ"*, and he *"has been trained for the kingdom of heaven."* This person has a storehouse of knowledge from which he can draw truths, both *"old and new."* It is *"new"* in the sense that, with the coming of Jesus Christ, the content of the treasure will be revealed; it is *"old"* in the sense that it was always present in the mind of God, but kept secret from the foundation of the world so that every Christian will be a teacher of the *"law of Christ"* and be prepared to instruct others in the ways and truths of God. The Holy Spirit leads us into all truth and understanding. This Spirit of God will reveal what we need to know for the ministry to which God has called and equipped us.

Among the questions that must be addressed are: *How are they to be trained for the kingdom? What is the content of what should be in the training? What is the purpose of the training?* They are to be trained in love, with perseverance, with commitment and with understanding. The *content* of the training should consist of the Word of God, the life of prayer, and the power of the Holy Spirit. They are to understand the significance of being a disciple so that they can be witnesses, ambassadors, fishers of men and shepherds. The *purpose* of the training is that everyone would be "... complete, equipped for every good work." (2 Tim. 3:16). "For we are his workmanship, created in Christ Jesus for good works, which God prepared beforehand, that we should walk in them." (Eph. 2:10)

Summary of Biblical Themes
Theme 2—The Kingdom of Heaven

To serve the kingdom of heaven requires training; in that way, Christians will be a faithful *"scribes"* to all whom we serve. That

Chapter Seven

training requires that we be in the Word of God, on our knees in prayer, and moving in the power of the Spirit.

A *secondary* theme deals with
Theme 4—The Christian Character
One measure of the Character of a Christian is the desire, a passion, to seek and to know the truths of God, and to make them evident in our lives. No truth can be considered fully understood until it has been *applied and active* in our life. We have a rich "*storehouse*", filled with "*great treasures*", the Word of God, a life of prayer and the power of the Holy Spirit. We are to make God's truths known in God's world.

Summary of God's Revelations
This parable has one truth; *we are to be trained for the kingdom. We should be open to the training, and we should be prepared to train others.*

Jesus leaves now the parables of the *character* of the kingdom of heaven and directs our attention to *the workers*.

2–7. The Parable of the Workers in the Vineyard: Matt. 20:1–16
"*For the kingdom of heaven is like a householder who went out early in the morning to hire laborers for his vineyard. After agreeing with the laborers for a denarius a day, he sent them into his vineyard. And going out about the third hour he saw others standing idle in the market place; and to them he said, 'You go into the vineyard too, and whatever is right I will give you.' So they went. Going out again about the sixth hour and the ninth hour, he did the same. And about the eleventh hour he went out and found others standing; and he said to them, 'Why do you stand here idle all day?' They said to him, 'Because no one has hired us.' He said to them, 'You go into the vineyard too.'*

God's Hidden Treasures

And when evening came, the owner of the vineyard said to his steward, 'Call the laborers and pay them their wages, beginning with the last, up to the first.' And when those hired about the eleventh hour came, each of them received a denarius. Now when the first came, they thought they would receive more; but each of them also received a denarius. And on receiving it they grumbled at the householder, saying, 'These last worked only one hour, and you have made them equal to us who have borne the burden of the day and the scorching heat.' But he replied to one of them, 'Friend, I am doing you no wrong; did you not agree with me for a denarius? Take what belongs to you, and go; I choose to give to this last as I give to you. Am I not allowed to do what I choose with what belongs to me? Or do you begrudge my generosity?' So the last will be first, and the first last."

Commentary

After His teachings about the *"new world, when the son of man shall sit on his glorious throne . . ."* (Matt. 19:28), Jesus returns to further teaching regarding the kingdom of heaven, this time with emphasis on the <u>workers</u> in the *"vineyard of God."* Although Israel was considered God's vineyard. The world has always been His vineyard.

The facts of the parable are simple and direct. The *"householder"* went out early in the morning and hired men to work in the vineyard and promised to pay them a denarius for the day. About the third hour (9:00 am), he went out again and promised to pay *"whatever is right."* He went again at the sixth, ninth, and the eleventh hour, again hiring workers for the vineyard. When evening came, he began to pay the workers, beginning with those who had been hired in the eleventh hour, paying them a denarius. He proceeded to do this with all the workers, paying a denarius also to those whom had been hired first. Those who had been hired first grumbled against the *householder* because they believed that they deserved more pay, particularly since they had *"borne the burden of the work and the heat of the day."* But the householder answered them with three questions, *"Did you not agree to work for a denarius? Don't I have a right to do what I want with my own money? Are you envious because I am generous?"*

Chapter Seven

It is significant that we recognize God's desire to bring workers into His vineyard. God offers us an opportunity to share in His plan for redemption. It is also interesting that no worker refused the call; instead, they all welcomed the opportunity. *The harvest is plentiful, the laborers are few, pray the Lord of the harvest to bring workers into the fields.*

Now before getting into the content of the text, we must first all recognize that there are not degrees of Christian workers. It is a dangerous thought that some Christians are better than others; that some Christians deserve greater honor than others. It is dangerous to consider that popes and bishops and certain Christian leaders rank higher in God's perspective than other Christians. Humility is an essential characteristic of all Christians. It is interesting that John Calvin left instructions that he be buried in an unmarked grave, because he did not want any special attention directed to him after his death. There is no differentiation in the mind of God. Instead, He has told us that we are His royal priesthood; we are all members of God's household; we are all children in His family; He loves us all the same, for God is generous and impartial.

There is so much work in the vineyard, and God calls everyone, including you and me. Did you ever wonder: why more people don't work for God? Don't they know how badly they are needed? Is it because we are too busy with the cares of this world and that we are more concerned with our interests than in the affairs of God? In the kingdom of heaven, the *"wage"* that we agree to work for is *eternal life*. That should be incentive enough; but most people are not convinced that God is *"serious"*, that there is another life, that there will be a final judgment, that there is a kingdom of heaven.

Further, for all those who work for God, should we be telling God how *"great we art"* rather than how *"Great Thou art"*? Should we be demanding greater *"pay"*, more recognition, and more attention because, in our minds, we believe that we have done more than others? Can't God distribute His *resources,* as He believes is right? Are Christians envious because some have been working in the vineyard, in Christian ministries, longer than others? Does that qualify them for greater reward? Don't Christians understand that all will receive the same reward?

We must keep in mind that work in the kingdom is a direct reflection of our faith. Salvation is not through works; but through faith alone in Christ alone. (Eph. 2:8). However, we are called to do good works; we have been empowered to do that, and so it is evident that we show our faith by bearing much fruit, which is the measure of our good works.

And so Jesus concludes, *"the last shall be first and the first shall be last."* Now this is the same phrase that Jesus used in Matthew 19:30 in His teaching about the end of the age. What Jesus is saying is that there is no difference in God's timetable, if you've worked a short time or a long time, the pay for *"working"* in His vineyard is the same, which *is eternal life*. Eternal life is an absolute term. The first are the same as the last, and the last are the same as the first. Christians should give thanks that God is generous and impartial.

Summary of Biblical Themes
Theme 2—The Kingdom of Heaven

God calls everyone to work in His kingdom; the *"pay"* is eternal life, the same for all. He is the "householder"; the kingdom is His; we are His faithful workers, welcoming everyone with whom we labor.

Jesus treats three additional themes in this parable:
Theme 1—The Character of God

God *"goes out"* to invite the *"idle"* to *"work"* in His vineyard. He pays everyone equally and generously, regardless of the time they work. He is *just, generous and impartial*.

Theme 3—The Alternatives in Life

Everyone is invited to work in, and for, God's kingdom. Those who work for God bring great joy and glory to God. We can serve and rejoice, or refuse and complain.

Theme 4—The Christian Character

We are to be *willing workers*, whenever God calls us. If He calls us early or late; we should respond and *work diligently*. We

Chapter Seven

should welcome our *"wages"* for He is a just God. Further, we should *rejoice that our fellow workers are many and equally rewarded.*

Summary of God's Revelations

This parable has messages regarding promises, truths and warnings. The promises are: *God calls everyone to work in His vineyard; He promised fair and equitable treatment for all. He chooses us.* The truth is: *God treats everyone equally and impartially.* The warning is: *Christians should not be concerned with the time spent in God's service; greater time is not the basis of greater reward.*

Ten (10) parables contain a *secondary* theme, regarding the Kingdom of Heaven:
2–8. *The Parable of the Sower*
2–9. *The Parable of the Wheat and the Tares*
2–10. *The Parable of the Good Samaritan*
2–11. *The Parable of the Approaching Hour*
2–12. *The Parable of the Lost and the Found*
2–13. *The Parable of the Two Sons*
2–14. *The Parable of God-given Talents*
2–15. *The Parable of the Wicked Tenants*
2–16. *The Parable of the King's Wedding Feast*
2–17. *The Parable of the Ten Virgins*

Summary of Biblical Themes
Theme 2—The Kingdom of Heaven

These 17 rich and powerful parables provide a summary picture of the kingdom of heaven. From these parables, we conclude:

In the Parable of the Mustard Seed, Jesus tells us that the kingdom may appear <u>small and insignificant</u>, but it will astonish many by its growth and the protection it offers.

In the Parable of the Leaven, the leaven will produce great and unexpected power, for <u>leaven symbolizes the penetrating power of the gospel</u> in this world.

In the Parable of the Treasure Hidden in a Field; the kingdom is no longer small and hard to discern; the kingdom is the <u>great treasure</u>

God's Hidden Treasures

that all should seek. The treasure is the gospel; the field is the world.

In the Parable of the Pearl of Great Value, the kingdom is of such value that some wise people will <u>sell</u> all their possessions and *"buy this great treasure."*

In the Parable of the Net Thrown into the Sea, in which all the fish caught in the net, will be brought ashore and the <u>good and the bad will be justly rewarded</u>.

In the Parable of the Training for the Kingdom, training is required, so that all Christians will be *"good scribes"* who will <u>preserve all godly truth and equip others in righteousness</u>.

In the Parable of the Workers in the Vineyard, the kingdom is like a householder, <u>who hires workers</u> for his vineyard. God gives eternal life to all faithful workers.

In the Parable of the Sower, the kingdom is reserved for those who have <u>good soil</u> in which the good seed can take root and bear much fruit.

In the Parable of the Wheat and Tares, they will co-exist until the End of the Age; at which time, the <u>wheat</u> will be gathered <u>into the "barn"</u>—*the kingdom*; the <u>tares will be burned</u>.

In the Parable of the Good Samaritan, Jesus reminds us that <u>the mark of the kingdom will be mercy</u>, for God blesses the merciful.

In the Parable of the Approaching Hour, Jesus is telling us that it is the Father's *good pleasure to give us the kingdom.* However, Jesus also warns us to be <u>prepared for the coming of the Son of man, at a time that is unexpected</u>

In the Parable of the Lost and Found, Jesus is reminding us that the kingdom is a place where there is <u>rejoicing over one sinner who repents</u>. God seeks the repentant sinner.

In the Parable of the Two Sons, those who "speak" through actions best serve the kingdom. We <u>serve God, not only with our lips, but also in our hearts</u>.

In the Parable of the God-given Talents, the kingdom is "home" for those who have <u>used</u> to the fullest, <u>the talents that God has given them</u>.

Chapter Seven

In the Parable of the Ten Virgins, the kingdom awaits those who have <u>prepared for the Second Coming of Christ</u>. We must be vigilant and be ready for His return.

In the Parable of the Wicked Tenants, the kingdom is for those who recognize and acknowledge the sovereignty of God and who <u>produce "good fruit."</u>

In the Parable of the Wedding Feast, many will be invited, but the invitation must be <u>willingly accepted</u>; we must also be clothed in garments of righteousness.

From these parables, there are three distinctive characteristics regarding the kingdom of heaven. The first characteristic deals with the *appearance* of the kingdom; the second with the *actions* relating to the kingdom; the third relate to the *people* called to be inheritors of the kingdom.

Regarding the *appearance* of the kingdom, we can see that it is almost insignificant, but it can produce great effects; it is like a hidden treasure; it is like a pearl of great value.

Regarding the *actions* relating to the kingdom, the kingdom is like a net thrown into the sea; it is like a vineyard, where all are invited to work for the householder; it is a kingdom which rejoices over one repentant sinner.

Relating to the *people* associated with the kingdom, the kingdom will only flourish in good soil; the people must learn to grow up among evil but with the knowledge that the wheat and tares will be separated in the Final Judgment; it is a kingdom in which mercy dominates; it is for people who await eagerly the coming of the King; it is a kingdom in which our actions speak louder than words; it is a kingdom for which we must be constantly prepared; it is a kingdom in which we must use our God-given talents for the ministry of the kingdom; it is a kingdom to which we are invited in the Wedding Feast of Christ and His church.

Summary of God's Revelations
Theme 2—The Kingdom of Heaven

From these seventeen parables, Jesus provides a rich series of God's promises, truths and warnings. The promises are; *the good "fish" will be welcomed into the kingdom; God gives fair and equitable*

God's Hidden Treasures

treatment for all who work in His vineyard; The truths are: *all fish (good and bad) will be brought into the nets; presently the kingdom appears small and hard to discern, however, it will become a great tree; the kingdom will permeate the entire world, just like leaven, until everyone is aware of the Bread of Life; the kingdom of heaven is priceless; we sell everything we own and buy this pearl of great value; there is no possession in the world as valuable as the kingdom of heaven; God treats everyone with equality and impartiality.* There are two warnings: *all evil fish will be cast into the furnace of fire; Christians must recognize that time in our ministry is not a measure of our rewards in heaven. It is the quality of that time and the manner in which we show love for God and our neighbor that is more important.*

Such are the rich messages regarding the Kingdom of Heaven.

CHAPTER EIGHT

Theme 3—The Parables of The Alternatives in Life

"See, I have set before you this day life and good, death and evil . . . choose life . . ." (Deut. 30:15, 19)

"Choose this day whom you will serve . . ." (Joshua 24:14)

"Set your mind on things that are above, not on things that are on earth." (Col. 3:2)

One of the classic marks of the Bible is that it sets before the world alternatives to do good or evil. The parables also present situations that demand decisions and present alternatives in life. Jesus talks of two houses (Matt. 7:24–27), two sons (Matt. 21:28–32), two types of virgins (Matt. 25:1–13) and two servants (Matt. 18:23–35). The Bible constantly presents examples of the alternatives; the following examples provide evidence:

- *In the Garden, the choice for Adam and Eve (Gen. 3:5)* This choice between obedience and rebellion is what God has presented to His people since the beginning of Creation. He told Adam *"not to eat of the fruit of the tree of knowledge in the Garden."* Adam had a choice; he could obey or rebel.
- *Moses, the choice before the people (Deut. 30:15–20),* "I have set before you this day life and good, death and evil . . . I call heaven

God's Hidden Treasures

and earth to witness against you this day, that I have set before you life and death, blessing and curse . . ."
- Joshua (Joshua 24:14f) sets before the people the choice to *"fear the Lord and serve him"* and *"if you are unwilling to serve the Lord, choose this day whom you will serve."*
- Elijah, before the priests of Baal (I Ki. 18:15–20–40) challenged the people who were *"limping with two different opinions."* (18:21). *"If God is God, then serve God; if Baal is god then serve Baal. But don't continue to go limping between two decisions."*
- In Psalm 1, David sets before the people the alternatives to life. Verses 1–3 tell of a righteous man who is like *"a tree planted by streams of water, in all that he does, he will prosper."* The wicked *"are like the chaff which the wind drives away . . . the way of the wicked will perish."*
- Paul, two options: the things of heaven or of this world (Col. 3:1–2), *"If then you have been raised with Christ, seek the things that are above . . . Set your minds on things that are above, not on things that are on earth."*

Jesus recognized the depth of the problems we face; He understood the alternatives in the Christian life and so Jesus provides us with guidance on how to judge and deal with life's secular temptations. He shows us how to recognize the alternatives and to choose those that are consistent with the will and purpose of God. Jesus also warned the world that the greatest alternative was the question of accepting or rejecting Him as Savior and Lord.

The Alternatives in Life are discussed in eleven (11) parables; one that is *primary*; ten (10) parables present this as a *secondary* theme. The *primary* parable is:

    3–1. The Parable of the Wheat and the Tares

The ten parables in which this is a *secondary* message are:

    3–2. The Parable of the House on the Rock
    3–3. The Parable of the Two Debtors
    3–4. The Parable of the Sower
    3–5. The Parable of the Good Samaritan
    3–6. The Parable of the Poor, Rich Fool
    3–7. The Parable of the Lost and Found

Chapter Eight

3–8. The Parable of the Rich Man and Lazarus
3–9. The Parable of God-given Talents
3–10. The Parable of the Wicked Tenants
3–11. The Parable of the Ten Virgins

3–1. The Parable of the Wheat and the Tares: Matt. 13:24–30

"Another parable he put before them, saying, 'The kingdom of heaven may be compared to a man who sowed good seed in his field; but while men were sleeping, his enemy came and sowed weeds among the wheat, and went away. So when the plants came up and bore grain, then the weeds appeared also. And the servants of the householder came and said to him, 'Sir, did you not sow good seed in your field? How then has it weeds?' He said to them, 'An enemy has done this.' The servants said to him, 'Then do you want us to go and gather them?' But he said, 'No; lest in gathering the weeds you root up the wheat along with them. Let both grow together until the harvest; and at harvest time I will tell the reapers, Gather the weeds first and bind them in bundles to be burned, but gather the wheat into my barn.'"

Commentary

This parable follows close on the heels of The Parable of the Sower. It is a further example of the judgment upon good and evil, as well as an example of the alternatives in life, consistent with The Parables of the Two Houses, the Parable of the Sheep and the Goats, etc. In this parable, there are six key components; the *man who sowed good seed, the sleeping men, the enemy who sowed weeds, the servants, the harvest,* and *the final judgment.*

First, the *man who sowed good seed* is God, for He is forever sowing His seed, which is His Word. Isaiah 55:11 states that it is *"his word that comes forth from his mouth . . . and it will not return to him void, until it accomplishes the purpose for which he sent it."* What is the *"good seed"*? It is the gospel; it is His commandments, His promises, His truths and His warnings, as well as His will for His people. For these are the good things that God wants to take root and to bring forth an abundant crop. The wheat represents the *"good crop"* that God has planted, and which He will nourish until the fullness of the harvest.

Second, the *men who were sleeping* are those who are not faithful in protecting God's *"vineyard."* It could be you and me, who fail to fulfill the stewardship responsibility that God has entrusted to us. *Sleep* means failure to be attentive, to be idle, at rest, to ignore sin and to be unconcerned with the evil around us. It is like the five virgins, who considered that there was always time to prepare for the coming of the Bridegroom (Matt. 25:1–13). Jesus said that the tares were sown *"while men were sleeping."* What do you think Jesus meant (13:25)? Is this case similar to that of the ten virgins; some awake and others not ready for the coming of the kingdom? Does this give you the impression that, when the children of God are *"asleep"*, then Satan seizes that opportunity to produce evil in the world? Does this send a message to the church today that *"sleeping"* does not mean literally so. However, it is that time, when we have the appearance of being alert and awake, but not fulfilling His will in this world.

Third, the *enemy who sowed the weeds* is *Satan,* who is constantly trying to tempt us, deceive us, and disrupt those who are trying to live a godly and faithful life. Why are there *"enemies"* to those who are trying to "produce a good crop"? The enemies are those who do not honor God as God, do not serve Him, who ignore and reject His Son—and do all they can to prevent the spread of the gospel. Wherever God's people are called to produce a good crop (e.g. in evangelism), Satan will be active. As long as God's people are inactive, Satan *"rejoices"* when he finds us sleeping. However, our positive actions for Christ will produce Satan's response and, most certainly, his antagonism. Like the wheat, we will face opposition, trials and suffering. The question is; how do we respond to opposition and are we prepared to suffer for His name's sake? Our faith demands it; our witness encourages it; our eternal life depends on it. The "enemy" is our enemy and God's

Chapter Eight

enemy. Jesus said that *"if they persecuted me, they will persecute you."* (Jn. 15:20) This is what they also did to the prophets.

Fourth, the servants are those who labor faithfully in God's vineyard. They seek to fulfill God's will; they are concerned that evil has come into the householder's field.

Fifth, the harvest is the end of the age, that time in which all will be called before the throne of grace and judgment to give an accounting of what has been done or not done.

Sixth, the final judgment will separate good and evil, the wheat into the barns, the tares to be destroyed by fire. All will be judged according to faith demonstrated and the works accomplished as evidence of that faith. Notice that Jesus said, it is *my* barn; this is evidence that we shall be with Him in eternity.

Now this parable outlines the difference between wheat and tares. The tares are the power of evil, which is among the wheat and actively trying to prevent the growth of the good wheat (*the sons of the kingdom*). The tares are not idle; they are intent on disrupting and destroying, if possible, the wheat. However, the tares will be permitted to grow along with the wheat until the End of the Age; then the tares will be separated from the wheat and cast into the fire for eternal destruction. This is a great truth, that, until the end of the age, there will always be evil present among the good. There will always be the sons of Satan, trying to destroy the good crop, which is *the good fruit* (Jn. 15:8), that the children of God are called to bear. Now tares are a poisonous grass, which closely resembles wheat, but with a slightly smaller seed. It looks enough like wheat to deceive the untrained; and the tares were usually left in the fields until harvest time, then separated from the wheat during winnowing. Jesus says that it is difficult to distinguish between wheat and tares, and we need to examine them carefully to know the difference. God knows the difference; He will separate the good from the evil, and the tares will be destroyed, to spend eternity without God.

If we are good fruit, the question is, are we prepared to grow along side the tares and continue to be the good wheat? Can we remain faithful and be a good crop, when evil is all around us? Are

God's Hidden Treasures

we prepared to remain awake and prevent the *"enemy"* from sowing even more evil among the good crop? Or are we "asleep" to the problems and issues of this age? Finally, are we prepared to suffer, to the same degree that Christ suffered, in order that a good "crop" may be produced?

God permits the evil in this world to grow along with the good. This is a great mystery; we would like to think that He would destroy evil, just as soon as it appears. But that has not been the history of God's people, and it will not be the case with us. He, in His justice, will separate the good and evil at the end of the age in His timing and according to His will. But God knows the heart of people (I Sam. 16:7) and what we would consider as tares will not be so with Him. In that way, we must recognize Saul of Tarsus, who may have appeared to be a *"tare"* is really one of the great seeds upon which God has built His church. The church, in which both good and evil may well exist, must always be alert to the prospect that the *"enemy"* will sow a poisonous crop among the good fruit that God is producing in His people. We must recognize the *"tares"* in this world, permit them to grow along with us, but knowing also that the evil in this world will eventually be judged and condemned.

Summary of Biblical Themes
Theme 3—The Alternatives in Life

Jesus tells us that there is good and evil present in most situations and in every *"field."* The Bible warns that the Antichrist will appear to be so much like Christ that many will have difficulty in telling them apart. Evil can be so attractive and can look so much like good that it is hard to distinguish. The alternative that we have is to be either wheat or tare. The wheat is genuine; and although the tares look like wheat, they are counterfeit. We also need to understand that those who are with us physically are not always with us spiritually.

Three other themes are presented in this parable:

Theme 1—The Character of God

God constantly seeks the sinner, that none should perish (2 Pet. 3:9). Therefore He permits the tares to grow along with the

Chapter Eight

wheat. The patience and forbearance of God is without measure. It is possible in God's grand design that what are tares today can become wheat tomorrow. He can make "*tares*" into wheat; perhaps He did that with you and me.

Theme 2—The Kingdom of Heaven

The kingdom of heaven is reserved for genuine fruit or grain; no *evil and poisonous* people will enter His kingdom.

Theme 10—The Final Judgment

Jesus tells us that, at the Final Judgment, the wheat and the tares will be separated; the tares will be gathered and *"burned"*, but the *"wheat will be gathered into His barn"* to spend eternity with God.

Summary of God's Revelations
Theme 3—The Alternatives in Life

There is a truth and a warning in this parable. The truth is: *good and evil (wheat and tares) will grow together until the Final Judgment. Then they will be separated.* The warning is: *while we sleep, the enemy sows weeds. While the church sleeps, evil will dominate.*

The ten (10) parables in which this is a *secondary* theme are:
- 3–2. *The Parable of the House on the Rock*
- 3–3. *The Parable of the Two Debtors*
- 3–4. *The Parable of the Sower*
- 3–5. *The Parable of the Good Samaritan*
- 3–6. *The Parable of the Poor, Rich Fool*
- 3–7. *The Parable of The Lost and Found*
- 3–8. *The Parable of the Rich Man and Lazarus*
- 3–9. *The Parable of God-given Talents*
- 3–10. *The Parable of the Wicked Tenants*
- 3–11. *The Parable of the Ten Virgins*

Summary of Biblical Themes
Theme 3—The Alternatives in Life

These parables identify the opportunities and challenges that each will face in this life. The alternative we choose will determine our eternal destiny.

God's Hidden Treasures

In the Parable of the Wheat and the Tares, we are called to be *"wheat"*, not *"tares"*; we are to be <u>faithful, not counterfeit</u>. At the final Judgment, the *"wheat"* will be stored in God's heavenly *"barn."* The *tares* will be burned, to spend eternity outside the Presence of God.

In the Parable of the House on the Rock, Jesus said that we could build on the <u>rock</u> or on the <u>sand</u>. The foundation determines the quality of our eternal home.

In the Parable of the Two Debtors, we need to recognize our sinful nature and seek the mercy of God. If we repent, He will forgive us. We can <u>confess or deny</u> our sin.

In the Parable of the Sower, the <u>type of</u> *"soil"* that we are determines the extent to which we will receive the *"seed"* and bear much fruit.

In the Parable of the Good Samaritan, the alternatives include <u>ignoring or showing mercy</u> to those in need. We can *"pass by on the other side,* ignoring a person in distress; or we can be like that Good Samaritan, who met the needs of a stranger.

In the Parable of the Poor, Rich Fool, Jesus emphasizes that <u>material riches are not true riches</u>; the things we cannot see (love, fellowship, peace, joy, etc.) really have eternal value, far greater than anything this world has to offer.

In the Parable of The Lost and Found, we can <u>seek the pleasures of this world</u>—or we can *"come to our senses"* and realize how much more wonderful it is to <u>spend our life in service to God</u>. The younger son initially sought his earthly inheritance; at the end of the story, he found his true inheritance was life with his Father.

In the Parable of the Rich Man and Lazarus, we can ignore the poor and destitute at our very door, while we <u>enjoy a self-centered life of material wealth—or we can reach out and help them now</u>. There will be the judgment, even after death, when God will bless and reward the poor, and the selfish rich will receive justice. In that Final Judgment, we will be held accountable for what we have done and not done.

In the Parable of God-given Talents, we <u>can *"multiply"* those God-given talents</u> for His interest and His glory. Or we can *"bury"* <u>our</u>

Chapter Eight

talent—<u>never use it for God's purpose</u>—and never produce the bountiful results that God means for us to achieve in this life.

In the Parable of the Wicked Tenants, we can have different views of the wealth of this world, either as <u>stewards of God's "vineyard"</u> or under the mistaken belief that <u>this Creation is ours</u>. Such beliefs ignore and dishonor the Sovereign God. If we believe that we are God's stewards, then we shall take great care that His vineyard reflects His values and standards and the vineyard produces great fruit.

In the Parable of the Ten Virgins, we can live, <u>prepared</u> for His coming or <u>unprepared</u>, and suffering the consequence of the decision for our unpreparedness.

The alternatives in life are that we can be either true or counterfeit; we can build on the firm foundation or on the sand; we can be grateful and righteous or ungrateful and self-righteous; we can ignore those in need or show mercy to the stranger *by the side of the road;* we can lay up treasures on earth or we can be rich in the things of God; we can fail to understand the difference in sin, whether it be obvious sin or hidden sin; we can be self-centered, ignoring the suffering of those at our doorsteps, and we suffer the judgment of neglect of those in need; we can use our talents for God's glory and His kingdom or we can bury our God-given talent; we can have a vision of Christian stewardship or we can believe that the things of this world are ours; we can be prepared or unprepared for the Second Coming of the Lord of all creation. We can enjoy eternal life or eternal damnation. These are representative of the alternatives in life that every one will face.

Summary of God's Revelations
Theme 3—The Alternatives in Life

There is both a truth and a warning in this parable. The truth is: *good and evil will grow together until the Final Judgment.* The warning is: *while we sleep, the enemy sows weeds. While the church sleeps, Satan spreads evil. The church must never "sleep."*

CHAPTER NINE

Theme 4—The Parables of The Christian Character

"He has shown you, O man, what is good; and what does the Lord require of you but to do justice, and to love kindness and to walk humbly with your God." (Micah 6:8)

"Love your enemies and pray for those who persecute you." (Matt. 5:44)

"But seek first his kingdom and his righteousness, and all these things will be yours as well." (Matt. 6:33)

"All men will know that you are my disciples if you love one another." (Jn. 13:35)

The fact that Jesus devoted eighteen (18) parables to this theme is a measure of its importance. In addition, the Bible in general has set before the world a mixture of the characteristics of non-believers and believers, over and above those listed in the parables.

Listen to these *negative* characteristics in the life of a non-believer. Paul wrote (Rom. 1:25, 29–31), *"They exchanged the truth of God for a lie, and worshiped and served things rather than the Creator . . . They have become filled with every kind of wickedness, evil, greed and depravity. They are full of envy, murder, strife, deceit and* malice. They are gossips, slanderers, God-haters, insolent, arrogant and boastful; they invent ways of doing evil; they disobey their parents; they are senseless, faithless, heartless, ruthless." Paul presents another litany of evil in Galatians 5:19–21, *"The acts of the sinful nature are obvious; sinful immorality, impurity and debauchery; idolatry and witchcraft; hatred, discord, jealousy, fits of rage, selfish ambition, dissensions, factions and envy; drunkenness, orgies and the like. I warn you . . . that those who live like this will not inherit the kingdom of God."* God says that this is not the way we are to live. In the Sermon on the Mount, Jesus summarized the sins of the nations and said, *"Do not do as they do."* (Matt. 6:8)

Conversely, on a *positive* note, Paul outlines the desirable characteristics of the Christian life, in at least two passages. In Gal. 5:22, Paul wrote, *"But the fruit of the Spirit is love, joy, peace, patience, kindness, goodness, faithfulness, gentleness and self-control."* Paul adds to these characteristics in other epistles (*e.g. Colossians 3:12–15*), *"Put on then, as God's chosen ones, holy and beloved, compassion, kindness, lowliness, meekness and patience, forbearing one another; as the Lord has forgiven you, so you also must forgive. And above all these put on love . . . And let the peace of Christ rule in your hearts . . . And be thankful."*

Therefore, these parables present further insight into the positive and negative characteristics of the Christian Life.

The Christian Character (Primary)

4–1. The Parable of the Two Debtors
4–2. The Parable of the New Wine and Old Wineskins
4–3. The Parable of the Good Samaritan
4–4. The Parable of the Poor, Rich Fool
4–5. The Parable of the Barren Fig Tree
4–6. The Parable of Humility
4–7. The Parable of the Great Banquet
4–8. The Parable of the Unworthy Servant
4–9. The Parable of the Response to Authority
4–10. The Parable of God-given Talents

Chapter Nine

The Christian Character (Secondary)
4–11. The Parable of the House on the Rock
4–12. The Parable of the Unworthy Servant
4–13. The Parable of the Friend at Midnight
4–14. The Parable of the Approaching Hour (Wedding Feast)
4–15. The Parable of the Lost and Found
4–16. The Parable of Workers in the Vineyard
4–17. The Parable of the Wicked Tenants
4–18. The Parable of the Ten Virgins

Many of these primary parables end with summary statements of great significance. For example, the first one ends, *"Your faith has saved you; go in peace."* The third provides insight regarding mercy, *"Which of these three, do you think, proved neighbor to the man who fell among the robbers? He said, 'The one who showed mercy on him.' And Jesus said to him, 'Go and do likewise.'"* The fourth closes with a warning to be rich towards God, *"But God said to him, 'Fool! This night your soul is required of you; and the things you have prepared, whose will they be?' So is he who lays up treasure for himself, and is not rich toward God.'"* The fifth identifies the need to be fruitful, *"And if it bears fruit next year, well and good; but if not, you can cut it down."* The sixth reminds us of humility, *"For every one who exalts himself will be humbled, and he who humbles himself will be exalted."* The seventh tells of God's anger against those who refuse His gracious invitations, *"For I tell you, none of those men who were invited shall taste my banquet."* The tenth warns of the rewards for faithfulness and the punishment for unworthy service, *"For to every one who has will more be given, and he will have abundance; but from him who has not, even what he has will be taken away. And cast the worthless servant into the outer darkness; there men will weep and gnash their teeth."*

With that introduction, let us examine the eighteen parables.

God's Hidden Treasures

4–1. The Parable of the Two Debtors: Lk 7:36–50

"One of the Pharisees asked him to eat with him, and he went into the Pharisee's house, and took his place at table. And behold, a woman of the city, who was a sinner, when she learned that he was at table in the Pharisee's house, brought an alabaster flask of ointment, and standing behind him at his feet, weeping, she began to wet his feet with her tears, and wiped them with the hair of her head, and kissed his feet, and anointed them with the ointment. Now when the Pharisee who had invited him saw it, he said to himself, 'If this man were a prophet, he would have known who and what sort of woman this is who is touching him, for she is a sinner.' And Jesus answering, said to him, 'Simon, I have something to say to you.' And he answered, 'What is it, Teacher?' 'A certain creditor had two debtors; one owed five hundred denarii, and the other fifty. When they could not pay, he forgave them both. Now which of them will love him more?' Simon answered, 'The one, I suppose, to whom he forgave more.' And he said to him, 'You have judged rightly.' Then turning toward the woman he said to Simon, 'Do you see this woman? I entered your house, you gave me no water for my feet, but she has wet my feet with her tears and wiped them with her hair. You gave me no kiss, but from the time I came in she has not ceased to kiss my feet. You did not anoint my head with oil, but she has anointed my feet with ointment. Therefore I tell you, her sins, which are many, are forgiven, for she loved much; but he who is forgiven little, loves little.' And he said to her, 'Your sins are forgiven.' Then those who were at table with him began to say among themselves, 'Who is this, who even forgives sins?' And he said to the woman, 'Your faith has saved you; go in peace.'"

Commentary

While a dinner guest of a Pharisee, named Simon, *"a woman of the city, who was a sinner . . ."* (7:37), came to Jesus where He was sitting. A woman of the city literally denotes a prostitute. Standing behind Him, the woman was weeping, and she wet His feet with her tears, wiped them with her hair, and kissed His feet, *and "anointed them with the ointment."* This is quite a scene, a prostitute doing such a thing. The Pharisee clearly disapproved of the actions of both Jesus and the woman—*"If this man (Jesus) were a*

Chapter Nine

prophet, . . . he would have known what sort of woman this was touching him, for she is a sinner." This Pharisee thought: Jesus, how could you associate with sinners? How could you let a woman like this touch you? Although Simon spoke to himself, Jesus knew what was in Simon's heart and *"answering him" told* Simon this parable about a certain creditor *"having two debtors." When they could not pay, he forgave them both."* Then Jesus asked Simon, *"Which of them will love him more?"* And Simon answered, *"The one . . . to whom he forgave more."* Jesus said—that is right. *"Simon,"* said Jesus, *"I entered your house, and you gave me no water to wash my feet; but this woman, whom you call a sinner, washed my feet with her tears and wiped them with her hair. You gave me no kiss, but she has not ceased to kiss my feet . . . Therefore I tell you, her sins, which are many, are forgiven, for she loved much; but he who loves little is forgiven little."* Jesus tells the woman two things, *"your sins are forgiven"* (7:48) and *"Your faith has saved you; go in peace."* (7:50). Jesus forgave her sins and acknowledged her faith. Fear will not produce faith; power will not produce faith; oppression will not produce faith; only love will produce faith. Her faith had saved her. Salvation through grace and faith is one of the great messages of the New Testament. Paul captures this thought in (Eph. 2:8), *"For by grace you have been saved through faith."* Our response in faith to the grace of God is the foundation of our salvation.

This woman was moved to tears by her sin; I have to wonder, when was the last time I was moved to tears by my sins?

Jesus did four things; He forgave her sin; He acknowledged her faith; He told her that faith leads to salvation; He told her that she had found peace and reconciliation with God.

Notice that Simon, the Pharisee, said *"if this man (Jesus) were a prophet . . ."* Recall also that this is what Satan said to Jesus in the wilderness, *"If you are the Son of God . . ."* (Matt. 4:3). Many in the world have always been saying to Jesus, *"if you are . . ."* Simon does not honor Jesus as God; but the woman does, there was no *"if"* about it. Jesus Christ is God Incarnate; Jesus Christ is the Son of God; Jesus Christ is God the Son. It is interesting to notice also in the parable that there is no evidence that the debtors ever asked for their debts to be cancelled. Yet God did it, and does it still without being asked, for God knows the heart of the truly repentant. In addition, there is no evidence that God was thanked for forgiving the debt. There is no evidence of request; there is also no evidence of thankfulness. What does that tell us about God? It tells us that God knows the heart. Sometimes *showing repentance* is far more significant than expressing it verbally. This woman was quietly, but deeply repentant. Deep down inside, with words too deep to utter, she recognized this Jesus of Nazareth as the One who could and would forgive her sins. On the other hand, Simon considered himself righteous and viewed the woman as a sinner. He did not express repentance, because, as a Pharisee, he believed that he had been a faithful keeper of the law, with no reason or need to repent. He undoubtedly believed that any debt he owed God was insignificant. So, in his self-righteous spirit, Simon ridiculed and condemned the woman, while overlooking the sin (failing to honor God) in his own heart. Unfortunately that could be the case with many today. When we repent, God forgives. *Repentance* is a key message throughout the parables. Later Jesus will tell the people, then and now, that *"unless you repent, you shall all perish."* (Lk. 13:3)

As long as the log is in our own eye, we can't see too well. In addition, it is dangerous to criticize the log in another's eye. *Forgiveness* is a vital Christian characteristic, because God is a God of forgiveness. We are forgiven people, and we come to God on our knees, *"Forgive us as we have forgiven others."* In one way or another, the lack of forgiveness can destroy the Christian church, for it can become an angry, cynical and depressed ministry. The only way to learn how to forgive is to come to the cross of Jesus Christ. *"Forgive them for they know not what they do."* On the cross, Christ forgives before we ever ask.

Repentance is our act; forgiveness is God's response. However, forgiveness is also our response to any who have offended us. *Forgiveness must be freely* given, it must be *full in application*. There is only one sin too great to be forgiven, and that is blaspheming the Holy Spirit, for such an act is rejection of Jesus Christ as God In-

Chapter Nine

carnate. If we blaspheme the Holy Spirit, then we are blaspheming God the Father and God the Son. Such actions blaspheme the basic doctrine of the Trinity; God in Three Persons.

Further, our forgiveness must be *final* in that we carry no bitterness in our spirits. The failure to forgive prevents us from being faithful witnesses. In forgiveness, we reflect the love of God through us. In Jer. 31:31f, God said, *"I will forgive their sins and I will remember them no more."* Our forgiving is a measure of being in His image. We have the evidence of the cross as the perfect expression of forgiveness. In addition, forgiveness is a divine characteristic; we would not know how to forgive unless we know Jesus Christ as Lord and Savior.

Let us return to the parable. Why would you forgive any debt for no reason? For God, it is simple; the debt is forgiven by grace, simply because God loves His people. In addition, God has said that the greater the debt, the greater the forgiveness. Without being asked, God runs to save and welcome home His people. This is almost a prelude to the story of the prodigal son. Look and see how much God loves sinners who repent! This theme is going to be repeated over and over again, particularly in the *Parable of the Lost and the Found* (the lost sheep, the lost coin, and the two lost sons).

Christ, God Incarnate, died on the cross for those in debt to sin. He didn't ask how much we owed; He didn't ask if we would be grateful; He just did it. Forgiveness is one of the most noble of Christian characteristics for it is an expression of the active working out of love. The expression of *repentance by the woman was an expression of her love*. The forgiveness of sins by God is an expression of His love. Love is redeeming a debt without being asked. That is God's nature; that should be ours. Everyone is in debt to Jesus Christ; "He paid a debt he did not owe; we owed a debt we could not pay" (Amazing Grace). Faith saves us; the result is peace and reconciliation with God. Kissing the *"feet"* is repentance; that is seeking forgiveness and that is what the woman did. God forgives because He loves the repentant.

God's Hidden Treasures

Summary of Biblical Themes
Theme 4—The Christian Character

Scripture tells us that we have been *"ransomed and redeemed"* (Matt. 20:28; Gal. 4:5) by Christ alone. To Him and to Him alone, we acknowledge our sin, repent of them and call upon God for mercy and restoration. To Him and to Him alone, we express our gratitude for such a wonderful redemption and the recognition of the enormous price God paid to redeem us. As He forgives us, we are called to forgive, *"forgive us as we have forgiven others."* Forgiveness, a noble Christian characteristic, is a measure of our life in the image of God. In addition, this parable speaks to the Christian characteristic of repentance; that is truly the mark of a Christian heart.

This parable treats two other themes:

Theme 1—The Character of God

Forgiveness is one of the great characteristics of God discussed in the beginning of chapter 6 (page 57). His great virtue must be our great virtue. God forgives without even being asked, and so should we. The righteous God forgives sinners; repentant redeemed sinners must forgive others.

Theme 3—The Alternatives in Life

We can be judgmental and critical of others without understanding the *"log in our own eye"* (Matt. 6:4). We can be like Simon, the Pharisee, ignoring our sinful nature, expressing self-righteousness or we can be like this woman, who repented of her sins and came to pay honor to the One to whom she repented and from Whom she received forgiveness. Her faith saved her; her faith led to peace, and God eternally forgives the repentant sinner.

Summary of God's Revelations
The Characteristics of the Christian Life

This parable has a promise, a truth and a warning. The promise: *If you love much, your sins are forgiven much.* The truth: *true repentance leads to forgiveness and salvation; love is the evidence of repentance.* The warning; *if you love little, you are forgiven little.*

Chapter Nine

4–2. The Parable of New Wine and Old Wineskins: Matt. 9:14–17

"Then the disciples of John came to him, saying, 'Why do we and the Pharisees fast, but your disciples do not fast?' And Jesus said to them, 'Can the wedding guests mourn as long as the bridegroom is with them? The days will come, when the bridegroom is taken away from them, and then they will fast. And no one puts a piece of unshrunk cloth on an old garment, for the patch tears away from the garment, and a worse tear is made. Neither is new wine put into old wineskins; if it is, the skins burst, and the wine is spilled, and the skins are destroyed; but new wine is put into fresh wineskins, and so both are preserved.'"

Commentary

This parable is too often overlooked; this is unfortunate for it has great messages and a great theme. First, it is interesting to examine the context in which this parable is given. In chapter 8, Matthew covers a broad range of subjects: *healing* (of people with leprosy, others who are demon-possessed) in fulfillment of Isaiah 53:4, the *faith* of the centurion, the *cost of discipleship* and the *calming of the storm* on the Sea of Galilee. This unusual sequence of events leads to this parable. In some regards, chapter 8 contains examples of the ministry of Jesus Christ, as He heals, as He recognized faith, as He calmed the natural elements and as He calls others to follow Him. Chapter 9 begins with further healing and the calling of Matthew and then we come face to face with this parable. The disciples of John asked Jesus a question regarding fasting, *"why do . . . your disciples not fast?"* Jesus answered that question about fasting and then moved to a discussion of *"old"* and *"new."* *Fasting* and *newness* will be examined, so that we can understand the connection between these two apparently unrelated subjects.

Now, the first subject deals with *fasting,* *"why do . . . your disciples not fast?"* Now, a few words on fasting is beneficial. Fasting

God's Hidden Treasures

has lost, to some degree, its Biblical basis and understanding. First, fasting is the act of abstaining from food and/or drink as evidence of private or public religious devotion. The purpose of fasting is twofold: *first by fasting, we open ourselves to God and second, we deny the material dimension of life.* Scripture says that man does not live by bread alone. As food and drink signify the physical life, with all its demands and pleasures, their absence permits the things of God to dominate our attention. Fasting represents a denial of the things of this world and expresses a single-minded devotion to God. (Col. 3:2) In general, fasting appears to be an expression of personal devotion linked to three different types of crises: *lamentation, mourning, and petition.* In *lamentation*, fasting is generally associated with confession (Dan 9:3) and the wearing of sackcloth (1 Kings 21:27). In the New Testament, Jesus rebukes the hypocritical Pharisees for disfiguring their faces when they fast (Matt 6:16–18). It became easy, however, for the outward appearance of repentance to take the place of a genuine, inner attitude and thus become an act of hypocrisy. Fasting is also a sign of *mourning*. In the example of the death of Saul, the people *mourned* his passing by fasting (1 Sam 31:13). In addition, fasting was frequently associated with *prayers of supplication*. Before Paul and Barnabas appointed elders for the various churches, they committed them to the Lord with prayer and fasting (Acts 14:23). In all these instances there is the clear implication that fasting is an effective means of making prayers of petition to God.

So, in this parable, Jesus said that this is not now the time for lamenting, mourning, or petitions. The time for fasting will occur after His death on the cross. So Jesus told the disciples of John, my disciples do not fast because *"I am still with them; there will be a true time to fast, when I have returned to my Father."* Now Jesus moves on to the next subject; the old and the new. He speaks of his departure from his disciples as a time of *mourning* when it will be entirely appropriate to fast (Matt 9:14–15).

Notice that Jesus begins the next section with *"And..."*, clearly indicating that the answer to fasting is closely coupled with the message regarding this comparison about an old garment and new wine in old wineskins. So we must understand the connection.

Chapter Nine

First, there is an old garment and an old wineskin; each needs change or renewal, which is to be improved with *new cloth and new wine*. If *"new"* or *"unshrunk cloth"* is attached to an old garment, it will pull away from the old cloth and ruin the garment. In the same way, if new wine is poured into old wineskin, it will cause the wineskin to burst, and the new wine will be lost. *So what is old and what is new?* The *old garment* and the *old wineskin* represent those who believed that Jewish heritage and the Law of Moses would be sufficient for salvation. The Jews considered themselves superior, by physical birth and race, to their pagan neighbors; the Jews believed that they already possessed the fullness of the grace of God. They claimed membership on their own terms. And Jesus said that that is the mark of a self-righteous and rebellious people. God's people must *seek* His righteousness and His kingdom (Matt. 6:33). God desires not self-righteous but *"heart righteous"* people. Jesus tells us that people need a new heart, a new soul, and a new birth. Paul said that true righteousness is of the heart (Rom. 2:28). And, if people are to uphold the Law, then it must be that Law which is written on their hearts. (Rom. 2:15) The old garment and the old wineskin represent the Old Testament, the old agreement, the old covenant. It also represents the old way that Israel defined the chosen people of God. In Romans 9:6–26, Paul outlines the theology that *"not all who are descended from Israel belong to Israel, and not all are children of Abraham because they are his descendants."* The true children of God are those who are righteous as Abraham was righteous. God will call His people from both Jews and Gentiles, *"those who were not my people I will call my people . . . they will be called 'sons of the living God.'"* Further, God said, *"I will one day make a new covenant with the House of Israel; I will write my laws on their hearts; I will forgive their sins and I will remember their iniquities no more (Jer. 31:33f)*

Now in saying that, the Old Testament (its commandments, truths, promises, and warnings) is still valid. On the contrary, the Old Testament sets the stage for the new agreement, the new covenant of grace. The Law and the gospel are eternally in effect. The Law was given to reveal sin; the gospel was given to provide

God's Hidden Treasures

forgiveness of repentant sin. God has made a New Agreement, a New Testament, with His people; in that regard, He has promised the forgiveness of sins. This is the *"good news."* Therefore, the *new cloth* and *the new wine* represent the gospel for the forgiveness of sins, which is to be proclaimed to all nations and for all people who receive Jesus Christ as Savior and Lord. The new garment and the new wine also represent the new covenant that salvation is through faith alone in Christ alone. Therefore a whole new cloth is needed, and a whole new wineskin is essential. The new cloth and the new wineskin are the *"true descendants of Abraham"*, not because of physical birth, but because they are righteous as Abraham was righteous. Jesus told the Jews then, and He is telling us now, that there is a new covenant for the forgiveness of sins that was instituted by His death on the cross. To become people of that new covenant, we must take on a whole new character; we must be a new creation, with a new heart and a new spirit—and a new vision of the kingdom of God. *"If anyone is in Christ, he is a new creation, the old has passed away . . ."* (I Cor. 5:17)

So how do we connect the elements of this parable, this idea of fasting and the concept of the new replacing the old? Well, I think that it is clear. There is to be no fasting until the new agreement, the new covenant for the forgiveness of sin has been put in place. That will be instituted by Christ's death on the cross. Then there will be sufficient time for fasting, when the new covenant is instituted by His death. It ties together very nicely: that the death of Jesus Christ will bring about the fulfillment of the new covenant, the new garment, the new wine which God proclaimed to His people through the prophet Jeremiah (31:31–33)

The gospel, the *"new message"* of salvation through faith alone in Jesus Christ alone comes directly into focus and against the *"old message"*, which the Jews had determined to be faithfulness to the Law. Jesus tells the world that the Law is eternally important, but it cannot save us. We need to be careful here; I am not implying that God has changed His message; instead it is clear that we now begin to understand the message that God had presented from the beginning of time. It is new in the sense that we understand what has been eternally on the heart of God. Jesus said; the new mes-

Chapter Nine

sage for all is that my people who have accepted Me are now under grace; His people are still to obey God's laws for these are eternal, but we are freed to obey it as God originally intended. Jesus Christ is the new wine; we are to be new wineskin. He is the new cloth; we are to be that new garment that gives glory to God.

Summary of Biblical Themes
Theme 4—The Christian Character

Jesus is the New Wine; we are the new wineskins. In the upper room, He said, this is my blood; I am the Perfect Sacrifice, freely given, for the sins of the world. Because of that act, Christians are people under grace; Christians are the true children of Abraham. We uphold the Law, for it is part of God's historical commandment, but under grace, we are free to fulfill the Law as members of a community of grace. We also understand that fasting is a meaningful part of our spiritual lives, when it is necessary for lamenting our sins, for mourning over the evil in this world and for offering prayers of supplication to God who welcomes our prayers. We are to put on the new garment of righteousness.

Summary of God's Revelations
Theme 4—The Christian Character

This parable presents commands, promises and truths. The commands are: *Do not put the new covenant of grace, in the old context of the Law; we must be a new creation.* The promises are: *Christ came to die for the forgiveness of our sins; the cross will institute the new covenant. Christ has died for the sins of the world.* The truths are: *Fast for the right reason; there is now a new covenant for the forgiveness of sins; there is a new standard of salvation by faith in Christ alone, instead of by faithfulness to the Law.*

God's Hidden Treasures

4–3. The Parable of the Good Samaritan: Lk. 10:25–37

"Then turning to the disciples he said privately, 'Blessed are the eyes which see what you see! For I tell you that many prophets and kings desired to see what you see, and did not see it, and to hear what you hear, and did not hear it.' And behold, a lawyer stood up to put him to the test, saying, 'Teacher, what shall I do to inherit eternal life?' He said to him, 'What is written in the law? How do you read?' And he answered, 'You shall love the Lord your God with all your heart, and with all your soul, and with all your strength, and with all your mind; and your neighbor as yourself.' And he said to him, 'You have answered right; do this, and you will live.' But he, desiring to justify himself, said to Jesus, 'And who is my neighbor?' Jesus replied, 'A man was going down from Jerusalem to Jericho, and he fell among robbers, who stripped him and beat him, and departed, leaving him half dead. Now by chance a priest was going down that road; and when he saw him he passed by on the other side. So likewise a Levite, when he came to the place and saw him, passed by on the other side. But a Samaritan, as he journeyed, came to where he was; and when he saw him, he had compassion, and went to him and bound up his wounds, pouring on oil and wine; then he set him on his own beast and brought him to an inn, and took care of him. And the next day he took out two denarii and gave them to the innkeeper, saying, 'Take care of him; and whatever more you spend, I will repay you when I come back.' Which of these three, do you think, proved neighbor to the man who fell among the robbers? He said, 'The one who showed mercy on him.' And Jesus said to him, 'Go and do likewise.'"

Commentary

This is one of the best known and best loved of all the parables and rightfully so. We begin by examining the context in which this parable is presented. It is interesting that Luke presents this parable in the midst of a passage where Jesus has sent out the seventy-two disciples to heal and to preach. They returned, rejoicing that the demons submitted to them in *"your name."* Then Jesus spoke to the Father *"through the Holy Spirit"* about the hidden things revealed to *"little children"* before Jesus turned to His disciples and said: *"blessed are the eyes that see what you see."* What did they

Chapter Nine

"see" that Jesus called them *"blessed"*? It is obvious; they truly saw Jesus Christ, God Incarnate. They were looking into *the face of God*. What a blessing!

Then Luke moves to this parable. It is interesting that Jesus was talking to the disciples, *privately,* when a lawyer stood up to *test* Jesus. These short statements prepare us for the parable that is to follow. Jesus is telling the world to use our *"eyes"* to see the world around us, and such spiritual sight makes a difference for the kingdom of heaven. We are to see with the *"heart"*, not just noticing the physical events around us, but with spiritual *eyes*, to see and perceive the things that God has on His heart. We cannot show mercy or be faithful children of God unless our *"eyes" see* the glory of God, the world around us, and its needs.

This parable introduces six major subjects: *eternal life, inheritance, the law, eyesight, grace and mercy*. Here there is also a sharp contrast between the lawyer, who speaks and lives according to the Law—and the Samaritan who acted according to grace. Christians honor and respect God's Law, but the Law can't save us; we are to fulfill God's Law, but we have the freedom to do so, and we are not in bondage to the Law. However, no human being can fulfill the Law, and the Law was given to reveal sin; the Law is not a means of salvation. The Law leads us to the gospel. The only salvation that we can possibly receive is that which comes through the grace of God. Paul understood this totally, *"For by grace you have been saved through faith . . ."* (Eph. 2:8).

This parable begins with a simple question from this Jewish lawyer: *"what must I do to inherit eternal life?"* Now, in an inheritance, there is someone who has a worthwhile possession that he chooses to bequeath to a beneficiary. To *inherit* means that the possessor of the gift must die, and certain individuals must be identified as the beneficiaries of that death. If the person dies and you are not a beneficiary, their death may have little significance to you. It is evident that the lawyer understands the term *"inherit."* A death must occur for any beneficiary to inherit the possession. So the lawyer asked, *"what must I do to inherit eternal life"?* What is *this eternal life* that he would want to inherit? Well, Jesus tells us

God's Hidden Treasures

that eternal life is the spiritual life that He came to give to us. He said *"I have come that you might have life and have it more abundantly."* Rom. 1:17, *"The righteous shall live by faith."* Jesus was not talking about an endless physical life with its mortal restrictions and boundaries. No, Jesus is telling the world that eternal life is a holy, divine life, lived in fellowship with God. To have eternal life, a person must be *"born again";* he must have experienced a new life in Christ, and the believer becomes a new creation *(2 Cor. 5:17)*. The basis of eternal life is acceptance of Jesus as the Christ (Jn. 20:30).

The lawyer understood the basis of inheritance, and it is obvious that he is confident of his greater intellect than this itinerant teacher from Nazareth. So the lawyer set out to *test* Jesus. Whatever his motivation, the lawyer asked a simple direct question *"what must I do to inherit eternal life?"*

However, Jesus takes his question and turns it around. He asked the lawyer, *"What is written in the Law?"* The lawyer quickly answers, because he knew what every good Jew knew, *"Thou shalt love the Lord your God with all your heart and all your soul and with all your strength and with all your mind"* and *"you shall love your neighbor as yourself."* (Lev. 19:18 and Deut. 6:5). The lawyer was convinced that fulfilling the law is evidence of our love for God; but we know that that is only part of the equation. It is hard to love God and to love our neighbor; anyone who doesn't believe that doesn't really understand the fullness of the dimension of love. Returning to the parable, Jesus said, *"that's correct—do that and you will live."* Jesus said to the lawyer and to the world; love God and love your neighbor, accept Me as the Son of God, than that is the evidence that you are *"born again"* and are a *"new creation"*, then you will inherit *eternal life.*

Now the lawyer had no difficulty with this part about loving God, but he wasn't so sure about this business of "loving his neighbor." Therefore, the lawyer does what so many of us do when faced with the uncomfortable truth; we ask for a definition of terms. And the term the lawyer asked Jesus to define was *my neighbor. Who is my neighbor*? Now, to answer that second question; *who is*

Chapter Nine

my neighbor?, Jesus told a parable that has four characters, a *"man coming down from Jerusalem to Jericho"*; a priest, a Levite, and a Samaritan.

First, the man, coming down from Jerusalem to Jericho, could be any person of any nationality. All we know is that robbers attacked him, and left him to die, *by the side of the road*. In that regard, he is any person and every person, who desperately needs help. A wounded, seriously injured man is too badly injured to help himself, and so he lies there *by the side of the road*, dependent only on someone who would come to his aid. Three people came down that road; perhaps help is on the way. Let us see how the parable unfolds.

Second, a priest. The first thought is that help has arrived. However, that is not the case, for Jesus explains that the priest *saw* the man and *passed by on the other side*. This priest does not even go to the man and determine his condition. Now this may seem surprising since the priests occupied a highly important role in the life of the Jewish nation. In general, the priestly functions were to make God's will known, to teach the law, and to conduct themselves in a morally correct manner. In summary, they were to represent and protect the purity and integrity of Israel. They were ministers of the Lord (Joel 2:17) and mediators between man and God; they were the spiritual leaders of the people. This was the kind of man who saw the injured man by the side of the road. For many reasons, it must be pretty hard to see a person in trouble, badly injured and ignore his need and *"pass by on the other side."* Why would a priest do such a thing? But before we are too harsh on the priest, he may have had a good reason. We are not told why he ignored a fellow human being in misery, but Pharisaic law required that, if a priest ever touched a dead man, he would be required to go to the temple, make an offering, and purify himself, and who knows, this man might die in his arms. Well, his reasons for ignoring this man are not given, and so we can only guess why *"he passed by on the other side."*

Next, a Levite came down the road, but he too *"saw"* the man and *passed by on the other side*. Now if the priest was too "busy" to

God's Hidden Treasures

stop and help this Samaritan, the Levites were even busier. Recall that the Levites were the descendants of Aaron. Later the Jewish priesthood was established, and the Levites became servants of the priests, leaving the priests free for what was considered the *"holy ministry before the tabernacle of witness."* Many of them were scribes and teachers of the Law. So, like the priest, the Levite knew the law, but, like the priest, the Levite also *"saw"* the injured man and *"passed by on the other side."* As with the priest, we don't know why the Levite passed by on the other side.

Now at this point there might be a great tendency on our part to condemn this priest and this Levite with the perspective that we would never do what they did! However, there is a tendency to overstate our position when we are just reading this story. No, in many regards, what they did would appear to many to be perfectly "normal", and that is the tragedy in the story and in our lives today. You see, by all standards, they didn't do anything wrong, according to *the law;* but, at the same time, they didn't do anything right, according to *grace.* The question is: how can we *"see"* a stranger, lying by the side of the road in desperate straits and not do anything about it. You would think that conscience would lead us to do otherwise. And if our conscience didn't bother us as we *"passed by on the other side",* you would certainly think that, in the days that followed, we would think back on what we had done or had failed to do. No, there are many of us today who might not be too much different from that priest and Levite. We may be more like them than we realize or are willing to admit. We might not *see* the man lying in blood by the side of the road, but there are people all over the world who desperately need our love and assistance, and they too are our neighbors.

Finally, a *Samaritan* came down the road. Now, keep in mind that Jesus is telling this parable to a group of Jews, who considered Samaritans to be unclean and impure. Over the years, a great schism had developed between Jews and Samaritans—and the Jews listening to Jesus must have been somewhat shocked when Jesus introduced a Samaritan into the story. All Jews were convinced that Samaritans were a people who had forsaken, at least in the

Chapter Nine

Jewish mind, the commands of God. The Jews referred to Samaritans as "dogs." Jews hated Samaritans, and yet Jesus attributed to this "unclean" Samaritan, a more noble and a greater sense of mercy for a stranger than a Jew. A strange set of circumstances; this was a hard message for the Jews—and even for the world today to grasp. The Jews of that age considered that their neighbor was their fellow Jew, whom they were to love; the pagans, they were permitted to hate. Jesus addressed this dilemma in the Sermon on the Mount (Matt. 5:44). He said that you are to love your enemy and pray for those who despitefully use, or abuse, you. In the vernacular of the Christian life, love includes both our friends and our enemies. Jesus said that, if you love only those who love you, don't the Gentiles, the pagans, do the same? But Christians are called to a wider love, a love that *includes* my enemy. My neighbor is every person, friend or enemy, whom God has put me in a situation to help. This Samaritan showed mercy; the priest and Levite *"passed by on the other side."* So, all three men *"saw"* the man by the side of the road, but only one really *"saw"* the desperate need of his neighbor.

Not only does the Samaritan see the need and respond to the need, but also he takes the man to an inn and provides for his present and future needs. This he does for a perfect stranger, who is helpless, yet needs a friend. And Jesus concludes the parable by asking the lawyer *"which of these three, do you think, proved neighbor to the man who fell among thieves?"* And the lawyer answered *"the one who showed mercy on him."* And Jesus said to him, *"Go and do likewise."* This parable addresses what everyone must do in order to obtain *"eternal life"*, *and that is to show mercy.*

What is this mercy that we are to show? In the simplest terms, mercy is sympathy with those in misery, and desiring to relieve the misery. It is striving to relieve those in distress; it is not simply possessed of pity but to be actively compassionate. God is rich in mercy (Eph 2:4), and has provided salvation for all men (Titus 3:5). *God is merciful; His mercy is evident by the fact that He does not give us what we deserve.* He is merciful to those who fear Him, who hold Him in awe and reverence (Luke 1:50), for He alone can comfort them. Therefore we are to pray boldly for mercy (Heb. 4:16) and we seek mercy for others (Gal 6:16). Mercy is to be shown by all people to all other people. Since God is merciful to us, we are to show mercy to one another (Matt 9:13). Wherever the words mercy and peace are found together they occur in that order. Mercy is the act of God; peace is the resulting experience in the heart of man. Grace describes God's attitude toward the lawbreaker and the rebel; mercy is His attitude toward those who are in distress. And that is exactly what the Samaritan showed the stranger lying wounded by the side of the road.

Jesus makes two significant points; *first,* don't be like the Jewish priest and Levite who *"passed by on the other side";* instead be like the Samaritan who gave comfort to a neighbor in need. This must have been shocking to His Jewish audience. Be like a Samaritan; don't be like the Jewish religious leaders. *Second,* don't just *"know"* the Law, or have knowledge of the Law; *live* the Law. The Priest and Levite had knowledge of the Law; but they did not live according to the Law. There is a basic Biblical truth, that no Law is fully understood until it is active in our lives. The lawyer had knowledge of the Law; but he did not understand the Spirit of God behind the Law.

So we conclude. A man traveled down from Jericho and was robbed and beaten; a Samaritan showed mercy. The parable began with the question: *what must I do to inherit eternal life?* And the answer is: *love your neighbor and show mercy.* That is what God does; that is what we are to do.

Summary of Biblical Themes
Theme 4—The Christian Character

Christians are to show *mercy* for everyone in need; mercy is God's characteristic that is to be our characteristic. We need to *"see"* so that we can bless others by the mercy that we show for them. Being in the image of God; we are to be a loving and compassionate people. Jesus said, *"if you have done it to the least of these, my brethren, you have done it unto me."* (Matt. 25:40). Mercy for the *"stranger"* in need, whom we don't know and never met, is to be one of the dominant characteristics of the Christian life.

Chapter Nine

Jesus sets before us three additional themes.

Theme 1—The Character of God

God is merciful and He calls for His people to exhibit the same characteristic. God would never pass by on the other side, when we are in difficulty. Jesus told us, *"lo, I am with you always, even to the end of the age."* His Presence with us is eternal, even when we are wounded *"by the side of the road."*

Theme 2—The Kingdom of Heaven

The Kingdom of heaven is for those who are *born again* and who have become a new creation in Christ. These are the *merciful*; these see the *"wounded"* of this world, by the side of each road, and come to their aid.

Theme 3—The Alternatives in Life

Jesus places before the world the choice that we can *help* people in need or we can *ignore* their cries for help. It is interesting that God never ignores the cries of His people, and neither should we. Our love for our neighbor is reflected in the mercy shown to strangers. There are people who *"see"* a need and make sacrifices to meet those needs; there are others who ignore them.

Summary of God's Revelations
Theme 4—The Christian Character

This parable has a command, a promise, a truth and a warning. The command is: *show mercy*. The promise is: *if you show mercy, you shall live. Here "live" means to be saved*. The truth is: *God loves the merciful*. The warning is: *do not neglect the needs of those whom God has called us to help* . . .

4–4. The Parable of the Poor, Rich Fool: Lk. 12:15–21

"And he said to them, 'Take heed, and beware of all covetousness; for a man's life does not consist in the abundance of his possessions'"

God's Hidden Treasures

"And he told them a parable, saying, 'The land of a rich man brought forth plentifully;' and he thought to himself, 'What shall I do, for I have nowhere to store my crops?' And he said, 'I will do this: I will pull down my barns, and build larger ones; and there I will store all my grain and my goods. And I will say to my soul, Soul, you have ample goods laid up for many years; take your ease, eat, drink, be merry.' But God said to him, 'Fool! This night your soul is required of you; and the things you have prepared, whose will they be?' So is he who lays up treasure for himself, and is not rich toward God."

Commentary

We begin by examining the context of this parable. Jesus had been asked to *"referee"* the division of an inheritance between two brothers, and He refused. Instead, He raises the subject of inheritance on a higher plane, for He explains inheritance according to spiritual terms, not according to material possessions. Jesus said; *"Beware of all covetousness; for a man's life does not consist in the abundance of his possessions."* (Lk. 12:15) Jesus probably refused the request because He knew that the distribution was meaningless and unimportant. After all, Jesus knew that all the possessions of this world belong to His Father. That is the concept essential to Christian Stewardship. The Maker of all things is the Owner of all things. Everything is God's by right; it is ours by responsibility. This is an important Christian doctrine.

This parable relates how a rich man seeks greater wealth. Four times, we see the phrase—*"I will . . ."*—all focused on him. At the conclusion of the parable, Jesus related *"treasures for himself"* in contrast to being *"rich towards God."* Here the emphasis is between material and spiritual possessions. For Christians, spiritual possessions are more important; for non-believers, material possessions are more important.

Jesus said that we could be *poor* and *rich* at the same time. We can be poor materially, but rich in the things of God. We could be poor in the things of God and rich materially. This is the alternative that Jesus presents to the world. God directed Moses to warn the people of the manner in which they value wealth, *"Beware lest you say in your heart, 'my power and my might have gotten me this*

Chapter Nine

wealth.' You shall remember the Lord your God, for it is he who gives you power to get wealth; that he may confirm his covenant which he swore to your fathers . . ." (Deut. 8:17–18). In the New Testament, James treats this subject of wealth on the basis that the wealthy are generally considered the worldly; it is difficult to be wealthy and not be worldly. In James 5:1–6, he wrote, *"Come now, you rich, weep and howl for the miseries that are coming upon you . . . you have laid up treasures for the last days . . . you have lived on the earth in luxury and pleasure."* James condemned the wealthy, when wealth leads to a disregard for the things of God and for the interests of others. Wealth in itself is not to be condemned; only when wealth is our focus and is worshipped.

Jesus explains this unusual combination, *poor and rich,* in this parable, by showing the self-centered concern for material possessions with little regard for the things of God or the interests of others. The parable can also be seen as a message of stewardship of the possessions of God and our view that the blessings of this life are richly earned and that God has little or nothing to do with our good *"fortune."* How we consider the question of possessions will shape how we view what are *"mine"* and what are God's. *"Rich towards God"* has the meaning of *"towards the things of God, with the things of God, in the things of God." "Rich toward God"* means being generous about those things, which are on the *"heart"* of God and which are important to God. *Poor* relates to the quality of a selfish spirit that results in being poor towards, and thoughtless of, the interest of God and our neighbor.

James emphasizes that fellowship with God is the only possession worth living for and dying for. The material possessions of this world must never be the focus of our lives or the emphasis of our ambitions. We should only be ambitious for the things of God (Matt. 6:33).

In this parable, the rich man relies on himself and his own materialistic good works to achieve the *"good life."* Christians are to do good works, as an expression of faith. However, Christians know that their good works are the result of a life committed to and dependent on Christ. By choice, we do not rely totally on ourselves nor do we believe that physical possessions will bring eternal life. Jesus came that all would *have life and have it more abundantly (Jn. 10:10).* Only Jesus can provide *"the good life"*, which is a life *"rich"* in the things of God.

Now Jesus doesn't specifically present these questions in this parable, but there are seven questions that we should wrestle with, e.g. *What does life consist of? What should the rich man have done? To what extent should he have shared his abundance? To whom does he show mercy? Whose possessions were they anyway? What can a person do with all the riches with which he has been blessed? Is the wealth of this world the possessions of a few; or is every person a steward of God's possessions?* Let's examine what Jesus has to say about these questions.

What does life consist of? In one sense, Jesus emphasizes what He had previously taught in the Sermon on the Mount; *"but do not be anxious about the things of this world, what to eat or what to drink or what to wear, for your Father in heaven knows that you need them all."* (6:31–32), but *"seek his kingdom and his righteousness, and all these things will be yours as well."* (6:33). This is what life consists of. Paul addressed this same issue (Col. 3:1–2) *"If you have been raised with Christ, seek the things that are above . . . set your mind on things that are above, not on things that are on earth."*

What should the rich man have done? It is evident that the rich man, every rich man, should share some of his abundance with the less fortunate. This is not an advocacy for a "welfare" state; that is not the Christian model. The Bible emphasizes that people must be responsible for their actions and for their needs in life. However, there are times and circumstances when Christians must help those facing permanent and temporary misfortunes. We cannot stand idly by; we cannot *"pass by on the other side of the road"* and ignore those whom we can and should help; we show mercy by providing love.

To what extent should he have shared his abundance? He should have shared what he had with the less fortunate and, like the Good Samaritan, he should not *"pass by on the other side."* Abundance suggests that we have far more than we need or can use.

Chapter Nine

To whom does he show mercy? Obviously to no one and that is the tragedy of his life and all others who view their *"possessions"* as theirs and they are not accountable to others in need. In the previous parable of the Good Samaritan, Jesus told the lawyer that a person inherits *eternal life by showing mercy.*

Whose possessions were they anyway? It is obvious that Christians acknowledge *"God Most High, Maker of heaven and earth."* (Psa. 14:19), so I can only conclude that the Maker is the Sovereign Owner; He is *"the King of all the earth."* (Psa. 47:7) The earth is the Lord's and everything that is within it. Everything belongs to God; we are His stewards. It is His by right; it is ours as stewards.

What can a person do with all the riches with which he has been blessed? Christians are commanded to be generous, loving, and sharing the goodness that God has showered on us. He has given us material treasures and wealth for a reason; we need to remember that and use them for God's glory, for the benefit of others and for the spread of His kingdom. God spoke through Malachi (3:10), encouraging the people to test Him, *"Bring the full tithes into the storehouse, that there may be food in my house; and thereby put me to the test, says the Lord of hosts, if I will not open the windows of heaven for you and pour down for you an overwhelming blessing."* God blesses us so that we would be His instruments for blessing others.

Is the wealth of this world the possessions of a few; or are all people stewards of God's possessions? Everyone is a steward of God's possessions. The author of Proverbs wrote, *"Honor the Lord with your wealth (3:9); Wealth is worthless in the day of wrath."* (11:4). Paul addressed this matter (I Tim. 6:17), *"As for the rich in this world, charge them not to be haughty, nor to set their hopes on uncertain riches but on God who richly furnished us with everything to enjoy."* The Bible teaches not to trust in material wealth. The man in this parable is the victim of idolatry; for the worship of money and the greed of believing it to be ours, is a deadly disease.

This parable has a message similar to that in the parable of the Good Samaritan. Only here the dimensions are changed slightly. In the parable of the Good Samaritan, three men actually *"saw"* the needs of another yet only one man showed mercy. In this parable, there are many with great wealth and great blessings, and all around us there is misery and physical poverty that we can't always *see,* but it doesn't take much imagination to know that it is present. Christians cannot *pass by on the other side* and ignore their plight. Christians cannot disregard the command to help those in need. Jesus said that when you do it to the least of these, my brethren, you do it unto Me. Jesus places before the world the question of who *"owns"* all with which we are blessed. If we truly believe that *"all gifts are thine, no gifts have we, Lord of all gifts to offer thee—and so with thankful hearts today, thine own before thy feet we lay."* The question is one of ownership and stewardship. If we believe that all that we have is by our own labor and is ours deservedly, then we will act like the rich young ruler, who was not *"rich towards God."* But, if we believe that all things are God's, then we will be anxious to share with the less fortunate the gifts with which God has blessed us. God knows what we need; Paul wrote (Phil. 4:19), *"And my God will supply every need of yours according to his riches in glory in Christ Jesus."* God knows what we need before we even ask (Matt. 6:8). The 23rd Psalm says, *"The Lord is my shepherd, I shall not want . . ."* David said, we shall not want. The message for David that he shall *not lack anything,* and the same is true for us today. God will meet our every need; that is His promise. We must not lay up treasures for ourselves, but be rich towards God.

Summary of Biblical Themes
Theme 4—The Christian Character

Here we have idolatry, worshipping that which we believe we have created. However, *"wealth"* is from God, and we can only have a blessing from wealth when we recognize its true source and when it does not dominate our lives. We must be rich in the things of God, then all these other things, which God knows we need, will be added to us. The warning throughout this parable is the danger of self-centered interest and the failure to see and meet the needs of others. God will give us what we need, not what we want. We must learn to be content in every situation, as Paul was (Phil. 4:12–13), *"I know how to be abased, and I know how to abound; in* any and all circumstances, I have learned the secret of facing plenty and facing hunger, abundance and want. I can do all things in Christ who strengthens me."

Jesus also directs our attention to two other themes with *secondary* messages.

Theme 3—The Alternatives in Life

Jesus places before us the choice; the things of this world verses the things of God. (Col. 3:1–2). We are *rich if* we seek and have found the treasures of God; we are *poor if* we place our trust in material possessions. This is also a parable about selfishness in which the things of this world *"choke"* out the seeds that the Sower is planting. Material possessions will rust and fade away, with no eternal value. The things of God, His righteousness, His love, His eternal protection and provision, they will never fade. The great message of Psalm 37 applies, *"Trust in the Lord, and do good . . . Take delight in the Lord, and he will give you the desires of your heart."*

Theme 7—Christian Stewardship

God is both the Maker and the Owner of all things. It is God's vineyard, and we are laborers in it. We are stewards of all His possessions, bringing forth good fruit for Him. In that way, we are able to show love for God and love for our neighbor. Paul wrote, *"Whatever your task, work heartily, as serving the Lord and not men, knowing that from the Lord you will receive the inheritance as your reward; you are serving the Lord Christ."* (Col. 3:23)

Summary of God's Revelations,
Theme 4—The Christian Character

This parable has a command, a truth and warnings. *The command is: Be rich toward the things of God.* The truth is: *Man's life does not consist in the abundance of his possessions.* The warnings are: *Do not lay up physical treasures for yourself. Seek the things of God; those are the only treasures worth seeking.* This message is also presented in the Parable of the Treasure hidden in the Field (2–3) and the Parable of the Pearl of Great Value (2–4).

God's Hidden Treasures

4–5. The Parable of the Barren Fig Tree: Lk. 13:6–9

"And he told this parable: A man had a fig tree planted in his vineyard; and he came seeking fruit on it and found none. And he said to the vinedresser, 'Lo, these three years I have come seeking fruit on this fig tree, and I find none. Cut it down; why should it use up the ground?' And he answered him, 'Let it alone, sir, this year also, till I dig about it and put on manure. And if it bears fruit next year, well and good; but if not, you can cut it down.'"

Commentary

The parable has perhaps the most unusual context of any. In addition, it has one of the more important messages of any of the parables. In the preceding section, Jesus had been told that Pilate had used the blood of some Galileans in Roman sacrifices. In response, Jesus told the crowd that the suffering and death of these Galileans was not related to any sin in their lives. There is a theology that says that bad things happen to bad people; good things happen to good people. However that is not the truth of the Bible, which is that bad things happen to good people and good things happen to bad people. *Here again is another strong warning.* Jesus describes the eighteen who died when the tower in Siloam fell on them, and He asked, do you think that their death was related to sin and guilt? Jesus said that their death had nothing to do with sin. Then Jesus repeats His previous warning, *"unless you repent, you too will all perish."* Many people search for the answer to the question: why do bad things happen to righteous people? And what does it have to do with this parable about the barren fig tree. Let us see how this ties together.

"And, he told them this parable." (13:5). Jesus said that bad things do not always happen because of sin in our lives. Bad things can, and do, happen to righteous people; but Jesus tells us that bad

Chapter Nine

things will happen, eventually, if we continue in sin. It does happen that the wicked prosper, but only for a time. God cannot abide sin, and there are eventual consequences and punishment for sin. The message of Psalm 1:6, *"for the lord knows the way of the righteous, but the way of the wicked will perish."* Do not believe that the wicked will go unpunished; the Bible makes that clear. Listen to the Word of God:

"Salvation is far from the wicked, for they do not seek thy statutes." (Psa. 119:155)

"The Lord is far from the wicked . . ." (Prov. 15:29)

"Woe to the wicked! It shall be ill with him, for what his hands have done shall be done to him." (Isa. 3:11)

Jesus sets the stage for two themes in the parable: *first*, death and misfortune are not always related to sin in our lives: the righteous do suffer. Job is the human evidence; Christ is the divine evidence. We have only to look at the cross to understand that. Consider that passage of faith (Hebrews 11) where the author described the suffering of the righteous. *Second*, repentance is the key to new life. So let us see how these two messages relate to this parable involving a barren fig tree. The righteous will suffer.

Jesus told us, *"Blessed are you when men revile you and persecute you and utter all kinds of evil against you falsely on my account. Rejoice and be glad, for your reward is great in heaven, for so men persecuted the prophets who were before you"* (Matt. 5:11–12).

"If they persecuted me, they will persecute you . . ." (Jn. 15:20)

The apostle James exhorted the brethren, regarding trials and persecution, *"Count it all joy, my brethren, when you meet various trials, for you know that the testing of your faith produces steadfastness. And let steadfastness have its full effect, that you may be perfect and complete, lacking in nothing"* (James 1:2–4).

Jesus tells the crowd that unless they repent, you too shall perish, just like the 18 who died when the tower of Siloam fell on them. Then using the example of the fig tree, Jesus tells the crowd that they, like the tree, will *"perish"* if they do not produce fruit. What is true for the fig tree is true for every person. Notice that the man is going to dig about it and fertilize it, to give it every chance to be *"fruitful."* Notice how patient Jesus is, for He is not anxious to cut down the fig tree, for He is prepared to give it sufficient time to bear fruit. Again the same is true with us. He is patient, but His patience has limits. Notice also that the time to bear fruit is *"three years."* Now the number *"three"* has Biblical significance, for it stands for that which is *"solid, real, substantial, complete and entire."* In the same context, three denotes divine perfection. Three is also the number of *"resurrection",* for the *"third day"* of creation was the time when the earth rose out of the water and that is a symbol of the resurrection life that we have in Christ. So the *"three years"* here is symbolic of the fact that the tree had time to become complete, but it had failed to do so. *"So every tree that does not bear good fruit will be cut down."* In many regards, we are *"trees"* in God's vineyard, and we are called to produce good fruit, as evidence of our works that are a direct reflection of our faith.

In John 15, Jesus presented the message that *"I (Jesus) am the vine, you are the branches. If a man remains in me and I in him, he will bear much fruit; apart from me, you can do nothing."* (Jn. 15:5). Like trees, we are to bear much fruit; but Jesus emphasizes that we can only do so by being *"in Him"*, which is the manner in which the branches are attached to the vine (Jn. 15). This is consistent with the message of Psa. 16:2, in which David wrote, *". . . I have no good apart from you."* We will be like the barren fig tree unless we are *"attached"* to the vine, Jesus Christ, and we can *do nothing* unless we maintain and preserve that relationship. Jesus is telling the world that we must be *"fruitful"* people, but that is the result of our dependence on Him. The key to our life as a *branch* on the *Vine* is that we acknowledge our sins, repent of them and confess Jesus Christ as Savior and Lord. As a result, we are forgiven of all unrighteousness, we are restored to fellowship with God, we become a child of God and we receive the gift of the Holy Spirit. The key to fruitfulness is abiding in Jesus Christ.

Jesus told His disciples that we must be ready for His return; and, while we prepare for that, we must be fruitful people. God is the source of the fruit; He *gives* life to the fruit, and we are to *bear* the fruit. The fruit of the Spirit is what we are to bear, which Paul

Chapter Nine

identified (Gal. 5:22) as *"love, joy, peace, patience, kindness, goodness, faithfulness, gentleness, self-control; against such there is no law."* We are to bear not just one or two of them; we are to bear them *all*. If we do not bear fruit, for whatever reason, than the tree will be cut down. Two key elements of bearing fruit are repentance and abiding in Jesus.

What is the fruitless fig tree? It is any nation, any ministry, and any individual that does not bear good fruit. God will not continue to nourish such a fruit tree.

In the letters to the Seven Churches in Revelation (chapters 2–3), Jesus Christ tells them that their *lamp stand* will be removed if they do not heed His warnings. Each of the seven churches contains some characteristic of the *"fruitless fig tree."* They have *lost the love* that they had at first (the church at Ephesus); the church *compromises* and will not suffer for the sake of his name (the church in Smyrna); the church is *not faithful to the Word* of God (the church in Pergamum); the church *compromises with evil* (the church in Thyatira); the church *seeks the approval of men and not of God* (the church in Sardis); the church is given an *open door to proclaim the gospel* and fails to do so (the church in Philadelphia); the church is filled with *indecision* regarding its relationship to God and men (the church in Laodicea).

God equips us and gives us time to be fruitful; if not *"fruitful"*, we face the danger of being *"removed"*.

Summary of Biblical Themes
Theme 4—The Christian Character

Bad things will happen to good people; good people will face trials and tribulation. In spite of such circumstances, the Christian life is one of *bearing fruit*, by being *"in Christ"*, and as knowing the fullness of the Spirit.

This parable has one *secondary* theme.
Theme 5—Repentance

Repentance is the key to bearing fruit, for good fruit can only be present and evident in a life that confesses sins, repents of them, is reconciled to God and is determined, in the power of the Holy Spirit, to lead a new life, following the commandments of God.

God's Hidden Treasures

Summary of God's Revelations
Theme 4—The Christian Character

This parable has a promise and a warning. The promise is: *God is patient and desires us to produce much fruit.* The warning is: *whoever does not produce fruit in due time will be "cut down."*

4-6. The Parable of Humility: Lk. 14:7-11

"Now he told a parable to those who were invited, when he marked how they chose the places of honor, saying to them, 'When you are invited by any one to a marriage feast, do not sit down in a place of honor, lest a more eminent man than you be invited by him; and he who invited you both will come and say to you, "Give place to this man," and then you will begin with shame to take the lowest place. But when you are invited, go and sit in the lowest place, so that when your host comes he may say to you, "Friend, go up higher"; then you will be honored in the presence of all who sit at table with you. For every one who exalts himself will be humbled, and he who humbles himself will be exalted.'"

Commentary

We begin by recalling the Old Testament passage: *"If my people who are called by my name humble themselves, and pray and seek my face, and turn from their wicked ways, then I will hear from heaven, and will forgive their sin and heal their land."* (2 Chron. 7:14) This passage reminds us that we are to do three things and God promises to do three things. We are to humble ourselves, pray and seek his face, and turn from our wicked ways; in turn, God promises that He will hear from heaven, forgive our sins and heal our land. What a great trilogy for God and for us.

This parable places before the world the central theme, *humility*, as one of the more noble characteristics of the Christian life. Humility stands in direct contrast to *self-exaltation*. Jesus teaches

Chapter Nine

that *humility can lead to exaltation and honor.* Since Jesus is speaking of these characteristics, *humility and exaltation*, we need to understand these qualities.

Humility is a most noble virtue; it is the divine virtue of Jesus Christ. The only time in Scripture where Jesus described Himself is in Matt. 11:28–30, *"Come to me, all who labor and are heavy laden, and I will give you rest. Take my yoke upon you, and learn from me; for I am gentle and lowly in heart, and you will find rest for your souls. For my yoke is easy, and my burden is light."* Three thoughts are important here. First, *rest* can mean a loosening of bonds, a freedom from slavery; it can also mean peace of mind; it can also mean a place (Heaven) of final rest. In this text, it can mean each of these and all of them together. That is the richness of the text. But look also at the manner in which Jesus described Himself, as gentle and lowly in heart. Gentle is the opposite of violence; violence is great energy out of control; gentle is great power totally under control. That is Jesus. In addition, He is lowly in heart; He is the divine Son of God, and He comes to earth as The Servant, who will suffer for the sins of the world. He willingly and freely laid down His life for our sins. Jesus is the evidence and the example of humility.

The Biblical view is that humility is not thinking badly of ourselves, nor is it thinking that we are useless and worthless human beings. That is false humility. No, true humility is actually seeing ourselves in contrast to the holiness and sovereignty of God. In that context, we are humbled. In teaching the lesson of humility, Jesus has in mind Micah 6:8, *"He has shown you, O man, what is good; and what does the Lord require of you but to do justice, and to love kindness (steadfast love) and to walk humbly with your God."* Again we have a choice to seek the honor of men and to be exalted among men, or to be humble so that God can exalt us. We are to seek first His Kingdom and His righteousness and all these other things will be added unto us. We do not seek honor. If honor is given, it is because it is earned, as the result of a humble life of giving and loving. Instead, we seek to do God's will and be faithful and wise managers. Humility is given a high place in the kingdom of God, as in Abraham (Gen. 18:27), Moses (Num. 12:3) and John the Baptist (Jn. 3:26–30). The Bible speaks at great length about humility (2 Sam. 12:28; Psa. 18:27; Matt. 21:5; I Pet. 3:8). Before God, man is humbled as creature (Gen. 18:27) and sinner (Lk. 18:9–14) having nothing to boast of (Rom. 7:18). We have ever before us the picture of the humiliation of Jesus Christ (Phil. 2:8; 2 Cor. 8:9). We begin to see that humility is the essence of saving faith (Rom. 3:27). In all our ministries, one of the principal keys is humility; it is the basis of the proper fellowship of the Christian church (Rom. 12:16; Eph. 4:2). God dwells with the humble; that is the greatest commendation. We have only to study the Beatitudes to get a glimpse of the humility that God approves.

Throughout the ages, Christians have ranked humility very highly. Augustine said, *"If you ask me what is the first precept of the Christian religion I will answer, first, second and third, humility."* Thomas À Kempis held humility necessary to the imitation of Christ. Martin Luther condemned exalting ourselves; he wrote, *"instead of being humble, seek to excel in humility. Unless a man is always humble, distrustful of himself, always fears his own understanding . . . and passions . . . and will, he will be unable to stand for long without offense. Truth will pass him by. Humility is aptness for grace, the essence of faith."* For Calvin, humility alone exalts God as sovereign; it is part of self-denial, the abandonment of self-confidence that constitutes faith, and of self-will. It is interesting that Calvin insisted on being buried in an unmarked grave, so that his followers would not show a human being special honor, but instead would focus on honoring God. Such appreciation of humility springs from prophetic conviction that man, made of dust, totally dependent, and sinful, *has nothing to be proud of* except God loving him and showering him with favor and redemption (Ps 8:4–5). God dwells with the humble (Isa 57:15), *"For thus says the high and lofty One who inhabits eternity, whose name is Holy: "I dwell in the high and holy place, and also with him who is of a contrite and humble spirit."*

Now *exalting* has a different flavor. Here the question is who shall exalt us or who shall humble us. If we exalt ourselves, we

Chapter Nine

will be humbled. If we are humble, God Himself will exalt us. Christians are to live a life characterized by humility. Now in the matter of exaltation, there are three types: *divine, human by God and human-by-human.* In the Bible, *divine exaltation* refers to the lofty position of God and of His Son, Jesus Christ. God is exalted over all the nations and above the heavens (Ps 46:10). As God Incarnate, Jesus Christ came to redeem mankind from sin. Through his death and resurrection Christ was *exalted* to the right hand of the Father. Both Isaiah 52:13 and John 3:14 speak of Christ's death as being both *"lifted up"* and being *"highly exalted."* By humbling himself and by being *"lifted up"* on a Roman cross, Christ paid the price for our sins. In doing so, Jesus Christ was *exalted* by the Father to the highest place and given *"the name that is above every name" (Phil 2:8–9).* At his second coming as King of kings and Lord of lords, His sovereign authority will be displayed, for *"every knee will bow and every tongue will confess that he is Lord" (Phil 2:10–11).* God honors and exalts those who are righteous (Ps 75:10); He takes special joy in raising up the poor and humble (1 Sam 2:7–8). Finally, the sin of mankind is shown in the third type of *exaltation, that of humans exalted by humans.* Such acts are an abomination to God and constitute the worse kind of idolatry. Sin entered the world when Adam and Eve rebelled against God, exalted themselves, desiring to become *"like God" (Gen. 3:5).* Human pride and arrogance lead to two sins; first, the failure to honor God as God; second, they represent direct rebellion against His Sovereignty. (See Romans 1). In that regard, human exaltation is conceit and arrogance. Divine exaltation is the result of humility.

So Jesus places before us the matter of humility and exaltation. Jesus required, for receiving the kingdom, that one humbles oneself as a child (Matt. 18:4). As the example of the Suffering Servant, Jesus humbled Himself, *"emptied himself"* (Phil 2:7–8). So, whoever would be first must be servant of all (Mark 10:43). Thus, from humility toward God followed humility toward others. Paul wrote often of this subject *"in humility count others better than yourselves," (Phil 2:3)* and also toward oneself *"not to think of himself more highly than he ought to think," (Rom. 12:3).* For the Christian knows he possesses nothing he has not received, is nothing but for

God's Hidden Treasures

the grace of God; and, apart from Christ, can do nothing. He remembers that God opposes the proud, gives grace to the humble. Christians always remember that they have been loved, justified and received as children of God, not through our own merits, but solely through His grace.

Summary of Biblical Themes
Theme 4—The Christian Character

One of the great characteristics of a Christian is a humble spirit and a contrite heart. Christians should not seek honor and prestige; instead they focus on honoring and serving God. If so, then God will exalt us. Divine humility is the mark of a Christian. We should have before us, the vision of Christ being exalted at the right hand of the Father.

This parable presents one *secondary* theme.
Theme 3—The Alternatives in Life

A person can exalt himself or be humble; the choice is clear. Humility shows the fruit of the Spirit (Gal. 5:22) evident in our lives.

Summary of God's Revelations
Theme 4—The Christian Character

This parable has both a truth and a warning. The truth is: *everyone who exalts himself will be humbled, and he who humbles himself will be exalted.* The warning is: *everyone who exalts himself will be humbled.*

4–7. The Parable of the Great Banquet: Lk. 14:12–24

"He said also to the man who had invited him, 'When you give a dinner or a banquet, do not invite your friends or your brothers or your kinsmen or rich neighbors, lest they also invite you in return, and you be repaid. But when you give a feast, invite the poor, the

Chapter Nine

maimed, the lame, the blind, and you will be blessed, because they cannot repay you. You will be repaid at the resurrection of the just.' When one of those who sat at table with him heard this, he said to him, 'Blessed is he who shall eat bread in the kingdom of God!' But he said to him, 'A man once gave a great banquet, and invited many; and at the time for the banquet he sent his servant to say to those who had been invited, 'Come; for all is now ready.' But they all alike began to make excuses. The first said to him, 'I have bought a field, and I must go out and see it; I pray you, have me excused.' And another said, 'I have bought five yoke of oxen, and I go to examine them; I pray you, have me excused.' And another said, 'I have married a wife, and therefore I cannot come.' So the servant came and reported this to his master. Then the householder in anger said to his servant, 'Go out quickly to the streets and lanes of the city, and bring in the poor and maimed and blind and lame.' And the servant said, 'Sir, what you commanded has been done, and still there is room.' And the master said to the servant, 'Go out to the highways and hedges, and compel people to come in, that my house may be filled. For I tell you, none of those men who were invited shall taste my banquet.'"

Commentary

Jesus describes a great banquet, possibly foreshadowing the great Wedding Feast in Heaven (Rev. 19:6–9). In another sense, Jesus is presenting a picture of the universal church, to which all are called. Some will accept and some will reject the invitation. There are similarities between this parable and that of the King's son (Matt. 22:1–10), but the differences are so distinctive as to suggest that these are two separate parables. In this parable, the invited decline the invitation; in Matthew, they ridicule the invitation and kill the messengers. As we shall see, the messages are complementary and unique.

Jesus said that we are to invite those who cannot repay us. Isn't that what God does! There is no way that I can repay God for all the wonderful blessings that He has given me, particularly His forgiveness secured for me on the cross.

If we invite kin or rich neighbor, Jesus said that they would repay you. But, Jesus said, if you invite the poor, they cannot repay you; however, God will repay you at the resurrection.

God's Hidden Treasures

We are to invite the poor, so that at the resurrection we will be blessed. That is only possible if we do *"good deeds"*, without the expectation of reward or repayment. *How will we be blessed?* By doing those things of which God approves. The Beatitudes define one measure of the Christian character that will ensure that God approves us. Blessed means to be *"approved by God."*

"Blessed are the poor in spirit, for theirs is the kingdom of heaven.
Blessed are those who mourn, for they will be comforted.
Blessed are the meek, for they will inherit the earth.
Blessed are those who hunger and thirst for righteousness, for they will be filled.
Blessed are the merciful, for they will be shown mercy.
Blessed are the pure in heart, for they will see God.
Blessed are the peacemakers, for they will be called sons of God.
Blessed are those who are persecuted because of righteousness, for theirs is the kingdom of heaven.
Blessed are you when people insult you, persecute you and falsely say all kind of evil against you because of me. Rejoice and be glad, because great is your reward in heaven, for in the same way, they persecuted the prophets who were before you."

In this text, Jesus refers to eight characteristics that define the Christian character. To begin with, Jesus talks of being *blessed* for many acts. Now these Beatitudes are a total combination of the Christian character; the Beatitudes are not to be separated or chosen at random. We are not at liberty to select only those that we like. All constitute a complete and integral part of the Christian character. So what is blessedness? There are three Greek words, which mean *"to speak well of or to think well of someone"*—*"to be fortunate or happy, or outwardly prosperous."* In both the Old and New Testament, it universally occurs in the sense that emphasizes God's approval, founded in righteousness that rests ultimately on love to God.

This parable describes the instruction to invite, not those who can repay you, but invite those who cannot repay, for, in their presence, you will be blessed. Jesus tells us to give invitations for the right reason, not for any benefit that we might receive in the fu-

Chapter Nine

ture. Our invitations are to be given out of love, expecting nothing in return and knowing that the invitation cannot be repaid. For isn't that what God has done for us? He has invited us to accept His Son as Savior and Lord. We are the *poor, the maimed, the lame, and the blind,* and there is no way that we can repay God for so glorious an invitation. In addition, Jesus speaks of *"blessed is he who shall eat bread in the kingdom of God."* Eating with one another is a sign of fellowship, and here that fellowship will be with God in His kingdom.

In this parable, people give a variety of excuses for not attending the banquet; some are busy with possessions; some busy with work; some with family. These are all important reasons, but they are not as important as the Wedding Feast to which God has called His people. Their excuses were based on personal and selfish interest; they have little regard for the person giving the banquet. Christians need to respond in a way that honors God's interests and God's will. God must be first in our lives. We have to get that right before we can deal with any other priorities. In addition, we must accept the invitation and be properly dressed. In ancient Israel, personal messengers delivered the invitations, and it was considered an insult to make an excuse. It was even a greater insult to show up in clothes, other than those generally provided by the host. Appearing in anything other than the wedding garment meant that the person would be *removed from the banquet,* i.e. not welcomed in fellowship with God.

It appears that the invitations went first to people in the city, and they may have been the wealthy, the elite of Israel. Excuses were made, reflecting the cares and concerns of the world. The refusal of the invitations made the *householder angry.* Therefore the invitation was given to those who were probably in the streets and alleys of the town, the *poor, the crippled, the blind, and the lame.* Note that the Gentiles are to be included *"so that my house may be full."* The householder then tells the servants that none of those to whom the invitation was originally given will be allowed to *"get a taste of my banquet."* *"Not to taste his banquet"* is a term that means that such people will not have fellowship with God. God seeks fellowship with His creation; to ignore His "invitations" has eternal consequences. Therefore, they will not enter the kingdom of heaven. In Scripture, it is clear that God has eternally extended His "invitation" to the Jews; God now says that many of those originally invited will not share in the banquet. It is uncertain how often the invitation will be offered; the invitation may be given, and many may fail to seize the moment. Many will be invited (God is *"forbearing towards you, not wishing that any should perish, but that all should reach repentance." 2 Pet. 3:9)*; but many will find excuses for not coming to Christ. The Jews were *"invited"* but they had excuses, e.g., such as the Law as the basis for their salvation. People are invited today, and there are more excuses. The message for us is that we should never refuse so great an invitation which might not be repeated.

Summary of Biblical Themes
Theme 4—The Christian Character

When God calls us to come to so wonderful a banquet, we should accept immediately. Obedience is what God asks of His children. The cares of this world must not govern our decisions and actions. God invites; He doesn't demand. He stands at the door and knocks. A second important message in this parable is that we should be dressed in the garments of righteousness, which God Himself has provided to His people.

Jesus also presents four *secondary* themes in this parable;
Theme 1—The Parables of the Character of God

God is patient that none should perish, but His patience has a limit. Continual rejection of His invitations will bring His judgment, wrath and His *holy anger* upon those who reject His fellowship and His Son.

Theme 2—The Parables of the Kingdom of Heaven

We are invited to *"eat bread in the kingdom of God."* Such an invitation includes eternal fellowship with God. The *"bread"* we shall eat is the body of Christ, and he who eats of this bread will never hunger. Christ is the "manna", the true bread that came down from heaven.

Chapter Nine

Theme 3—The Parables of the Alternatives in Life

The invitations are given, sent by God, and we have the option of making excuses or attending a banquet in which we shall have eternal *fellowship with God*. The physically healthy are the ones who make excuses; it is those in *need, the poor, the maimed and blind and lame*, who welcome the invitation. Jesus said that the tax collectors and harlots would enter the kingdom before the Pharisees.

Theme 10—The Parables of the Final Judgment

People who refuse God's invitation to have fellowship with Him will not taste the banquet prepared for all believers at the End of the Age. The demands of the present should not prevent the joy of the future.

Summary of God's Revelations
Theme 4—The Christian Character

This parable has a command, truths, and warnings. The command is: *invite those who cannot repay you*. The truths are: *Blessings come from those acts in which people cannot repay; this is the fullness of giving, when nothing can be given in return*. The warnings are: *Do not anger the householder by refusing so wonderful an invitation; those invited and who refuse shall not taste the banquet; don't ignore or refuse fellowship with God; the consequences of such refusal are eternal.*

4–8. The Parable of the Unworthy Servant: Lk. 17:7–10

"Will any one of you, who has a servant plowing or keeping sheep, say to him when he has come in from the field, 'Come at once and sit down at table'? Will he not rather say to him, 'Prepare supper for me, and gird yourself and serve me, till I eat and drink; and afterward you shall eat and drink'? Does he thank the servant because he did what was commanded? So you also, when you have done all that is

God's Hidden Treasures

commanded you, say, 'We are unworthy servants; we have only done what was our duty'."

Commentary

This continues the series of parables regarding faithfulness to the commands of God. There is no special context in which this parable was told. Rather, Jesus has been discussing a series of themes; sin, faith and duty. In the preceding verses, the disciples had asked Jesus to *"increase our faith."* . . . *"He replied that if you have faith as small as a mustard seed, even a mulberry tree will obey you."* He is setting the tone for the discussion of faith, by saying that faithfulness is more than duty. Faith is willingness; duty is obligation, perhaps even under compulsion. Duty is doing what is demanded of us; faith is performing willingly and graciously the will of God out of love for and a desire to please the Father.

In addition to duty and faith, Jesus also sets the tone for the character of a servant. Let us look briefly at these terms: *duty, faith, and servants.*

The New Testament concept of *duty* emphasizes service and piety. Jesus says that when a servant has done his best, serving his master, he is only performing his duty (Luke 17:10). We should not expect any reward or recognition for doing our duty; for duty is being faithful and obedient to the commands of God. Instead, we are to do far more than duty. Further, Christians are to anticipate the interest and will of God. We are to do the work of God which *"is to believe in him whom he has sent."* (Jn. 6:29). Our belief in the Son of God is the foundation of our duty.

Faith is well defined in Hebrews 11, which is one of the great chapters in the Bible regarding faith. The author of Hebrews wrote *"now faith is the assurance of things hoped for, the conviction of things not seen. For by it the men of old received divine approval."* Faith is confidence, conviction and belief. It is the basis of divine approval. It is the expectation and prospect of great good. Faith leads to accepting the commands of God, and following them; duty is fulfilling the commands. Without faith, it is impossible to please God (Heb. 11:6). We must have faith to perform our duties and be a worthy servant.

Chapter Nine

The theme of *servants* has been extensively discussed in many excellent commentaries. One of particular merit is that by Walter M. Dunnett (Evangelical Dictionary of Biblical Theology). Dr. Dunnett emphasized that people are servants of other human beings as well as servants of God. The Biblical texts emphasize two key ingredients: *action* (the servant as "worker") and *obedience*. Abraham (Gen. 26:24), Jacob (Gen. 32:4), Moses and Joshua (Josh 24:29), David and Daniel (Dan 9:17) are prime examples of Old Testament servants. Perhaps the greatest examples of servants are those contained in The Book of Isaiah, where the *"Servant Songs"* (42:1–4; 49:1–6; 50:4–9; 52:13–53:12) identify Jesus Christ as the Suffering Servant and the Mediator of salvation. These prophetic passages relate to the suffering, death, and new life of the Servant; which becomes fully exemplified in Christ. The passage in Isa. 52:13 sets the stage for Acts 3:13; the passage in Isa. 61:1 relates to Acts 4:27; the passage in Isa. 53:7–8 relates to Acts 8:32–33; the passage in Isa. 53:4–5,7,9–1 relates to Peter 2:22–24. These are a few examples of the Old Testament prophecies regarding Jesus Christ as the Suffering Servant. In the New Testament, the word for *"servant"* is frequently used to designate a master's slave but also a follower of Christ (a *"bond slave"* of Christ). The term points to a relation of absolute dependence, in which the master and the servant stand on opposite sides, the former having a full claim, the latter making a full commitment. The servant can exercise no will or initiative on his own. Paul (Titus 1:1) and James (1:1) both refer to themselves as servants of God; Paul also calls himself the *"servant of Christ"* (Rom. 1:1). Christ took upon himself the *"form of a servant"* (Phil 2:7). As the Son of man, Jesus *"did not come to be served, but to serve, and to give his life as a ransom for many"* (Matt 20:28). Through the cross, believers have moved from being slaves to sin to become slaves of righteousness (Rom. 6:17–18).

This parable identifies faithfulness to the commands of God as required if we are to be worthy servants. Service to and for God is an everlasting responsibility; we should never get weary nor fail to fulfill all that lies before us. There are a variety of both direct and indirect ways that we serve. Duty is demanded of us, and we should be prepared and content to perform whatever duty the Lord requires of us, and we should not seek attention or recognition as justifiable reward. When we serve the Lord Jesus, that service is recognition enough. In Acts 4 and 5, Peter and John *"rejoicing that they were counted worthy to suffer dishonor for the name (of Jesus)."* They were not looking for approval from their friends or condemnation from their enemies. They sought only the approval of God. The true sign of service is maturity (Col. 1:28). This is the attitude which Paul encouraged for Timothy (2 Tim. 2:15), *"Do your best to present yourself to God as one approved, a workman who has no need to be ashamed, rightly handling the word of truth."* What is true for Timothy is true for us today. Paul also wrote to the church at Thessalonica (1 Thess. 2:4), *"but just as we have been approved by God to be entrusted with the gospel . . ."* Like Paul, we have been approved by God and entrusted with the gospel. The question is: how well have we discharged that responsibility? The Christian is to seek and provide service to God and others. That is the measure of our love.

When laboring in the Father's vineyard, we should not look for God, or anyone else, to serve us. To do so would reflect our desire for special treatment and special recognition. In serving God, we have been doing only what is commanded of us. However, Jesus makes another interesting comment at the end of this parable, *"we are unworthy servants; we have only done what was our duty."* Just doing what is required in not sufficient; instead, we must do more that our duty. A worthy servant does not need to be commanded to do something; he looked for opportunities for service to others, and he does so willingly. A worthy servant does not seek self-interests; instead he is committed to his master's interest, his purpose, and his will. *Service and love are interconnected and inseparable.* Therefore Jesus sets a new and higher standard for Christian service. We are to do more than what is commanded; we are to seek opportunities to serve God and our fellow man; this is the measure of our understanding and commitment to the Two Great Commandments in our love for God and love for our fellow man.

Chapter Nine

What does God command us to do? Well, the list is staggering. God has given commands to believers, to individuals, such as Adam and Eve, to Joshua, to David and to the nation of Israel. H. L. Willmington (Book of Bible Lists) has compiled a summary of almost 200 commands, ranging from those given in the Shema (love your God and love your neighbor) to the Ten Commandments, and to a broad range of commands dealing with every aspect of the Christian life. Fulfilling our duty is important; going further than duty is the measure of Christian service.

Summary of Biblical Themes
Theme 4—The Christian Character

God desires obedience and faithfulness in our response to His commands and warnings. We must have an inner desire, a passion, a deep motivation, to do more for God and His kingdom than what is commanded of us. We should want to live a life so fruitful that God would call us *"blessed and approved for every good work."* When our interests are subordinate, at all times and in every situation, to those of our Lord, only in that way will we be considered *"worthy."*

Jesus presents two *secondary* themes in this parable.

Theme 3—The Alternatives in Life

We can seek rewards and commendation in our efforts for God, or we can only seek to be obedient to His commands. We must know His will and do more than He commands us.

Theme 7—Christian Stewardship

Our stewardship requires that we do more for God than that which is commanded of us. Good stewards know the Master's heart and His will even before He expresses it.

Summary of God's Revelations
Theme 4—The Christian Character

This parable provides several truths: *We should do more than what is commanded of us. Commanded acts are under compulsion; Christians are to act out of love and faith.*

4–9. The Parable of Response to Authority: Matt. 21:28–32

"What do you think? A man had two sons; and he went to the first and said, 'Son, go and work in the vineyard today.' And he answered, 'I will not'; but afterward he repented and went. And he went to the second and said the same; and he answered, 'I go, sir,' but did not go. Which of the two did the will of his father?" They said, "The first." Jesus said to them, "Truly, I say to you, the tax collectors and the harlots go into the kingdom of God before you. For John came to you in the way of righteousness, and you did not believe him, but the tax collectors and the harlots believed him; and even when you saw it, you did not afterward repent and believe him."

Commentary

Jesus told this parable immediately after His authority was challenged by the *"chief priests and elders of the people."* (Matt. 21:23) When Jesus refused to tell them by what authority He did these things, He addressed, not His authority, but the response of the Jews to the authority of God. The two passages are closely linked. The distinction is made between those who serve God with their lips and those who serve God with their hearts and hands. God spoke against those who *"honor me with their lips, while their hearts are far from me."* (Isa. 29:13) By their lifestyle, the tax collectors and harlots first rejected the will and commands of God; then later they said, *"yes"*, because they repented.

This parable discussed two issues: first, *repentance and* second, *response and respect for authority*. Repentance is a change of heart and can be expressed by words and actions. Respect for authority is based on the recognition of God as Sovereign.

In this parable, the two *"sons"* take on distinctive characteristics; the first son is representative of the tax collectors and harlots; the second is representative of the Pharisees and other Jewish authorities. The question is the authority we honor and the man-

Chapter Nine

ner in which we show respect for the things of God. God called both to work in His vineyard. The first son initially refused but *"afterwards he repented and went." The* second son said that he would go and did not *go.*

This parable is about people who say one thing and do another. One son respected his father; the other apparently showed respect for the authority of his father, but then was hypocritical by failing to do what he had promised to do. Although the basic theme here is repentance and the response to authority, there is emphasis on *hypocrisy*. This subject is discussed by Dr. G. W. Parsons (Evangelical Dictionary of Biblical Theology). The Old Testament identifies hypocrisy as primarily insincere worship. The Lord rejects sacrificial offerings and temple attendance (Jer. 7:4–11) when worshipers have no intimate knowledge of Him or genuine love (Isa 1:11–17). Hypocrisy is disclosed in a godless heart (Job 36:13) that rebels against God's laws (Jer. 7:21–24) and results in injustice and oppression (Isa 1:10–17). In contrast, the true worshiper must come before the Lord with a pure heart (Ps 15:2; 24:4). The hypocrite is also an ungodly rebel. The New Testament combines the Old Testament concept of the godless rebel with religious performance to impress men (Matt 23:5). Hypocrites make an outward show of religion, whether in giving alms, praying, or fasting. The hypocrite pretends goodness, but beneath a religious veneer is a malicious or deceitful heart (Matt 22:15–18). Though hypocrites justify their religious activity, their hearts are not true to God (Matt 15:7–9,18–19). Thus, the term *"hypocrite"* (Matt 24:51) is a synonym for *"unfaithful unbeliever."* Such "hypocrites" hinder others from coming to Christ and even make converts to their godless lifestyle (Matt 23:13,15). Genuine faith and sincere love from a pure heart is a mark of godly character (1 Tim 1:5); it is the absence of hypocrisy.

Continuing with the theme of authority, we acknowledge that we are under the authority of Jesus Christ, who is the Head of the body, the church (Col. 1:18). Only through the power of the Holy Spirit is it possible to fulfill God's commandments. The self-righteous scribes and Pharisees refused to accept the teaching of the prophets, the apostles and Jesus Christ. They had the witness of

God's Hidden Treasures

John the Baptist; they refused to change even when they saw the repentance of the tax collectors and prostitutes. Tax collectors, harlots, and any one else who has initially said *"no"* to God can be saved, if they confess their sins, repent, and return to Him. Such people, the forgiven repentant, are the more productive workers in the kingdom of heaven. Some people today initially refuse to serve God and later *repent*. The apostle Paul is the classic example of a person who first denied Christ and then later became Christ's chosen vessel to take the gospel to the Gentiles. God calls everyone into the kingdom of heaven and rewards his or her service. However, those who profess that they will serve God, and do not do so, unfortunately, will not enter the kingdom.

Summary of Biblical Themes
Theme 4—The Christian Character

His authority must be honored, and our response in actions speaks louder than words. By our deeds, we shall be known. Hearing the *"truth"*, responding in faith, repenting of sins are all necessary preludes to entering the kingdom of heaven (Acts 26:20; Matt. 5:16; James 2:20; I Pet. 2:12).

In this parable, Jesus treats the following *secondary* messages:
Theme 1—The Character of God

God is sovereign, and His authority must be dominant in the life of the Church. Secular interests must not compromise His authority and His truths. The church of God is called to work in God's vineyard, faithfully responding to God's authority and obeying faithfully His commands.

Theme 2—The Kingdom of Heaven

The kingdom of heaven is for those who have accepted Jesus Christ; who *"receive"* and *"believe"* in Him (Jn. 1:12). To *"receive"* Him is to acknowledge Him as Savior and Lord. *"Believe"* means trusting in Him, completely and without limit or reservation. Repentance must occur prior to *"belief"*; for Jesus has stated, *"Unless you repent, you shall all perish."* (Lk. 13:5). The converse of that is, if we do repent and turn to Christ, we will be saved.

Chapter Nine

Theme 3—The Alternatives in Life

God has called everyone to work in His vineyard. Some will say that they will serve and not do so. Others may refuse to serve and later repent and serve. The two sons present an interesting example of the alternatives in our lives. We can promise and not fulfill the promise; instead, we must ensure that our actions exceed our words.

Theme 5—Repentance

God knows the hearts of His people (I Sam. 16:7). If we first refuse to accept His call, and later repent, God forgives us and brings us into His kingdom. Response to God's grace and repentance are important keys to entering the kingdom of heaven.

Summary of God's Revelations
Theme 4—The Christian Character

This parable deals with a promise, a truth, and a warning. The promise is: *Those who hear the message and repent will enter the kingdom of heaven.* The truth is: *The harlots and tax collectors will enter the kingdom before the self-righteous.* The warning is: *a person who continues in spiritual adultery and idolatry will never enter the kingdom of heaven.*

4–10. The Parable of God-given Talents: Matt. 25:14–30

"For it will be as when a man going on a journey called his servants and entrusted to them his property; to one he gave five talents, to another two, to another one, to each according to his ability. Then he went away. He who had received the five talents went at once and traded with them; and he made five talents more. So also, he who had the two talents made two talents more. But he who had received the one talent went and dug in the ground and hid his master's money. Now after a long time the master of those servants came and settled accounts with them. And he who had received the five talents came

God's Hidden Treasures

forward, bringing five talents more, saying, 'Master, you delivered to me five talents; here I have made five talents more.' His master said to him, 'Well done, good and faithful servant; you have been faithful over a little, I will set you over much; enter into the joy of your master.' And he also who had the two talents came forward, saying, 'Master, you delivered to me two talents; here I have made two talents more.' His master said to him, 'Well done, good and faithful servant; you have been faithful over a little, I will set you over much; enter into the joy of your master.' He also who had received the one talent came forward, saying, 'Master, I knew you to be a hard man, reaping where you did not sow, and gathering where you did not winnow; so I was afraid, and I went and hid your talent in the ground. Here you have what is yours.' But his master answered him, 'You wicked and slothful servant! You knew that I reap where I have not sowed, and gather where I have not winnowed? Then you ought to have invested my money with the bankers, and at my coming I should have received what was my own with interest. So take the talent from him, and give it to him who has the ten talents. For to every one who has will more be given, and he will have abundance; but from him who has not, even what he has will be taken away. And cast the worthless servant into the outer darkness; there men will weep and gnash their teeth.'"

Commentary

We have here a continuation of the theme of *servants*, as shown in two previous parables (4–8 and 4–9) and now here. The context for this parable is that Jesus has been speaking to His disciples regarding His Second Coming and the need to be prepared spiritually for His return, *"for you know neither the day nor the hour."* (Matt. 25:13). Further, the previous parable (4–8) described two sons who responded in different ways to the commands of their father. Similarly, in this parable, we have two types of servants, who respond differently to their stewardship responsibilities.

Regarding Christ's return, He has instructed us to be productive in all that He has entrusted to us. There will be an accounting for the *"good"* we have done with the *"talents"* that have been entrusted to us. There will be a final judgment of all believers, not on the basis of sin, but on the basis of works and stewardship.

Chapter Nine

So now, we come to this parable of the *"talents."* Although the term is used for money, but it is obvious that Jesus has a much higher and broader perspective in mind. As in most of these parables, there is again a contrast and the explanation of the alternatives in life. We are to choose the right direction with the right conduct, based upon the right attitude. Our attitude leads to our acts; our acts lead to our habits; our habits lead to our character; and our character defines our destiny.

The facts of the story are direct and simple. A master is going on a journey and entrusts some of his property to his servants. He gives to the first five talents, to the second two talents and to the third one talent. The issue is not so much the quantity of the talents that are given to a person but what each would do with the talents entrusted to him. The first took the five talents and doubled them. The second took the two talents and also doubled them. The third buried his one talent and returned it to his master; the third servant did nothing with the talent. He not only did nothing with it, in fact, he *"buried"* the talent. The master was pleased with the first two servants; he was angry because of the unbelief and lack of faith of the third. To the first and second servants, the master said, *"well done, good and faithful servant. You have been faithful with a little; I will set you over much. Enter into the joy of your master"* To the third servant, the master said—*"you wicked, lazy servant . . . cast the worthless servant into the outer darkness."*

There are two interesting aspects to this parable. First, there is the *characteristic* of the two types of servants: second, there are the two types of *rewards* experienced by the servants. The two characteristics are *"good and faithful"* and *"wicked and slothful."* The two types of rewards are *"enter into the joy of your master"* and *"cast the worthless servant into the outer darkness."* Two types of servants; two types of rewards. Now to understand and appreciate the fullness of this parable, there are key words that we need to examine e.g., *good, faithful and wicked*. These are words that we should examine, for knowledge of these words is important in understanding the parable.

God's Hidden Treasures

First, consider the word *good*. God's goodness is a bedrock truth of Scripture. <u>The Evangelical Dictionary of Biblical Theology</u> offers considerable insight into this subject. God's goodness is praised in the Psalms (e.g. 25:8), while Jesus affirms the Father's goodness when speaking to the rich young ruler (Matt 19:17). In 1 Peter 2:3, Peter echoes the language of Ps 34:8: *"Taste and see that the Lord is good;"* God's nature is not only *"good"*, but He is good to us (Ps 23:6; Rom. 2:4; Eph 2:7). Because we are to be in the image of God, our goodness is a reflection of divine goodness (Matt 5:48). For us, our goodness consists of love, joy, peace, righteousness; it includes avoiding evil. A good God is good to his people; good people behave decently toward each other and reflect God's goodness to them. In the New Testament, many words describe the specific characteristics and behaviors of good people, including *"just," "righteous," "holy," "pure," "gentle" and "kind "*. The choice between good and evil has been placed before people since the Garden of Eden when Adam and Eve ate fruit from the *"tree of the knowledge of good and evil"* (Gen. 2:9). Since then, God's curse has fallen on *"those who call evil good and good evil, who put darkness for light and light for darkness,"* (Isa 5:20). Those who serve God will *"seek good, not evil, . . . hate evil, love good"* (Amos 5:14–15). For Christians, goodness is from within. In the same way, a good person's good behavior shows a righteous heart (Matt 12:33–35). In the New Testament, goodness is a fruit of the Spirit (Gal 5:22). In summary, Jesus told the world, that *"only God is good."* (Mk. 10:18) We would not know goodness, if we do not know God.

The second important term is *faithful*. Faithful involves the sense of *steadfast, unchanging, constant in all situations, and committed to promises*. God is faithful because that is His nature, and He cannot go against His nature. As He is faithful, we, in His image, are likewise to be faithful. In the Old Testament, God's faithfulness and covenant love are interrelated (e.g. Deut 7:9; Ps 25:10). His covenant love is an expression of His faithfulness; conversely His faithfulness is expressed in His covenant love. Just as God is both faithful and loving, all that believe in God are to exhibit faithfulness and steadfast love in our lives. In the New Testament, His

Chapter Nine

faithfulness is evident, because He supplies "rain" to both the just and the unjust (Matt 5:45); He rewards those who do his will (Matt 6:4); He remains faithful as He fulfills His promises (2 Cor 1:18–19). Paul reminds us that God is faithful even when we are faithless, *"If we are faithless, he remains faithful—for he cannot deny himself."* (2 Tim 2:13). John declares that Jesus is the faithful and true witness (Rev 3:14), and *"is called the Faithful and True"* (Rev 19:11). Throughout the New Testament, faithfulness is one of the outstanding characteristics of Christians; it is the Spirit of God that enables Christians to remain *faithful* to both God and other believers (Gal 5:22). Since faithfulness is a divine virtue; our faithfulness is a measure of our fellowship with God.

The third term is *wicked (which is being sinful)*. Sin is lawlessness, for it is a clear transgression of God's laws. Sin includes both a failure to do what is right, and a decision to do what is clearly wrong. Sin has its foundation in idolatry. Although sin involves acts of rebellion and disobedience against God, it also includes acts against our fellow human being. Sin means missing the mark or the target, or the standard; and the target missed, and the standard violated is that established by God. Sin is rebellion in the heart, which refuses to accept the authority of God. The result of sin, if never confessed or repented of, is alienation from God and an eternity far removed from God. According to Dr. J. P. Payne, the Bible teaches that sin is the result of actions by a heart that is corrupt and inclined toward evil. Jesus deepened the understanding of sin in two ways. *First,* Jesus said that God requires obedience to His standards, values and commands. Jesus' harsh denunciations of sin show that sin must be confronted; we must do everything in our power to restore the unrepentant (Matt 18:15–20). Otherwise, the sinner dies in his sins, if he fails to acknowledge Jesus as the Christ. (John 8:24). However, Jesus Christ came to forgive sin. His name is Emmanuel because he will deliver his people from their sins (Matt 1:21; Luke 1:77). Jesus was a friend of sinners (Matt 9:9–13), He forgives sins, and He frees those suffering from its consequences (Mark 2:1–12). We cannot understand the gravity of sin until we stand at the foot of the cross and realize the price that God paid for the sins of the world. My sins put Christ on the cross.

We are called to be a good *"workman who has no need to be ashamed, rightly handling the word of truth."* (2 Tim. 2:15). *"We are his workmanship, created in Christ Jesus for good works, which God prepared beforehand, that we should walk in them."* (Eph. 2:10) *"All Scripture is inspired by God . . . that the man of God may be complete, equipped for every good work"* (2 Tim. 3:17) *"Now may the God of peace . . . equip you with everything good that you may do his will, working in you that which is pleasing in his sight."* (Heb. 13:20f) We are to do *"good works"* for we shall be judged by our works. Works are not the basis of salvation, but our good works are the evidence of faith and our love for God and for our neighbor. *"But be doers of the word, and not hearers only, deceiving yourselves."* (Jam. 1:22). Because works are the evidence of our faith, James wrote, *"You see that a man is justified by works and not by faith alone."* (Jam. 2:24)

This parable concludes with the judgment on the *"wicked, lazy servant"* being cast *"outside, into the darkness, where there will be weeping and gnashing of teeth."* The darkness is the absence of light, and therefore darkness is that region in which God is absent, for God is light. It may seem that God's judgment on the third servant is harsh; it is. However, it is just, because the servant failed to honor God; the servant failed to be a good steward; he failed to use God's possessions that were *"entrusted"* to him. Jesus closes this parable with the result of wickedness; in the darkness, there will be weeping and gnashing of teeth. However, for those in the light (Rev. 21:4), there will be no more weeping, for God *"will wipe away every tear from their eyes, and death shall be no more."* (Rev. 7:17)

Summary of Biblical Themes
Theme 4—The Christian Character

Everyone has God-given *"talents"*, which are to be multiplied. Our *"talents"* are not for our own use and pleasure; we have a higher purpose and a greater vision. God tells us that to those to whom much has been given, much will be required. Good and faithful servants make good use of their God-given talents.

Chapter Nine

In this parable, Jesus presents three *secondary* themes.

Theme 2—The Kingdom of Heaven

We will be judged on the manner in which we have used our talents and the degree to which we have been fruitful. Good and faithful servants will inherit the kingdom.

Theme 3—The Alternatives in Life

The choice is either to use our talents for God and others or for ourselves. We can be *good and faithful servants*, or we can be *wicked and lazy servants*.

Theme 7—Christian Stewardship

We are called to be good stewards of God's *"talents"* which He has entrusted to us; we are to use them for His glory and for the benefit and welfare of others.

Summary of God's Revelations
Theme 4—The Christian Character

This parable treats promises, truths and a warning. The promises are: *Faithfulness leads to the joy of our master; more will be given to those who use wisely the talents given by God.* The truths are: *If we are faithful over little, we will be entrusted with more; there is judgment for all.* The warning is: *wicked, slothful and worthless servants will be cast into outer darkness and spend eternity separated from God.*

The following eight (8) parables provide a *secondary* message:
4–11. *The Parable of the House on the Rock*
4–12. *The Parable of the Unworthy Servant*
4–13. *The Parable of the Friend at Midnight*
4–14. *The Parable of the Approaching Hour (Wedding Feast)*
4–15. *The Parable of the Lost and Found*
4–16. *The Parable of Workers in the Vineyard*
4–17. *The Parable of the Wicked Tenants*
4–18. *The Parable of the Ten Virgins*

God's Hidden Treasures

Summary of Biblical Themes
Theme 4—The Christian Character

These eighteen (18) parables can be summarized as follows:

The Parable of the Two Debtors remind us that we must *recognize our sinful* nature; *express sorrow for sin* in our lives; *repent* and turn to Jesus Christ as Savior and Lord. Then He will say, *"your sins are forgiven . . . your faith has saved you; go in peace."*

The Parable of the New Wine and Old Wineskins tells all Christians that we are children of God under the new covenant of grace: we must live a life worthy of such a New Testament, for the *forgiveness of sins:* we are to be *people thankful* for every blessing.

The Parable of the Good Samaritan is to instruct us that we must *show mercy* to everyone. We are to help the person by the *"side of the road."*

The Parable of the Poor, Rich Fool tells us that we must not seek material possessions at the expense of being *"rich towards God."* God-centered people will inherit the kingdom of heaven.

The Parable of The Barren Fig Tree identifies the *patience* of God towards His children who presently do not bear much fruit. It is God's desire that every *"tree"* be *"fruitful"*; each tree is given every opportunity to bear much fruit.

The Parable of Humility describes *humility* as one of the most necessary and valued characteristics of the Christian life.

The Parable of the Great Banquet calls Christians to be *responsive and obedient to God;* the demands of this world cannot dictate the time we spend serving God.

The Parable of the Unworthy Servant tells us that, if we do only what is commanded, then we will fail to live the full Christian life. We need to seek for *ways of doing more* than what God requires of us. Then we will be *worthy servants.*

The Parable of the Response to Authority calls us to be *faithful in our response to God.* Our *actions,* even more than our words, measure our obedience to God.

The Parable of God-given Talents identifies *good and faithful servants,* as those always seeking the spread of His kingdom. We are to multiply our God-given talents.

Chapter Nine

The Parable of the House on the Rock encourages us to build a *strong foundation on the Rock,* Jesus Christ (I Cor. 10:1–3). Doing so will ensure that we can survive the trials and tribulations of this life.

The Parable of the Ungrateful and Wicked Servant leads us to understand that we are forgiven people who express the image of God in the degree to which we *forgive others.*

The Parable of the Friend at Midnight is to encourage us to *pray diligently for the interests and welfare of others.*

The Parable of Christ's Return: the Unexpected Hour tells us that we must be *constantly vigilant and prepared* for the Second Coming of Christ.

The Parable of the Lost and Found is to teach us that we must *"seek the lost"* until they are found. This will result in great rejoicing in heaven over every sinner who repents.

The Parable of the Workers in the Vineyard calls us to be *generous and loving* in our relations with all other Christian workers who labor in God's vineyard. We rejoice that all receive the same wage, which is *eternal life.*

The Parable of the Wicked Tenants is to encourage us to be *good stewards of this world,* knowing that it is God's world and His possessions, not ours.

The Parable of the Ten Virgins warns us to be *constantly prepared* for the Second Coming of Jesus Christ.

Eighteen parables summarize the Christian life as: one of forgiveness towards others; as thankful people, living in the new covenant of grace; as showing mercy in every situation; of being rich towards the things of God, who is the God of patience, waiting for us to be fruitful; as people with a humble and contrite spirit; a people responsive and obedient to God; a people faithful and worthy servants, doing more than is commanded of us; a people faithful and bold in the use of our talents; a people who know that our true foundation is the Lord God; a people forgiving as we have been forgiven; a people who pray for the will of God and the interest of others; a people alert and prepared for the Second Coming; a people seeking the lost; a people loving and generous to our fellow

God's Hidden Treasures

laborers in God's vineyard; good stewards of God's vineyard; above all, to live a life fully prepared for the Second Coming of our Lord and Savior, Jesus Christ.

Summary of God's Revelations
Theme 4—The Christian Character

The commands are: *show mercy; do not put the new covenant of grace, in the old context of the Law; be rich towards the things of God; invite those who cannot repay you.* The promises are: *if you love God, your sins are forgiven; Christ died for the sins of the world; if you show mercy, you shall live (be saved); God is patient and desires us to produce much fruit; those who hear the message and repent will enter the kingdom of heaven; faithfulness leads to the joy of our master; more will be given to those who use wisely the talents given by God.* The truths are: *true repentance leads to forgiveness and salvation; love is the product of repentance; fast for the right reason; there is now a new covenant for the forgiveness of sins; there is a new standard of salvation (by grace) instead of the Law; we must be a new creation; the Law was given to reveal sin; God loves the merciful; man's life does not consist in the abundance of his possessions; everyone who exalts himself will be humbled, and he who humbles himself will be exalted; blessings come from those acts in which people cannot repay; we should do more than what is commanded of us; commanded acts are under compulsion; Christians are to act out of love and faith; the harlots and tax collectors will enter the kingdom before the self-righteous; if we are faithful over little, we will be entrusted with more; there is judgment for all.* The warnings are: *if you love little, you are forgiven little; do not neglect the needs of others; do not lay up physical treasures for yourself; seek the things of God; if we do not produce fruit in due season, we shall be "cut down"; never exalt yourself, for you shall certainly be humbled; do not anger the householder by refusing so wonderful an invitation; the consequences of refusal are eternal; one who continues in spiritual adultery and idolatry will never enter the kingdom of heaven; wicked, slothful and worthless servants will be cast into outer darkness and spend eternity separated from the Father.*

CHAPTER TEN

Theme 5—The Parable of Repentance

"Repent and turn away from all your transgressions, lest iniquity be your ruin." (Eze. 18:30)

"They went out and preached that people should repent." (Mk. 6:12)

". . . unless you repent, you shall all likewise perish." (Lk. 13:3)

Repentance is a theme that permeates every parable, even though there is only one parable in which this theme is *primary*. Jesus began His earthly ministry by preaching, *"Repent, for the kingdom of heaven is at hand." (Matt. 4:17)*. Since His first earthly word is *repent,* it is not surprising that repentance would play such a dominant role in the parables. Not only must people repent, but Jesus went on to say, *"unless your righteousness exceeds that of the scribes and the Pharisees, you will never enter the kingdom of heaven." (Matt. 5:20) Therefore repentance is the first and vital step towards righteousness in the journey to the kingdom of heaven.* The kingdom *is at hand* because Jesus Christ, the King, *is at hand*. Obedience is our response to the command to repent.

But what is *repentance?*. It is a fundamental and thorough change in the hearts of people, to turn from sin and towards God. Repentance and faith are two sides of the same coin: by repentance, one turns away from sin; by faith, *turning toward* God and His glory (Acts 20:21), eternal life (Acts 11:18), and knowledge of the truth (2 Tim. 2:25). Although faith alone in Christ alone is the condition for salvation (Eph. 2:8–10), repentance is representative of faith and inseparable from it, for repentance is not possible without expressing our faith. Repentance means a change of mind (Gen. 6:6–7), regret for past conduct (Matt. 27:3) and a desire to be conformed to God. It expresses a genuine sorrow to God (2 Cor. 7:9–10); it is a humble self-surrender to the will and service of God (Acts 9:6). Repentance is not an act that arises from fear of the consequences or penalty of sin. It is an act, expressing sorrow and regret for past sin; a willingness to recognize and accept Jesus Christ as Savior and Lord; and a commitment to obey and serve Him. Such a twofold turning, or conversion, is necessary for entrance into the kingdom (Matt. 18:3). *"Unless you repent,"* said Jesus, *"you will all likewise perish"* (Luke 13:3,5). The positive, or merciful, side is seen in these words: *"There is joy in the presence of the angels of God over one sinner who repents" (Luke* 15:10). After Jesus' crucifixion and resurrection, His disciples continued His message of repentance and faith (Acts 2:38).

Jesus told the world, then and now, that you will perish unless you repent. Therefore, we need, in like measure, to understand *"perish."* The Greek word is used of the *"eternal doom of the sinner, to be utterly and finally ruined and destroyed, to be lost or put to death, even to disappear or vanish or to decay completely."* (A Critical Lexicon and Concordance of the English and Greek New Testament—Bullinger). This casts the word *"perish"* in its proper light and therefore anyone who ignores the necessity of repentance faces the future that this word implies.

The Parable of the Lost and Found (21) is the single parable in which Jesus stresses this theme of repentance. It is one of the best known and most beloved of all the parables; everyone is familiar with the story. In addition, it has been the subject of extensive study by many people, e.g. Martin Luther, Charles Haddon Spurgeon, Dr. John Stott, Dr. Haddon Robinson, Dr. Carol Wilcox, including information in Vincent's Word Study of the New Testa-

Chapter Ten

ment. All of these insights have influenced my thinking. Further, It is a parable of such breath and depth that it relates to almost all the Ten Biblical Themes.

5–1. The Parable of the Lost and Found: Lk. 15:1–31
(The lost sheep, the lost coin, and the two lost sons)
"Now the tax collectors and sinners were all drawing near to hear him. And the Pharisees and the scribes murmured, saying, 'This man receives sinners and eats with them.' So he told them this parable:

What man of you, having a hundred sheep, if he has lost one of them, does not leave the ninety-nine in the wilderness, and go after the one which is lost, until he finds it? And when he has found it, he lays it on his shoulders, rejoicing. And when he comes home, he calls together his friends and his neighbors, saying to them, 'Rejoice with me, for I have found my sheep which was lost.' Just so, I tell you, there will be more joy in heaven over one sinner who repents than over ninety-nine righteous persons who need no repentance.

Or what woman, having ten silver coins, if she loses one coin, does not light a lamp and sweep the house and seek diligently until she finds it? And when she has found it, she calls together her friends and neighbors, saying, 'Rejoice with me, for I have found the coin which I had lost.' Just so, I tell you, there is joy before the angels of God over one sinner who repents.'

And he said, 'There was a man who had two sons; and the younger of them said to his father, "Father, give me the share of property that falls to me." And he divided his living between them. Not many days later, the younger son gathered all he had and took his journey into a far country, and there he squandered his property in loose living. And when he had spent everything, a great famine arose in that country and he began to be in want. So he went and joined himself to one of the

God's Hidden Treasures

citizens of that country, who sent him into his fields to feed swine. And he would gladly have fed on the pods that the swine ate; and no one gave him anything. But when he came to himself he said, 'How many of my father's hired servants have bread enough and to spare, but I perish here with hunger! I will arise and go to my father, and I will say to him, "Father, I have sinned against heaven and before you; I am no longer worthy to be called your son; treat me as one of your hired servants." And he arose and came to his father. But while he was yet at a distance, his father saw him and had compassion, and ran and embraced him and kissed him. And the son said to him, "Father, I have sinned against heaven and before you; I am no longer worthy to be called your son." But the father said to his servants, "Bring quickly the best robe, and put it on him; and put a ring on his hand, and shoes on his feet; and bring the fatted calf and kill it, and let us eat and make merry; for this my son was dead, and is alive again; he was lost, and is found." And they began to make merry.

Now his elder son was in the field; and as he came and drew near to the house, he heard music and dancing. And he called one of the servants and asked what this meant. And he said to him, "Your brother has come, and your father has killed the fatted calf, because he has received him safe and sound." But he was angry and refused to go in. His father came out and entreated him, but he answered his father, "Lo, these many years I have served you, and I never disobeyed your command; yet you never gave me a kid, that I might make merry with my friends. But when this son of yours came, who has devoured your living with harlots, you killed for him the fatted calf!" And he said to him, "Son, you are always with me, and all that is mine is yours. It was fitting to make merry and be glad, for this your brother was dead, and is alive; he was lost, and is found.'"

Commentary

This is generally acclaimed as the greatest of the parables, for it contains three excellent stories, with a multitude of themes and messages. Its greatness lies in its simplicity, the power of the message, and the depth of the degree to which Jesus treats the subject. For that reason, it is important to understand its context. Recall that the parable begins with, *"now the tax collectors and sinners were gathering around to hear him."*

Chapter Ten

They were gathering around—why? Well, recall that in the previous chapter, Jesus was teaching on the conditions of being His disciples. He summarized it by stating, *"Whoever does not bear his own cross and come after me, cannot be my disciple"* (Lk. 14:27). So Jesus has been talking about *discipleship*, and what is required of those who would follow him. So they were gathering around to understand more of what that meant, and what was involved in being His disciple. Typical of the questions they might have asked were; what would be required of them as disciples?; what does it mean to *follow him*?; what is involved in doing so?; if they were to follow him, where is he going?; finally, what is the personal price of being a disciple? They were probably seeking answers to these and other questions; that is why *they gathered around*.

Jesus is telling them, and us, that what is required to be His disciple is to be willing to *seek the lost*. This is an important aspect of being a disciple of Jesus Christ. Oswald Chambers (*My Utmost for His Highest*) presents some interesting insight into being a disciple of Jesus. In his September 25th meditation, Chambers wrote, *"No amount of enthusiasm will ever stand up to the strain that Jesus Christ will put upon His servant. Only one thing will bear the strain, and that is a personal relationship with Jesus Christ Himself—a relationship that has been examined, purified, and tested until only one purpose remains and I can truly say 'I am here for God to send me where He will.' . . . If we are to be disciples of Jesus Christ, we must be made disciples supernaturally. And as long as we consciously maintain the determined purpose to be His disciples, we can be sure that we are not disciples. Jesus says, 'You did not choose me, but I chose you . . .' (Jn. 15:16). That is the way the grace of God begins. We are drawn to God by a work of His supernatural grace, and we can never trace back to find where the work began . . . He does not build on any natural capacity of ours at all. God does not ask us to do the things that are naturally easy for us—He only asks us to do the things that we are perfectly fit to do through His grace, and that is where the cross we must bear will always come."*

Oswald Chambers has it right; being His disciple is an unselfish willingness to spend whatever time and effort is necessary to serve God and to find the lost. In following him, He is going to lead us in a deliberate search for the lost of every generation. The personal price for them and, for us, is a willingness to seek the Father's heart, to be obedient to His will, to rejoice over sinners who repent and not to rest until the lost have been found.

Now in the parable, two actions are in process; first, by those who are interested in hearing what it means to be a disciple; second, by the Pharisees and scribes who *murmured, "this man receives sinners and eats with them."* And Luke continues, *"So he told them this parable."* The parable has two purposes; *first,* is to tell one group (*tax collectors and sinners*) what is involved in being His disciple; *second,* to tell the Pharisees and scribes why Jesus *"receives sinners and eats with them."* In another sense, Jesus has a single message that is relevant to His earthly ministry. He is saying He has come to *"seek and to save the lost"*, while at the same time telling His disciples that His ministry must become their ministry. This relates to Matthew 11:19–20, when Jesus confronts the crowds because many said of Jesus," *Behold, a glutton and a drunkard, a friend of tax collectors and sinners . . . then he (Jesus) began to upbraid the cities where most of his mighty works had been done, because they did not repent."* Jesus had been called previously a *"friend of tax collectors and sinners",* so the charge was not new to Him. But it is interesting that that is what we must precisely be, friends to sinners and tax collectors. That is the ministry of the Christian Church.

So to explain further this message of discipleship, Jesus told *one parable with three closely interrelated stories*; each "*story*" sets the tone for the following until the full message of His teaching in this parable is set before the hearer. *One parable; three stories.*

In the first story, Jesus looked at the *"Pharisees and the scribes"* and said, suppose one of you were a shepherd. Now, to begin with, that is a disgusting thought; in Judaism, the shepherd was an outcast in his own society. They were not permitted to worship in the temple; people were discouraged from having any dealing with them, and the Midrash (23rd Psalm) said, *"there is no position in the world as despised as that of a shepherd."* And Jesus said to the Phari-

Chapter Ten

sees, suppose one of you were a shepherd. Suppose you were an outcast and despised! The Pharisees would have been insulted by such a supposition.

The first story concerns a shepherd who had 100 sheep *and loses* one of them. Jesus said that the shepherd leaves the 99 and searches until he *finds* it. Then he joyfully calls his neighbors to rejoice with him. *"In the same way, said Jesus, there will be more rejoicing in heaven over one sinner who repents than over 99 righteous persons who do not need to repent."* Why did the shepherd have to go and seek the lost? Was it all that important? And I guess the answer is: yes, it was important, and he sought the lost sheep simply because he cared for him. In the first story, the emphasis is on *rejoicing,* in heaven, rather than repentance. That is what a disciple does, said Jesus; a disciple seeks the lost, and he rejoices, and heaven rejoices, when the lost are found.

The second story deals with a woman who had 10 coins and *lost* one of them. The small coin may not have been of great value, but it was extremely important to this woman. So she searched for that lost coin until she found it; then, she invites her neighbors to *rejoice* with her. Jesus concludes this part of the parable with these words, *"in the same way, there is rejoicing in the presence of the angels of God over one sinner who repents."*

At this point, we can begin to get a sense that God is persistent in seeking and finding the lost. That is the great message of Luke 19:1–10, where Jesus told Zacchaeus and the crowd in Jericho, *the "Son of man came to seek and to save the lost."*

Jesus now moves from a story about a *lost sheep* and a *lost coin* to that of *two sons.* Now, the first son, the younger, asks for his inheritance, which he takes and wastes in riotous living in a far country. There is a famine in the land, and he is reduced to feeding pigs with the husks that he would gladly have eaten. Then it said that *"when he came to himself",* which is to say *"when he came to his senses."* By the way, isn't that a wonderful way to describe repentance, when we come to our senses! The younger son determines that he will return to his father's house and say to him, *"Father, I have sinned against heaven and before you; I am no longer worthy to be called your son; treat me as one of your hired servants."* And he arose and came to his father. Think of what it would mean to be no longer a son but to be a hired servant. Slaves had privileges, for the master was required to care for them, but a hired man had no standing with the master. However, the hired man could be paid, and perhaps the son was looking for a way to repay his father. Perhaps that is what he had in mind.

But while he was yet at a distance, his father *saw* him and *had compassion* on him and *ran* and *embraced* him and *kissed* him. What a symphony of actions! That is what God does, *when a repentant sinner comes home.* So the father welcomes the son home. He had the servants put the best robe on him, a ring on his hand, sandals on his feet and had a feast arranged because *"my son was dead and is now alive; he was lost and is found."* Is that the way that you would use those words, dead and now alive; lost and is found? Wouldn't you just say that he was lost and is found? But the father had it right; his son was dead, separated from the father; now he's alive; he is home with the father.

Now it seems that Jesus might well conclude the parable at that point; the younger son has come home and is reinstated as a son. But Jesus continues, *"the elder son was in the fields",* and he was unhappy to hear that his brother has returned. In addition, he did not even recognize him as his brother. The elder son also refuses to come and join in the celebration. Further, the elder son does not act like a son. Instead he acts like a hired servant. Listen, *"Lo, these many years, I have served you, and I have never disobeyed your commands. But this son of yours (not my brother), who has devoured your living with harlots . . ."* and he would not listen to his father nor share in the joy of a sinner who has come home. The father tells the elder son, *"Son, you are always with me, and all that is mine is yours. It was fitting to make merry and be glad, for this brother of yours was dead and is alive; he was lost and was found."* That is the story.

When we examine the story, we begin to understand that the younger son was lost in a far country, while the elder son was lost at home. The elder son was lost, because he never understood the father's heart; he never understood the grace of God. You see, Jesus is telling us that we can spend a lifetime in the father's vineyard and never truly understand what is on the Father's heart.

The sheep was lost in the far country; the younger son was lost in the far country.

The coin was lost at home; the elder son was lost at home.

We can be just as lost at home as we can be lost in a far country.

And Jesus is saying; heaven rejoices when a repentant sinner *comes to his senses* and comes home. We can be dead and are now alive; we can be lost and are now found. And one reason for our life is to bring joy to a heavenly God: by pleasing Him in all that we do and say. King David (Psa. 19:14) understood this well, *"Let the words of my mouth and the meditations of my heart be acceptable in thy sight, O Lord, my rock and my redeemer."* Isn't that a great summary of just how we should live for God in this life! We are in the business of pleasing God, and we do so by demonstrating our faith in Him for *"Without faith it is impossible to please God . . ."* (Heb. 11:6)

This great parable about repentance, when all the temptations of this world are before us, teaches us to remember how good it is in my father's house. When we come to our senses, the true measure of repentance, we return to the Rock of our salvation. This is a parable about being lost and found and the joy in heaven when a sinner repents.

Summary of Biblical Themes
Theme 5—The Necessity of Repentance

Repentance is one of the keys to discipleship and the fullness of the Christian life. Jesus addressed the subject of being His disciple by defining one of the crowning marks as bringing the lost to repentance. When we *"come to our senses"*, we remember our loving Father, and we return to Him, in a humble and contrite spirit. It began with the younger son asking for a share of his inheritance; it concludes with him receiving his true inheritance, eternal life with his Father. Repentance was the key. What is true for him is true for us.

God's Hidden Treasures

There are five *secondary* themes:

Theme 1—The Character of God

God searches for the repentant sinner, *"for there is more joy in heaven over one sinner who repents than over ninety-nine righteous persons who need no repentance."* (Lk. 15:7) It is God's character that He constantly looks for the sinner to "*return*", to *repent;* when that happens, the *"father saw him and had compassion on him, and ran and embraced him and kissed him."* (Lk. 15:20) God seeks the lost; He rejoices when they are found. And when the sinner returns, the Father *reclaims him as his son, who was dead and in now alive, who was lost and is now found.* God *"receives sinners and eats with them."* That is the mark and the glory of His fellowship with us.

Theme 2—The Kingdom of Heaven

The kingdom of heaven is a place of joy over one repentant sinner.

Theme 3—Alternatives in Life

This parable emphasizes that we can seek the pleasures of this world and spend all their material resources for the things that give us physical pleasure; but, *when we come to our senses*, we begin to realize how wonderful everything is in our Father's house.

Theme 4—The Christian Character

The characteristic of the Christian life is to know that sometimes we may deliberately leave our father and be lost. When we come to our senses, we return, repentant and confident of His everlasting love. We are lost when we sin; we are *"found"* when we repent.

Theme 6-Our Role in Evangelism

Evangelism is one of the more important themes of this parable. The parable begins with the shepherd *"searching"* for the lost sheep; the woman *"searching"* for the lost coin and then *heaven rejoicing* when the lost sheep is found and when the lost coin is found. The *Father rejoices* when his son returns, who was *"dead and is now alive, was lost and was found."* Evangelism is seeking the lost and rejoicing when a sinner comes home.

Chapter Ten

Summary of Biblical Themes
Theme 5—Repentance

Repentance is the great message of Jesus as He began His earthly ministry, *"Repent, for the kingdom of heaven is at hand."* (Matt. 4:17) Repentance is a dual act, of turning away from sin and turning to the righteousness of God. It is a change similar to baptism, where we die to the old self, the old allegiances, and we rise up out of the *"water"*, committed in a new allegiance to Christ. Repentance represents a change from bondage in sin to freedom and reconciliation with God. *The Parable of the Lost and Found (Lk. 15)*, presents two messages regarding repentance, the first regarding God and heaven, the second regarding ourselves. The first message is that *"there is more joy in heaven over one sinner who repents than over ninety-nine people who need no repentance."* The second message is that repentance begins, *"when we come to our senses."* Repentance is the act required for the forgiveness of our sins and our acceptance as a child of God. Therefore, repentance is the key to discipleship that, in turn, is the key to entering the kingdom of heaven. Repentance leads to our eternal inheritance.

Summary of God's Revelations
Theme 5—Repentance

This parable has promises, truths, and warnings. The promises are: *the Father welcomes the repentant sinner and restores him to his previous position; once a son; always a son; God searches for and seeks his own.* The truths are: *there is more joy in heaven over one sinner who repents than over 99 persons who need no repentance; a person can be lost "at home", even doing the work of God; you don't need to go to the far country to get lost.* The warnings are: *the lost are dead; the found are alive; the lost will be eternally separated from the Father; if you are lost, come to your senses and return to your father's house.*

CHAPTER ELEVEN

Theme 6—The Parables of The Responsibility for Evangelism

"Seek the welfare of the city where I am sending you . . . for in their welfare, you will find your welfare." (Jer. 29:7)

I must preach the good news of the kingdom of God to the other cities also; for I was sent for this purpose." (Lk. 4:43)

"you will receive power when the Holy Spirit has come upon you, and you will be my witnesses . . . to the ends of the earth." (Acts 1:8)

    We now come to evangelism, one of the most significant themes for the Christian church. It is one of the hardest and one of the most challenging. However, for the Christian Church to fulfill its true calling, then evangelism must be one of its principle ministries. Evangelism is the proclamation of the *"good news"*, a message that includes the *presentation* of the Person of Jesus Christ, in the Power of the Holy Spirit, and the *invitation* for the hearer to accept Jesus Christ as Savior and Lord, leading to *reconciliation* with God the Father. The purpose of evangelism is to bring about such reconciliation and to present *"everyone mature in Christ."*

    The <u>Evangelical Dictionary of Theology</u> defines evangelism as *"The proclamation of the good news of salvation in Jesus Christ with a view to bringing about the reconciliation of the sinner to God the Father through the regenerating power of the Holy Spirit."* Luke takes up the theme with the angel Gabriel predicting the Savior's birth *"therefore the child to be born will be called holy, the Son of God." (Lk. 1:35)* Other angels announced the Savior's birth (Lk. 2:10), as well as *"evangelized"* the shepherds, by bringing them *"good news of a great joy which shall come to all people."*

Throughout the New Testament, Jesus taught one great message about evangelism: that world evangelism must occur between His Ascension and his Second Coming (e.g. Matt 24:14): *"And this gospel of the kingdom will be preached in the whole world as a testimony to all nations, and then the end will come."* World evangelization is certain in its occurrence and universal in its scope. We cannot ignore so specific a responsibility.

Jesus said that evangelism is sowing the *"seed"*; in this regard, Jesus defined the *"seed"* to be sown as the *"word of the kingdom"* (Matt. 13:19). For this reason, every disciple of the Lord Jesus Christ is committed to fulfilling the commission to *"go into all the world and make disciples of all nations, baptizing them . . . and teaching them to observe all that I have commanded you."* (Matt. 28:19f). The process of sowing seeds is, first, to understand and *accept* the gospel, to *"live"* it and then *"witness"* (Acts 1:8) to it in our lives. Christians are to prepare the *"soil" (the hearts of people)* to receive the seed; we must be willing to *"fertilize and nourish"* the growth and *"water"* and protect the plant, so that the growth is consistent with God's plan. In presenting the gospel to others, our role is to be faithful in presentation and to rely on the power of the Holy Spirit to convince and convict. We are constantly reminded that the seed will fall on different types of soil; in some cases, our role might be to soften *"hardened hearts"* to receive this *"good news."*

There is one parable in which this is the *primary* message, but it is of such significance and so explicit as to make the message abundantly clear.

Chapter Eleven

6–1. The Parable of the Sower: Matt. 13:1–9, 18–23

"That same day Jesus went out of the house and sat beside the sea. And great crowds gathered about him, so that he got into a boat and sat there; and the whole crowd stood on the beach. And he told them many things in parables, saying: 'A sower went out to sow. And as he sowed, some seeds fell along the path, and the birds came and devoured them. Other seeds fell on rocky ground, where they had not much soil, and immediately they sprang up, since they had no depth of soil, but when the sun rose they were scorched; and since they had no root they withered away. Other seeds fell upon thorns, and the thorns grew up and choked them. Other seeds fell on good soil and brought forth grain, some a hundredfold, some sixty, some thirty. He who has ears, let him hear . . .'

"Hear then the parable of the sower. When any one hears the word of the kingdom and does not understand it, the evil one comes and snatches away what is sown in his heart; this is what was sown along the path. As for what was sown on rocky ground, this is he who hears the word and immediately receives it with joy; yet he has no root in himself, but endures for a while, and when tribulation or persecution arises on account of the word, immediately he falls away. As for what was sown among thorns, this is he who hears the word, but the cares of the world and the delight in riches choke the word, and it proves unfruitful. As for what was sown on good soil, this is he who hears the word and understands it; he indeed bears fruit, and yields, in one case a hundredfold, in another sixty, and in another thirty."

Commentary

Jesus now presents one of the more significant parables relating to His earthly ministry and that of His disciples. Matthew 13:1–9 presents the parable; Matthew 13:18–23 is its explanation.

God's Hidden Treasures

Now, we should understand the context in which this parable is given. Matthew concluded chapter 12 with Jesus speaking to the people and addressing the question of *"who is my mother, and who are my brothers? And stretching out his hand towards his disciples, he said, 'Here are my mother and my brothers. For whoever does the will of my Father in heaven is my brother, and sister, and mother.'"*

The phrase, *"that same day"* relates now to the matter of kinship with Jesus for all those who *"do the will of my Father in heaven . . ."* He has defined those who are His brothers and sisters and mother as the ones who do the will of His Father. The will of God is that every knee would bow and every tongue confess that Jesus is Lord to the glory of God the Father. (Phil 2:11) The will of the Father is that all would come to salvation through faith alone in His Son alone. Presenting this message is the purpose of evangelism and that is the subject Jesus now addresses.

When Jesus spoke publicly in parables, He often, in private, explained the meaning of the parable to His disciples. This is the situation now as Jesus describes four types of people who will *"hear"* the message and the result that follows.

- The seed fell along *the path*; birds came and *ate* it,
- The seed fell on *rocky soil*; the plants *withered* because they had no roots.
- The seed fell *among thorns*, which *choked* the plants.
- The seed fell *on good soil*, and it brings forth an *abundant crop*.

The message is similar to that in the Parable of the House on the Rock (1), in which Jesus stresses that the wise is one who *"hears these words of mine and does them."* Now Jesus states that the wise is he who *receives* the *seed* (my words) and is *fruitful* (does them).

In three cases in this parable, the seed is sown, but there is no growth and no fruit. The secret to growth is that the soil must be *"good"*, it must be willing, perhaps even anxious, to receive the seed. Good soil *"receives"* the seed and produces an abundant crop. The soil is the *"heart"* of those who hear the message and give the seed the opportunity to bear fruit in their lives. One question is, how do we identify the *good soil* in this world? Maybe we never

Chapter Eleven

can; therefore, we must keep sowing as if all soil is good. We can never judge the character of the soil, until we have seen the fruit in people's lives. How does a person become *"good soil"*? Well, that is the result of the power of the Holy Spirit, leading us into all truth, convicting us of all sin, and leading us to confession and repentance. The soil gets better as our relationship and fellowship with God grows. In some ways, this parable brings to mind Isaiah 55:10–11, *"For as the rain and the snow come down from heaven, and return not thither but water the earth, making it bring forth and sprout, giving seed to the sower and bread to the eater, so shall my word be that goes forth from my mouth; it shall not return to me empty, but it shall accomplish that which I purpose, and prosper in the thing for which I sent it."* The seed, God's Word, goes forth to accomplish God's purpose.

We must understand what the seed is. The seed in Isaiah and the seed in the parable are one and the same. The seed is the Word of God, sent by God to nourish His people; it is *His word that goes forth from His mouth.* It shall not return to Him until it accomplishes the purpose for which He sent it. What is that purpose? It is that there would be *"peace"* or reconciliation of the world to its Creator. It is that people would hear the word and would bear much fruit (Jn. 15:8) *"by this my Father is glorified, that you bear much fruit."*

In this passage, Jesus presents four messages. The *first* concerns the Sower of seeds; the *second* relates to evangelism; the *third* describes the result of evangelism; and the *fourth* identifies the fruitful life of a Christian.

First, there are two different Sowers and two different seeds. *"He who sows the good seed is the Son of man"*; this is obviously Jesus Christ. However, there are *"weeds . . . and the enemy who sows them is the devil."* Two sowers; two seeds, Jesus Christ sows the good seed; Satan sows seeds of deceit and lies and temptations to trap the unwary. Christ is sowing seed that brings forth truth, righteousness, peace, joy and love. What a difference there is in the two sowers and in the results of their seed.

God's Hidden Treasures

The second theme relates to *evangelism*. Recall that Jesus described His earthly mission in His encounter with Zacchaeus (Lk. 19:10), *"the Son of man has come to seek and to save the lost."* In this parable, Jesus is giving renewed emphasis to that ministry. In this passage, Jesus tells the world and His disciples that He has come to sow much seed. The intent is to call out His disciples who will be the righteousness of God, so that, at the close of the age, they *"will shine like the sun in the kingdom of their Father."* This parable describes the world as the field, where both Jesus Christ and Satan sow seeds. Jesus said that one seed produces the *"sons of the kingdom"*, while the other seed produces *"sons of the evil one."* To produce the sons of the kingdom, the seed must also contain the Word of God. However, God has had two Words, the Revealed Word (the Bible) and the Living Word (Jesus Christ). God's Words are two complementary elements of the one seed; both Words have authority, but Jesus Christ is the higher authority.

The *third theme* relates to the purpose of evangelism. Jesus explains the reason for sowing the seed; that people would commit their lives to Him and become children of God in the kingdom of heaven. The seed is the gospel, which is the good news of the forgiveness of sin. This purpose of sowing the seed is to bring people into a committed and personal relationship with Jesus Christ and into the kingdom of heaven.

Fourth, our responsibility in evangelism is to preach the gospel (2 Tim. 4:2) and to spread the Word of God by sowing seeds. Jesus warns us that the seed will fall on a variety of soils, and we should be prepared for a variety of responses. However, we are to be faithful in sowing the *"seed"*, knowing that the Holy Spirit will convince and/or convict the hearer to receive the Word. Our stewardship requires that we preach the word with power and conviction. Regardless of the reaction of the *"soil"*, we are to be *"good and faithful workers."* We are to remember the experience of Jesus Christ, who taught, who healed, who gave many signs, and yet only eleven believed. The cross is the greatest example of love and the greatest demonstration of the rejection of the "good news." We remember Paul, in his joyful ordeals to take the *"seed"* to an unbelieving world. We are to remember the faithful (Heb. 11:1–40),

Chapter Eleven

who never looked back, but were faithful in receiving the *"seed."* And we remember also that, if we don't suffer for the cross of Christ, then perhaps we are not fulfilling the will of God, that the *seed* be spread throughout the world. We must evangelize with passion, compassion, conviction, and courage. As Paul wrote to Timothy (2 Tim. 2:15), *"Do your best to present yourself to God as one approved, a workman who has no need to be ashamed, rightly handling the word of truth."* In evangelism, we are to be such a workman, a good and faithful worker. James wrote, *"count it all joy, my brethren, when you meet various trials, for you know that the testing of your faith produces steadfastness . . ."*

We must keep before us the reasons that Jesus spoke in parables to the crowds, but later explained them to His disciples. First, Jesus knew that only the *"born again"*, a child of God, would understand the deep truth of the parables. He spoke to His followers, because they had *"been given to know the secrets of the kingdom of heaven, but to them it has not been given."* (Matt. 13:11) Only those who believe in Him; accept Him, follow Him and serve Him would truly understand the message of the parables. To everyone else, there is limited understanding of their secrets. Secondly, Jesus spoke of the hardness of people's hearts, quoting from Isaiah 6:9–11, in which God said, *"the people will hear without understanding; see without perceiving; their hearts will grow dull."* God is saying, then and now, that we should hear and understand, that we should see and perceive, and that our hearts would receive the Word with gladness and not be hardened, or grow dull, or become calloused. God sows seeds; He is seeking good soil in which His word will take root and grow and bear much fruit. Finally, it is important to understand the phrase *"he who has ears, let him hear"*, since Jesus repeats this phrase both to the crowd in general and to His disciples in particular. The Greek word for *"hear"* has a series of meanings. *"Hear"* can mean to hear imperfectly, hear incorrectly and misunderstand, not to listen to, or pretend not to hear. Hear can also mean following a suggestion, believing a promise, or obeying a command but more importantly, it means personally to *accept the speaker*. It is in the latter sense that the term is used here. Jesus wants us to hear perfectly, and, more importantly, to accept Him personally.

God's Hidden Treasures

Summary of Biblical Themes
Theme 6—The Responsibility for Evangelism

The Parable of the Sower defines God as the sower of seeds; in like manner, we are to be *faithful sowers* of the same seed, the gospel, with the certainty and conviction that the *seed* will take root in the hearts of people. Our responsibility is to sow the seed; it is the work of the Holy Spirit to convince and convict. Regardless of the reaction of the *"soil"*, we are to be *"good and faithful workers."* We remember Paul, in all his ordeals, taking the *"seed"* to an unbelieving world. We are to remember the faithful (Heb. 11:1–40), who never looked back but were faithful in receiving and sowing the seed. We remember also that, if we don't suffer for the cross of Christ, then perhaps we may be doing far less than fulfilling the will of God. We must evangelize with passion, compassion, conviction, and courage. Evangelism is one of the greatest trials and greatest opportunities we face; God will richly reward our faithfulness.

In addition, Jesus presents four other *secondary* themes:
Theme 1—The Character of God

God wants everyone to hear and believe; God offers salvation to all. It is His perfect patience that none should perish (2 Pet. 3:9) *"The Lord is not slow in keeping His promises, as some understand slowness. He is patient with you, not wanting anyone to perish, but everyone to come to repentance."* The Lord spoke through Ezekiel (18:32) *"For I take no pleasure in the death of anyone, declares the Sovereign Lord. Repent and live!"*

Theme 2—The Kingdom of Heaven

The righteous receive the seed with joy; they are faithful in becoming good wheat; they will shine like the sun in the kingdom of heaven. They truly are the light of the world.

Theme 3—The Alternatives in Life

The *"seed"* is to be spread, so that all would know that God's perfect patience is that none should perish. There is only one *"seed"* but there are different types of *"soil.* Some will reject the seed; others will accept the seed and produce great fruit.

Chapter Eleven

Theme 4—The Christian Character

Christians are to be *"good soil"* so that the seed of God will flourish in their lives. The cares of this world must not distract us from life with God, the Word of God, our life of prayer, and the power of the Holy Spirit. We are to hear the word, treasure it in our hearts and demonstrate its power in our lives.

Summary of God's Revelations
Theme 6—The Responsibility for Evangelism

This parable has a promise and a warning. The promise is: *if you hear the word, understand it and do it, you will bear much fruit. The fruit is in doing the will of God.* The warning is: *don't be rocky soil; don't let the cares of the world choke the seed.*

I would like to close with a great message of evangelism:

Give us a watchword for the hour, a thrilling word,
a word of power;
A battle cry, a flaming breath, a call to conquest or to death;
A word to rouse the church from rest,
to heed the master's high behest,
The call is given, ye hosts arise, the watchword is Evangelize!
To fallen men, a dying race, make known the gift of gospel grace,
The world that now in darkness lies,
O Church of Christ, Evangelize!
(Author Unknown)

CHAPTER TWELVE

Theme 7—The Parables of our Role as Christian Stewards

"Everything comes from you (God), and we have given you only what comes from your hand." (I Chron. 29:14b)

"Moreover, it is required of stewards that they be found trustworthy." (I Cor. 4:2)

"So each of us will give account of himself to God." (Rom. 14:12)

"Each one should use whatever gifts he has received to serve others, faithfully administering God's grace in its various forms." (I Pet. 4:10)

This theme is presented in two of Jesus' most powerful parables. However, that should not surprise us, for Christian stewardship has its foundation in the recognition that *"the earth is the Lord's and the fullness thereof, the world and those who dwell therein; for he has founded it upon the seas, and established it upon the rivers."* (Psalm 24:1–2). Christians acknowledge this truth and have surrendered themselves completely to Him as Savior and Lord. This dual understanding, Savior and Lord, is fully accepted by all Christians. Jesus cannot be one without the other. Stewardship is only possible and will only bear fruit when such surrender is complete.

God's Hidden Treasures

God is the Creator, Sustainer, and Redeemer of His creation; we are His stewards, and our stewardship responsibilities are to care for God's people and God's *"vineyard."* The proper understanding of stewardship is an important Christian concept that demands increased emphasis in the Christian Church.

In Scripture, stewardship literally means a manager or superintendent of another's household, and the household that we *"manage"* is the Lord's; we are to be faithful in its management and preservation. The people are the Lord's, and we are to be faithful stewards and witnesses to them. The Old Testament examples of stewardship are Eliezer, over the house of Abraham (Gen. 15:2) and Joseph as steward to Potiphar (Gen. 43:19). The selection as a steward reflected the great confidence that was placed in him. In the New Testament, Paul describes Christian ministers as the *"stewards of God over His church"* (1 Cor. 4:1–2). Also stewards should be viewed as those given a trust. According to Lk 12:42, the steward was responsible for the overall management of all of the affairs of his master. In like manner, the disciples of Jesus were responsible for His gospel and were to proclaim this message until His return. In the gospel ministry, Paul and the other apostles considered themselves as *"stewards of the mysteries of God"* (1 Cor. 4:1–2). Peter considered himself and all other Christians as *"stewards of the manifold grace of God"* (1 Pet 4:10). Stewards are those to whom a trust has been given, who have overall management for the things of God, who are blessed to manage the overall *mysteries of God* that have been revealed to us. However, we are both stewards of physical and material possessions as well as stewards of the mysteries of God; we need to understand both concepts.

This subject of the *"mysteries of God"* is worth exploring more fully. The subject has been extensively studied by many leading scholars, among them Dr. Frank Thielman, Dr. G. Bornkamm, Dr. R. E. Brown, Dr. A. E. Harvey and Dr. J. A. Robinson.

The *"mysteries of God"* describe God as the One who knows all things, including that which the human mind cannot understand nor could ever know. He knows the mysteries of the universe (Job 38–39); most importantly, He directs human history. As Sovereign,

Chapter Twelve

He wills all that happens, and does so to accomplish His own purposes (Dan 2:37; 5:21; Rom 11:25–36). Therefore, God graciously reveals His purpose to His people, through His prophets and lastly through His Son. When God's purpose is revealed in this way, the Bible frequently refers to it as a *"mystery."* It is evident in the Old Testament, it takes on greater detail in the gospels, and it declares its fullest revelation in Paul's letters. In Daniel, the mystery refers to God's understanding of the symbols in Nebuchadnezzar's dream that represent the rise and fall of human empires and to the eventual establishment of God's eternal kingdom (Dan. 2:44). The *mystery of God's purposes* is emphasized in the gospels, where Jesus, particularly in His parables, reveals the *"mystery of the kingdom of God"* (Mark 4:11). Paul also identifies the divine mystery with the revelation of God in Christ (Col. 2:2) but expands the idea in three ways. *First,* he equates the divine mystery with the gospel of *Christ's atoning death on the cross* (1 Cor 2:1); *second,* he describes it as God's plan, through Christ's atoning death (Eph 2:13–16), to *include the Gentiles among his chosen people;* and *third,* he defines it as the *reconciliation of all things to God (Eph 1:9–10).* Thus, Daniel described the divine mystery in general terms as the eventual establishment of God's eternal kingdom; Jesus defined it more specifically as his proclamation of God's kingdom; and Paul described it more specifically still as the constitution of a new people, from among both Jews and Gentiles, through the atoning death of Christ on the cross.

We are to be stewards of these great mysteries; that is we are to guard them, live them, preach them. This is the basic concept that defines the stewardship of God's people, not solely to material and physical stewardship, but far more importantly to the great mysteries of God, revealed through His prophets, His Son and finally through His apostles.

With this introduction, Jesus presents two parables, explaining this responsibility:

7–1 .*The Parable of the Faithful and Wise Manager*
7–2 .*The Parable of Stewardship (the Shrewd Manager)*

God's Hidden Treasures

The first parable is direct and straightforward; the second is complex, often misunderstood and generally neglected. However, it is a parable with great messages for the Christian Church in every age. There are no parables in which this theme is secondary.

The parables end with two great truths; the first is: *"Every one to whom much is given, of him will much be required; and of him to whom men commit much they will demand the more."* The second ends: *"You are those who justify yourselves before men, but God knows your hearts; for what is exalted among men is an abomination in the sight of God."*

7–1. The Parable of the Faithful and Wise Manager: Lk. 12:42–48

"And the Lord said, 'Who then is the faithful and wise steward, whom his master will set over his household, to give them their portion of food at the proper time? Blessed is that servant whom his master when he comes will find so doing. Truly, I say to you, he will set him over all his possessions.' But if that servant says to himself, 'My master is delayed in coming,' and begins to beat the menservants and the maidservants, and to eat and drink and get drunk, the master of that servant will come on a day when he does not expect him and at an hour he does not know, and will punish him, and put him with the unfaithful. And that servant who knew his master's will, but did not make ready or act according to his will, shall receive a severe beating. But he who did not know, and did what deserved a beating, shall receive a light beating. Every one to whom much is given, of him will much be required; and of him to whom men commit much they will demand the more.'"

Commentary

In the preceding passages, Jesus has been talking about being *"ready for service"* (Lk. 12:35), *"because the Son of man will come at an hour when you do not expect him."* At the conclusion of that

Chapter Twelve

parable, *"Peter asked, 'Lord, are you telling this parable to us, or to everyone?'" (Lk. 12:41)*. Jesus does not answer Peter's question directly; instead, He continues with this parable of the *"faithful and wise manager."* The NIV text says, *"The Lord answered . . ."* It is interesting to see how this parable can be an *"answer"* to the previous parable (Lk. 12:35–40). This parable has eight significant messages;

1. Wise and faithful stewards are always put in charge of God's possessions;
2. The better the steward performs, the greater is the responsibility given to him;
3. Any steward who abuses his authority and mistreats the master's servants will be severely punished;
4. The steward does not know the day or the hour when his master will return;
5. Any steward who knows the master's will and refuses to acknowledge or honor that will, then that steward will be severely punished;
6. The steward who does not know the master's heart will be punished less severely;
7. A steward to whom much is given, much will be required;
8. A steward to whom men commit much, they will demand more.

In this parable, Jesus takes up the matter of *stewardship*, which we are to provide in a *"faithful and wise"* manner. Jesus identifies three types of stewards; the first is *"faithful and wise"*, and he is richly rewarded. The second *"knew his master's will . . . but did not act . . . according to his will—this servant shall receive a severe beating."* This second manager thought primarily of himself; he ate and drank and got drunk; there is no mention of any concern for the household. This is the same situation in Ezekiel 34, of the self-centered shepherds of Israel, the leaders, who do not provide for the sheep, the people of God. The third *did not know his master's will and did not do it;* he shall receive a light beating. However, his error was in not seeking to know the master's will. He acted more out of ignorance rather than out of selfishness. However, ignorance of God's laws is not an excuse for sin. The theme is that each will be treated and judged according to the revelation given them

God's Hidden Treasures

and their response to that revelation. The faithful and wise steward will be set over all his possessions; the other two will receive punishment according to the degree that they knew their master's will and failed to do it.

The first is the *faithful and wise steward*, who *"feeds"* the household and cares for them. His emphasis is on *others*. This relates to the message of Jesus to His apostles (Jn. 21:15 –16) to *"Feed my sheep"* and *"Tend my sheep."* Feeding and tending means more than the physical acts; it broadly and rightfully includes all spiritual *"feeding"* and *"tending."* We *"feed"* His flock with His truth about salvation; we *"tend"* His flock by teaching them, protecting them and safeguarding them against false teachings. The message here is to know the master's will and be faithful and wise in fulfilling that will. That is preferable to those people who know the master's will and do not act accordingly. Understanding these terms, *faithful and wise,* will help us to appreciate the significance of this parable. The first steward is called *faithful and wise*. The questions arise: *What is the measure of his faithfulness? What is the evidence of His wisdom?*

This term, *faithful,* had been previously discussed, in the Parable of the God-given Talents (Lk. 19:11–27) on page 163. Faithfulness has its origin in God, and it therefore is a divine characteristic. When we are faithful, we live in His image. We would not know nor understand *faithfulness*, if we did not know God. In the Bible, God's faithfulness and covenant love are directly interrelated. *"Know therefore that the Lord your God is God, the faithful God who keeps covenant and steadfast love with those who love him and keep his commandments, to a thousand generations . . ."* (Deut 7:9). In the same way, our faithfulness is a reflection of our love for God and for our fellow man. If we love, we are faithful; if we are faithful, we love. David, a prime example of godly faithfulness, wrote *"I have chosen the way of faithfulness, I have set thy ordinances before me."* (Ps 119:30). As God is both faithful and loving, those who believe in God are to demonstrate faithfulness and steadfast love in their lives. In the New Testament, God demonstrates His faithfulness by His provision for all people (Matt 5:45) and by

Chapter Twelve

remaining faithful as He fulfills His promises (2 Cor 1:18–19). John declares that *Jesus is the faithful and true witness* (Rev 3:14); Jesus is identified as the *Faithful and True* (Rev 19:11). So faithful represents knowing God's will, loving God's will, acting willingly in accordance with His will in every situation and doing so without counting the cost that such faithfulness demands.

Next, the term *wise or wisdom* is indicative of the way of viewing and approaching life, which involves morality and living a life based on that morality. Wisdom means deep insight into life and the proper way of dealing with its problems. Further, the terms *"wisdom"* and *"wise"* apply to individuals who represent a way of thinking and type of conduct that is *morally upright*. Therefore, the major thrust of wisdom in the Old Testament was a code of moral conduct, based on the commandments of God. Wisdom was the evidence of keeping the law; keeping the law produces wisdom. Therefore, wisdom and the law were interconnected. Those who kept the law were *"wise"*; *conversely* those who were *"wise"* kept the law. The Old Testament emphasized that God *spoke* the law to the nation of Israel. The characteristic that best defined the wise person is summed up in the phrase *"the fear of the Lord."* Job (ch. 42) began to understand that the *"fear of the Lord is the beginning of wisdom."* Fear means being in awe of and having reverence for God; it does not mean being *afraid of God*. Reverence for God is the beginning of wisdom; reverence is the foundation by which an individual matures.

In the New Testament, there are several examples of *"wisdom literature"* as providing moral advice for Christian living. The Beatitudes (Matt 5:3–12) and the parables are prime examples of the wisdom of God. The *"wisdom of men"* was human understanding as compared with the *"hidden wisdom of God,"* which was a knowledge of God's plan for salvation through Jesus Christ, foreordained before the world began. The ultimate manifestation of wisdom is Jesus Christ; God revealed His *wisdom* in the *Person of his own Son, Jesus Christ* (1 Cor 1:21–24, 30). *"For since, in the wisdom of God the world through its wisdom did not know him, God was pleased through the foolishness of what was preached to save those who*

God's Hidden Treasures

believed. *Jews demanded miraculous signs and Greeks looked for wisdom, but we preach Christ crucified: a stumbling block to the Jews and foolishness to Gentiles, but to those whom God has called, both Jews and Greeks, Christ, the power of God and the wisdom of God. He is the source of your life in Christ Jesus, whom God made our wisdom, our righteousness and sanctification and redemption."*

The only way that we can be good stewards is simply by being faithful and wise.

This parable poses significant questions for us. For example: Do we *know* our Lord's will? Have we *searched* the Scriptures to understand it? Have we *prayed* for faithfulness, wisdom and understanding? Do we *act* according to His will? If we know His will and act accordingly, then are we *"faithful and wise stewards"?* The message is that we will be held accountable for what we know about God and the manner in which we obey and fulfill the will of our Father. The truth in this parable is that God holds us accountable for the stewardship that He has committed to us. He calls us to be faithful and wise.

Summary of Biblical Themes
Theme 7—Our Role as Christian Stewards

We are to be faithful and wise servants of God so that we will secure an eternal habitation. To do so requires that we make specific plans, in the power of the Holy Spirit, for the manner in which we live in this life. We will be trusted with the true righteousness only when we have learned to handle well the lesser responsibilities of life. Much is required of a good and faithful steward; however, His grace and our faith lead to salvation.

The *secondary* themes presented in this parable are:

Theme 1—The Character of God

God will punish the wicked and reward the wise and faithful stewards.

Theme 3—The Alternatives in Life

Jesus tells us that we can be *good and faithful* stewards or we can be unfaithful *stewards* of God's *possessions*. There are consequences for all of our actions in this life. If we are faithful in little, God will put us in charge of even greater things.

Chapter Twelve

Theme 4—The Christian Character

Much is required of those to whom much is given; certainly Christians have been given blessings beyond measure. We need to be good and faithful stewards, workmen approved by God.

Summary of God's Revelations
Theme 7—Our Roles as Christian Stewards.

This parable has a command, truths and a warning. The command is, *know your master's will and act according to his will.* The truths are: *everyone to whom much is given, of him much will be required; and to him to whom men commit much they will demand the more.* The warning is, *everyone who knows the master's will and fails to fulfill his will will be severely punished.*

7–2. The Parable of the Shrewd Manager: Lk. 16:1–15

"He also said to the disciples, 'There was a rich man who had a steward, and charges were brought to him that this man was wasting his goods. And he called him and said to him, 'What is this that I hear about you? Turn in the account of your stewardship, for you can no longer be steward.' And the steward said to himself, 'What shall I do, since my master is taking the stewardship away from me? I am not strong enough to dig, and I am ashamed to beg. I have decided what to do, so that people may receive me into their houses when I am put out of the stewardship.' So, summoning his master's debtors one by one, he said to the first, 'How much do you owe my master?' He said, 'A hundred measures of oil.' And he said to him, 'Take your bill, and sit down quickly and write fifty.' Then he said to another, 'And how much do you owe?' He said, 'A hundred measures of wheat.' He said to him, 'Take your bill, and write eighty.' The master commended the dishonest steward for his shrewdness; for the sons of this world are more shrewd in dealing with their own generation than the sons of light. And I tell you, make friends for yourselves by means of unrighteous mammon,

God's Hidden Treasures

so that when it fails they may receive you into the eternal habitations. He who is faithful in a very little is faithful also in much; and he who is dishonest in a very little is dishonest also in much. If then you have not been faithful in the unrighteous mammon, who will entrust to you the true riches? And if you have not been faithful in that which is another's, who will give you that which is your own? No servant can serve two masters; for either he will hate the one and love the other, or he will be devoted to the one and despise the other. You cannot serve God and mammon.' The Pharisees, who were lovers of money, heard all this, and they scoffed at him. But he said to them, 'You are those who justify yourselves before men, but God knows your hearts; for what is exalted among men is an abomination in the sight of God.'"

Commentary

This immediately follows the Parable of the Lost and the Found (page 175), so this passage may be rightly viewed as a continuation of Luke 15, for some texts read, "He also said to the disciples . . ." as if this was given to the same audience at the same time. When we read it in that context, we can get possibly a better understanding of what Jesus is about. Therefore, consider that the audience still included, among others, the Pharisees and other wealthy Jews of that day. Jesus had been explaining what it means to be His disciple; if one would follow Him, then they would be called to seek and save the lost. His concluding remarks in that parable deal with the great joy in heaven when a sinner repents and comes home. The last verse of chapter 15 concludes with, *"it is fitting to make merry and be glad, for this your brother was dead, and is alive; he was lost and is found."*

Now Jesus turns to a most unusual subject, one that does not seem to relate too closely to Luke 15. The subject is still how to be one of His disciples and so Jesus adds a further dimension to the Parable of the Lost and the Found. The message is that my disciples are to be good stewards who use their worldly possession (our mammon) so that we will be received into the eternal habitation. Another way of saying it is that we need to be shrewd managers of our possessions in the time that we have so that we can reign with Him when He returns to earth. This is a truly powerful parable.

Chapter Twelve

From the message regarding repentance (Lk. 15), Jesus now presents perhaps one of the more controversial and most difficult of all of the parables. Despite the controversy and confusion, its sheer length demands our attention. Therefore, we must face the questions and the issues head-on. *First* of all there is the danger of taking the events too literally. *Second*, many people argue that Jesus is commending dishonesty and that the *sons of light* should be devious. This is far from the truth. Jesus is instructing Christians in *Christian stewardship* and our faithfulness as stewards of the things of God.

Here, Jesus is talking about a steward who is clearly dishonest. It is not certain, but he apparently has embezzled funds, possibly misapplied them and has caused significant loss for the master. Informed of this, the master dismissed the steward. The steward wonders what he shall do, because he has forfeited a good job by his unfaithfulness. So he begins to take stock of the situation.

- He "*is not strong enough to dig.*" The truth is that he is probably lazy; his "*cannot*" is a "*will not.*"
- He is "*ashamed to beg.*" He is too proud; this is the language of his *pride*.
- Therefore, he is determined to make friends with his master's debtors. He decided that he would treat them well, so that they will be indebted to him. He did this quickly; his treachery and deceit are obvious. This is true both for those who encourage and those who participate; many people cannot find honorable methods in dealing with difficult situations.
- Notice that the debtors were no more honorable than the steward. They were more than willing to accept such a bargain. Evil sometimes finds its greatest ally in evil.

The facts are plain; the steward is faced with dismissal because of corruption. He has one last avenue to save himself. He still controlled the books, and he could reduce the debt owed to his master. This he did.

Jesus makes eight points in this parable:
1. The master commends the dishonest manager, commended not because he was dishonest, but because he acted shrewdly;

God's Hidden Treasures

2. The master recommended using unrighteous mammon (wealth) to gain friends for yourself, so that when the wealth is gone, you will be welcomed into the eternal habitation;
3. The person who is faithful in little will be faithful in much;
4. The person who is dishonest with little will be dishonest with much;
5. If you have not been trustworthy with other people's property, who will entrust to you the true riches?
6. No servant can serve two masters; either you will hate the one and love the other or you will be devoted to one and despise the other; you cannot serve God and mammon;
7. God knows our hearts;
8. What is exalted among men is an abomination to God.

First, the master commends the dishonest manager. Now, the master recognized his dishonesty, but also he approved of his actions. Jesus said, I approve of a man who knows how to face a present difficulty and to provide for a future need. Jesus does not commend him because he has been *dishonest,* but because he has done *wisely*. Christians need to recognize the difference between the two. Jesus said that the children of this world are wiser, act more considerately, and take steps to improve their situation more than the *"children of light."* Jesus said that His disciples should imitate the wisdom of the worldly people, who recognize their opportunities, do what is most needed and to prepare now for the future. *Jesus is encouraging us to be wise in both our material and spiritual affairs.* Jesus said that the *"sons of light"* are not as shrewd as the children of this world. However, we must be careful, for the children of this world are *not truly wise*. There is a great difference between being shrewd and being dishonest. Being dishonest represents an evil nature; dishonesty can be used to accomplish wicked plans. Shrewdness can be both good and evil; it can mean being dangerous, but it can also be a person who has good ability in practical matters, in other words, very astute. It implies cleverness in practical matters. A shrewd person may also have penetrating discernment and might have a great degree of wisdom. So shrewd

Chapter Twelve

does not imply evil in all circumstances. Jesus does not commend evil thoughts and evil acts. He does encourage shrewdness.

Second, Jesus tells His disciples that they should *"make friends for yourselves by means of unrighteous mammon."* Now what is this *mammon of unrighteousness* that Jesus speaks of? The word, *mammon*, represents the Aramaic word for riches or wealth. The term, *"the mammon of unrighteousness"* (Luke 16:9) relates to the *"evils of money."* Most people equate money with power. The more money; the greater the power. Jesus is not condemning money in itself, but He does condemn the pride of money, the love of money, the power of money, the quest for money, the priority that is attached to money and the worship of money. Jesus tells His disciples that they should show wisdom and foresight in the use of *"the mammon of unrighteousness"* that is at least comparable, if not superior, to the unrighteous steward's. If worldly possessions are misused, one cannot expect the real and genuine riches to be committed to him. And, of course, it is morally impossible to serve God and mammon at the same time. The mammon is unrighteous simply because wealth is the representative object of a selfish and unrighteous world. *What is the unrighteous mammon?* Wealth in general is not unrighteous mammon. Instead, it is that wealth that leads to unrighteous thoughts and unrighteous acts. Any *"wealth"* that separates us from the things of God and any *"priority"* that we make higher than the will of God is *unrighteous mammon*. Now although this mammon is not the foundation for peace or happiness, it may be used to accomplish and serve the interest of God. Though we cannot find true peace and happiness in it; yet we may use it to accomplish many goals, for the glory of God. Therefore, we must use the possessions that God has given us for the benefit of those less fortunate. Good stewardship of *"unrighteous mammon"* on earth is a measure of faith. Good works will follow and good fruit will be the evidence of faith and works. In addition, Christians must properly handle worldly and secular interests in order that they can handle with confidence the spiritual aspects of life. The Christian use of material possessions is a measure of the Christian character. God is the Maker of all; Jesus challenges us to make good use of

God's Hidden Treasures

our possessions in this world. The things of this world are the mammon of unrighteousness, particularly if fraud and unrighteousness are the means of obtaining them. To trust in them for satisfaction and happiness is a great deception, for riches are perishable and will disappoint those who put their trust in them. Jesus tells His followers that we should use God's blessings to form bonds of lasting friendship and fellowship with other Christians. We should not fail to achieve the greatest good through the use of God's gifts in our dealing with one another. We will be judged by the use of the talents and possessions that God has given us. Paul wrote to Timothy, *"As for the rich in this world, charge them not to be haughty, not to set their hopes on uncertain riches but on God who richly furnished us with everything to enjoy, . . . They are to do good, to be rich in good deeds, liberal and generous, thus laying up for themselves a good foundations for the future, so that they may take hold of the life which is life indeed."* (I Tim. 6:17–19)

Third, Jesus states that the person *"who is faithful in little will be faithful in much."* Faith is an absolute term; there are not degrees of faith. If faithful, we will be faithful in all things, in all situations, in all relationships. This is the measure of being in the image of God, who is the true Faithful One. Since faith is absolute, then if faithful in little, we will be faithful in much.

Fourth, the person who is dishonest with little will be dishonest with much. Dishonesty is an ingrain characteristic. Again dishonesty is an absolute term; dishonest people will be dishonest in every situation, because it is their nature.

Fifth, If you have not been trustworthy with other people's property, who will entrust to you the true riches? How can we be faithful to that which belongs to another? Good stewards recognize that everything belongs to God. Remember that great hymn, *"all things are thine, no gifts have we, Lord of all gifts, to offer thee and so with grateful hearts today, thine own before thy feet we lay."* However, we can be trustworthy in that which belongs to another when we understand that we are but caretakers and stewards of the *"wealth and vineyard"* of God. *How is it possible that, by being faithful to the unrighteous mammon, we are qualified to receive the true riches?* This is strange and not at all what we might expect. What Jesus tells us

Chapter Twelve

is that if we are not faithful to the possessions that have little value, how can we expect faithfulness to those things that are far more difficult to understand and to grasp. Being faithful to wealth and power and all the aspects of *unrighteous mammon* teaches us the wisdom of faithfulness; it prepares us for the important riches that God has in store for us.

Sixth, No servant can serve two masters; either you will hate the one and love the other or you will be devoted to one and despise the other; you cannot serve God and mammon. This is a major conflict, between the things of God and mammon. We continually face the conflict between the things of this world and the things of God; how we resolve this eternal dilemma determines our eternal destiny. Paul understood this conflict, and he wrote (Col. 3:2), *"set your mind on things above, not on things that are on earth."* We must seek the things that are above, in heaven, for that is where all true riches are. We should serve God and not men (Col. 3:23). We must obey God and not men (Acts 4:19). The questions that we must ask ourselves are: Do economics dictate my relationship to God? Do we worship physical possessions? Does the church bow to secular demands that compromise Christian doctrines, principles and values? Do we truly worship God or do we have an idol somewhere called money? We cannot serve two masters; Christians are called to love God with all their heart and all their soul and all their mind.

Seventh, God knows our hearts. This is consistent with the Old Testament message (I Sam. 167), *". . . for the Lord sees not as man sees; man looks on the outward appearance, but the Lord looks on the heart."* The Pharisees love for money distorted their love of God and their love for their neighbor. Dishonesty was recognized and was not necessarily condemned. Therefore, the Jews would have agreed with Jesus completely, up to the final condemnation in 19:13–15. Jesus points that out directly and aims His concluding remarks at them. Jesus said that your vision is too low; your greed is to high; you seek to justify yourselves before men. Jesus said that you must seek God's approval, not men's. Again in this passage, Jesus tells the Pharisees, and all other lovers of money, that God knows your heart; He knows if your allegiance to Him is true; He

God's Hidden Treasures

knows that your lips may not speak the truth. God knows our hearts, from which come our thoughts, our words and our deeds.

Eight, what is exalted among men is an abomination to God. Jesus again directs our attention to humility and exaltation, the same theme He discussed in the Parable of Humility (Lk. 7–11: page 146). In this parable, Jesus makes the statement even stronger by stating *"that what is exalted among men is an abomination in the sight of God."* Men exalt money, power and prestige which are abominations to God.

What is the eternal habitation? Heaven is our eternal habitation. Scriptures tell us that we are aliens and sojourners in a foreign land; this earth is not our eternal home, for that is in heaven. The Christian hearts are restless until we are home with our Lord.

The theme of the parable is that good stewardship on earth is a measure of faith. Good works will follow and good fruit will be the evidence of faith and works. In addition, Christians must properly handle secular interests in order that they can handle with confidence the spiritual aspects of life. Failure to be faithful with worldly matters may also mean that we will be unfaithful with spiritual responsibilities.

This parable has three lessons regarding Christian stewardship:
1. Christians must understand the difficulties in which we find ourselves, even if they are not of our own making. We should recognize the problem so that we have a positive plan for the future.
2. We must use worldly possessions (unrighteous mammon) to gain friends so that *"when it is gone, you will have an eternal dwelling."* We are to feed the hungry, clothe the naked; we are to be like the Good Samaritan, who laid out worldly possessions for a wounded stranger by the side of the road. We are to use our worldly possessions for the benefit of others and the glory of God. This is one measure of the works by which we will be judged. Saved through faith; we are to be judged by our works.

3. We must be trustworthy in handling worldly possessions, so that we will be entrusted with the true riches, which are the Word of God and the Gospel.

We are to live a godly life in this world so as to ensure an eternal habitation. We must believe God, obey Him and serve Him. We must recognize the difficulties of this life, make plans for the next, and use our worldly possessions to ensure our eternal habitation.

Summary of Biblical Themes
Theme 7—Our Role as Christian Stewards

Our earthly stewardship is to do good works, as evidence of our faith; if so, we will receive the crown of righteousness that the Lord will award us. We are to be faithful and good stewards of God's possessions. We are to be shrewd in the use of unrighteous mammon. As stewards, we are to feed the hungry, clothe the poor, and be a light in the darkness. For those who persevere, *"There is laid up for me the crown of righteousness, which the Lord, the righteous Judge, will award to me on that Day, and not only to me, but also to all who have loved his appearing."* (2 Tim. 4:8)

There are three *secondary* themes:
Theme 1—The Kingdom of Heaven
Our stewardship in this life determines our eternal habitation.
Theme 3—The Alternatives in Life
The great lesson here is that we are to be faithful in unrighteous mammon, so that we can be trusted with true riches. We cannot serve God and mammon.
Theme 4—The Christian Character
Christians serve the living God; however, we are to use our "*unrighteous mammon*" to secure an eternal habitation. We must be faithful in handling our possessions. We must not justify ourselves before men; we must not seek to be exalted among men. God's will should be our will; God's ways should be our ways; God's ministries should be our ministries.
Summary of God's Revelations
This parable has both a truth and three warnings. The truth is: *the sons of this world are shrewder in using unrighteous mammon*

than are Christians. The warnings are: *You must be faithful in dealing with the things of this world, the unrighteous mammon; otherwise no one will commit to you the things of God; no servant can serve two masters.*

Summary of Biblical Themes
Theme 7—Our Role as Christian Stewards

Jesus calls us to be *"faithful and wise"*, not wicked and lazy, servants. We are to take the initiative in stewardship, doing more than what is commanded of us. Much has been given to us and much is demanded of us. Handling well the unrighteous mammon equips us to handle the more righteous and spiritual matters of God. As stewards, we must seek the things that are above, knowing that *"whatever your task, work heartily, as serving the Lord and not men."* (Col. 3:23). We should use our worldly possessions to prepare us for our heavenly home. We must make plans now for that home, because we will one day be *"released"* from our stewardship here on earth, and we must make preparations for the next. We must be trustworthy in handling earthly things as a prelude to being trustworthy in handling heavenly things. Whatever gifts we have are to serve God and others. Christ in us is not only the hope of glory, it is the measure of our service to others. Finally, Christ is the example of the servant that we are called to be in Christian stewardship. The character of a steward of God is bound up in faithfulness, obedience, being trustworthy, single-minded, loving, giving, generous and thankful. Good stewards seek the things that are above (Col. 3:1–2).

Summary of God's Revelations
Theme 7—Our Role as Christian Stewards

These parables have a variety of commands, truths and warnings. The commands are: *know your master's will and act according to his will; use our unrighteous mammon to bring others to Christ.* The truths are: *everyone to whom much is given, of him much will be required; to him to whom men commit much they will demand the more; the sons of this world are shrewder in dealing with problems and preparing for the future than are Christians; God knows our heart* (I Sam. 17:6). The warnings are: *everyone who knows the master's*

Chapter Twelve

will and fails to fulfill his will will be severely punished; be faithful in dealing with the things of this world, the unrighteous mammon, otherwise no one will commit to you the things of God; no servant can serve two masters.

CHAPTER THIRTEEN

Theme 8—The Parables of The Power of Prayer

"What other nation is so great as to have their gods near them the way the Lord our God is near us whenever we pray to him?" (Deut. 4:7)

"If my people, who are called by my name, will humble themselves and pray and seek my face and turn from their wicked ways, then will I hear from heaven and will forgive their sin and will heal their land." (2 Chron. 7:14)

"It is written, he said to them, 'My house shall be called a house of prayer...'" (Matt. 21:13)

"Be joyful always; pray continually. Give thanks in all circumstances, for this is God's will for you in Christ Jesus." (I Thess. 5:16–18)

We now come to the theme of the Power of Prayer, which is a measure of our fellowship and our personal communion with the loving and living God. In our prayers, the Spirit of God provides us with the *"wisdom"* to pray (Romans 8:26, 28), "Likewise *the Spirit helps us in our weakness; for we do not know how to pray as we ought, but the Spirit himself intercedes for us with sighs too deep for words..."*

God's Hidden Treasures

Because God is a personal God, who is near (Psa. 119:151), anyone can pray to Him, and God has promised that He will answer prayers, in the fullness of His time and according to His purpose. Although everyone can offer prayer, it is only the true children of God (Jn. 1:12), who have a full and rewarding experience in prayer.

Unbelievers can and do pray, but Scripture identify seven reasons for prayers not being answered. Sinners who have *not repented and trusted Jesus Christ for their salvation* remain alienated from God. <u>Sin</u> is the major impediment to prayer, for sin is *iniquity in the heart,* "If I had cherished iniquity in my heart, the Lord would not have listened." (Psa. 66:18); <u>refusal to hear God's law</u>, "If one turns away his ear from hearing the law, even his prayer is an abomination." (Prov. 28:9); <u>empty words from an unloving heart</u>, "Because this people draw near with their mouth and honor me with their lips, while their hearts are far from me . . ." (Is. 29:13); <u>sinful separation from God</u>, ". . . your iniquities have made a separation between you and your God." (Is. 59:2); <u>praying to be seen by men</u>, "And when you pray, you must not be like the hypocrites; for they love to stand and pray in the synagogues . . . that they may be seen by men." (Matt. 6:5–6); <u>pride</u>, the example of the Pharisee in Luke 18:11–14, who prided himself on his self-righteousness, "that he was not like other men."; <u>lack of faith</u> "And without faith, it is impossible to please him. For whoever would draw near to God must believe that he exists and that he rewards those who seek him." (Heb. 11:6). A meaningful prayer life is not possible when there is sin in our lives, when there is a refusal to hear God's law, when there are empty words from an unloving heart, when we pray to be seen by men, when pride rules our lives, and when faith is lacking.

However, in their prayers, Christians recognize and express their dependence upon their Creator; in prayer, they express gratitude for God's blessings. They pray in response to the love of God for them and for the rich blessing He has showered on them. They pray because they abide in Jesus Christ and know that only through union with Him are they able to bear much fruit (Jn. 15:7). *Prayer is a measure of our dependence upon God.* If a person doesn't

Chapter Thirteen

pray, our silence is a *"statement"* that God is not necessary in our lives and that we are *independent* of our Father. The most meaningful prayer comes from a heart that places its trust in the God who has acted and spoken through His Son and His Word. As God *"speaks"* to us through the Bible and the Holy Spirit, we in turn speak to Him in trustful, believing prayer. We are assured by Scripture that God is personal, living, active, all knowing, all wise, and all-powerful; we know that God hears and answers us.

Consider a few examples of prayer in the Bible. Some of the great treasures in prayer are Solomon's prayer at the dedication of the temple (I Ki. 8:12–61); Jehosaphat's prayer in time of peril (2 Chron. 20); Daniel's prayer in seeking the face of God (Dan. 9:4–19); Paul's great prayers in all of his writings (e.g. Phil. 3:3f). Above all, consider the prayer life of Jesus Christ, God Incarnate, who has lived an earthly life of prayer, particularly as evident by the great priestly prayer of John 17.

Prayer and good works are two sides of a single coin. Christians are to do good works but such works can never replace prayer, for good works can only bear much fruit when they are grounded in faith and prayer. Prayer is seeking communion with God with a pure heart; therefore we must confess our sins to God, and to God alone, to be reconciled to Him. When we confess them directly to God, He has promised to forgive us of all our unrighteousness (1 John 1:9). Recall also (Jeremiah 31:31) that God promised that He would forgive our sins and remember them no more. For many reasons, God's holy and wise purpose prevents Him from granting every petition as it is asked. God will give us not what we ask, but what is best for us. As such, prayer is one of the greatest gifts that God has given His children. The prayers of His children bless God, for our prayers are in the *"golden bowls, full of incense, which are the prayers of the saints." (Rev. 5:8)*. James wrote (5:16), *"The prayers of a righteous man has great power in its effect."* Prayer removes all fear (Psa. 118:5–6); it strengthens the soul (Psa. 138:3); it provides guidance (Isa. 58:9–11), wisdom and understanding (Dan. 9:20–27) and the fullness of God's peace (Phil. 4:6–8). Finally, our prayer life must be balanced; it should include a proper mix of adoration,

God's Hidden Treasures

petition, praise, thanksgiving, and intercession. It should also involve periods of silence, for how can we hear God speak if we are always *"talking"*? Remember the example of young Samuel, who said to God, *"Speak Lord, for your servant hears."* (I Sam. 3:9). Prayer is in the midst of our silence and quiet time, when we focus on God.

Finally, we are commanded to pray; Jesus told us that we do not receive because we do not ask. *"And I (Jesus) tell you, Ask, and it will be given you; seek, and you will find; knock, and it will be opened to you. For every one who asks receives, and he who seeks finds, and to him who knocks it will be opened."* The apostle John (I Jn. 3:22) wrote, *"and we receive from him whatever we ask, because we keep his commandments and do what pleases him."*

There are many great Biblical examples of prayer that are already mentioned; however there are equally great examples of prayers written by many saints over the ages. I should add that every Christian is a saint, for a saint is a redeemed child of God. One of the great saintly prayers is that of John Baille (A Diary of Private Prayer); he wrote:

". . . Let me not forget, when this morning prayer is said, think my worship ended and spend the day in forgetfulness of You. Rather from these moments of quietness let light go forth, and joy and power, that will remain with me through all the hours of the day;

>Keeping me chaste in thought,
>Keeping me temperate and truthful in speech,
>Keeping me faithful and diligent in my work,
>Keeping me humble in my estimation of myself,
>Keeping me honorable and generous in my dealings with others,
>Keeping me loyal to every hallowed memory of the past,
>Keeping me mindful of my eternal destiny as a child of Yours,
>Through Jesus Christ, my Lord. Amen."

Prayer keeps our hearts focused on the Lord.

Chapter Thirteen

Three parables present the *primary* message on the Power of Prayer.

8–1. *The Parable of the Friend at Midnight*
8–2. *The Parable of the Persistent Widow; Persistence in Prayer*
8–3. *The Parable of our Perspective in Prayer*

These three parables are most unusual, for each of them deals with human interactions and then conclude with a significant message regarding God and our relationship to Him. These parables test our *"hearing", "he who has an ear to hear, let him hear."* The first parable concludes with these words, *"how much more will the heavenly Father give the Holy Spirit to those who ask him."* The second with this question, *"when the Son of man comes, will he find faith on earth?"* The third with this message, *"everyone who exalts himself will be humbled, but he who humbles himself will be exalted."*

8–1. *The Parable of the Friend at Midnight: Lk. 11:5–13*

"And he said to them, 'Which of you who has a friend will go to him at midnight and say to him, 'Friend, lend me three loaves; for a friend of mine has arrived on a journey, and I have nothing to set before him'; and he will answer from within, 'Do not bother me; the door is now shut, and my children are with me in bed; I cannot get up and give you anything.' I tell you, though he will not get up and give him anything because he is his friend, yet because of his importunity (note—persistence) he will rise and give him whatever he needs. And I tell you, Ask, and it will be given you; seek, and you will find; knock, and it will be opened to you. For every one who asks receives, and he who seeks finds, and to him who knocks it will be opened. What father among you, if his son asks for a fish, will instead of a fish give him a serpent; or if he asks for an egg, will give him a scorpion? If you then, who are evil, know how to give good gifts to your children, how much more will the heavenly Father give the Holy Spirit to those who ask him!"

God's Hidden Treasures

Commentary

Again, the context is important in order to appreciate this parable. Luke began this chapter by telling us that *"He (Christ) was praying in a certain place, . . ."* That *"certain place"* must have been known to His followers, as a place where He went often to pray. Now, their request (11:1) is, *"Lord, teach us to pray; as John taught his disciples."* The disciples of Christ came to the Master of prayer for Him to teach them. So Jesus answered, by instructing them in this life-giving spiritual role, in much the same manner as He had in Matthew 6:9, where Jesus had taught them to pray *after this manner*. They had not forgotten it, but apparently they felt a need to have further and fuller instructions. Jesus knew that, when the Spirit would be poured out upon them, they would express every need and would be able in their own words to come to the throne of grace. So Christ's teaching contained a type of formula for the elements of a prayer from the heart. In that manner, they may come with more *boldness to and greater love* for God.

Perhaps more than any other of the evangelists, Luke takes particular notice of Christ's praying. Luke records that Jesus prayed when He was baptized (Lk 3:21), when He went into the wilderness and prior to the beginning of His earthly ministry (Lk. 5:16). Jesus often went out to a mountain to pray; He would continue all night in prayer (Lk. 6:12). At His transfiguration, Luke wrote of Jesus' deep time of prayer (Lk. 9:28–29). Now Jesus is *praying in a certain place*. In some regards, this does not immediately seem to be a parable regarding prayer, but that is the condition that Luke is describing in this chapter.

In one sense, the introduction to this parable is somewhat unusual and tends to lead the reader possibly in another direction. However, Jesus quickly makes it clear that this passage concerns prayer, which is one of the great Christian virtues. The message of the parable is *persistence in prayer* and the threefold statements of Jesus (*ask-receives, seek-finds, knock-opens*) are promised to all believers. A person who prays and gives glory to God will know God's pleasure and, by prayer, will acknowledge his dependence upon Him. Such a person will have fellowship with His Maker. This entire chapter is a beautiful dissertation on prayer.

Chapter Thirteen

This parable *encourages* us to be persistent in prayer. If persistence could affect a man who was angry, how much more will our loving God accept our persistence. God accepts it, welcomes it and encourages it. We must not only ask, but we must seek; and, in asking and seeking, we must continue pressing, knocking at the door, that God would hear and answer. The Bible says, "*This poor man cried, and the Lord heard him,*" (Psa. 34:6). When we ask God for those things that Christ has commanded us, then His kingdom will come, and His will will be done on earth as it is in heaven.

In this parable, his asking came because of a need. Needs are fulfilled, not always because of the need, but more likely because of *boldness* and because they *are consistent with the will and power of God*. We must pray for the needs of others as well as for ourselves. In this parable, this man would not have wanted bread if his friend had not come in unexpectedly. Notice the boldness of the request. *Boldness* is the measure of Peter and John (Acts 4:13), "*Now when they saw the boldness of Peter and John, and perceived that they were uneducated, common men . . .*" They were warned not to speak "*to any one in this name.*" (4:17). But Peter and John questioned their authority, "*Whether it is right in the sight of God to listen to God or to you, you must judge . . .*" "*And now, Lord, look upon their threats, and grant to thy servants to speak thy word with all boldness . . .*" (Acts 4:29). *Boldness* is the total disregard for self in the service of God. Boldness generally means "*boldness of speech before men*"; but many times in the New Testament, it means boldness of believers before God *(Eph. 3:11–12; Heb. 10:19; I Jn. 4:17)*. This boldness is the confidence that we have from our faith in Christ. When we speak boldly for ourselves and for the needs of others, then the evidence is that boldness will be rewarded.

Finally, we must address the closing statement of this parable, "*how much more will the heavenly Father give the Holy Spirit to those who ask him.*" Although the emphasis In this parable is on prayer, there is also the example of God as Father compared to a human father. If human fathers, *who are evil,* give good gifts to their children; how much more will our heavenly Father give the Holy Spirit to those who ask him! God desires to give good gifts to His children, if we only ask. And the greatest gift He can give us is the

God's Hidden Treasures

Holy Spirit, which is the Presence of God in our daily lives. God is Spirit (2 Cor. 3:17), and He means for His Spirit to dwell in us so that, through Him, we can do all things. In Peter's speech at the First Pentecost, when the crowd asked what they should do after hearing his powerful appeal, Peter told them, *"Repent and be baptized every one of you in the name of Jesus Christ for the forgiveness of sins: and you will receive the gift of the Holy Spirit."* (Acts 2:38). At baptism, we are washed *"clean"*; our sins are forgiven, we become a child of God, and we receive the gift of the Holy Spirit. It is a gift, but we have an obligation to accept the gift. So here we have instruction in prayer, the encouragement to pray, the admonition to be persistent, and the command to be bold. Jesus presents a wonderful combination of Christian acts.

Summary of Biblical Themes
Theme 8—The Power of Prayer

Jesus challenges the world with promises, but our response and actions are required. We are to *ask, to seek, to knock*; He promises that, when we ask, we will *receive*; that when we seek, we will *find*; that when we knock, it will be *opened*. We are to be *persistent* in seeking the face of God. We are to be *bold*; one of the greatest gifts that we can receive is the Holy Spirit which we shall receive from *"the Heavenly Father"* to *"those who ask him."*

Three *secondary* themes are contained in this parable.

Theme 1—The Character of God

God desires to give good gifts to His children, particularly the gift of the Holy Spirit, to those who ask Him. We "ask" by accepting Jesus Christ as Savior and Lord.

Theme 3—The Alternatives in Life

The choice is by taking action, by *asking, seeking, and knocking or* denying the power of prayer.

Theme 4—The Christian Character

In this life, we are to persist in *asking, seeking, and knocking*. Christians are to *persevere*, in full confidence that our loving Father desires only the best for His children. Paul wrote, *"We know that in everything God works for good with those who love him, who are called according to his purpose."* (Romans 8:28)

Chapter Thirteen

Summary of God's Revelations

This parable has a command, a promise and a warning. The command is: *we are to be persistent in prayer; we are to ask, seek, and knock.* The promises are: *Our heavenly Father answers the prayer of His children; God desires to give the gift of the Holy Spirit to those who ask Him.* The warning is: *everyone who exalts himself will be humbled.*

8–2. The Parable of Persistence in Prayer: Lk. 18:1–8

"And he told them a parable, to the effect that they ought always to pray and not lose heart. He said, 'In a certain city there was a judge who neither feared God nor regarded man; and there was a widow in that city who kept coming to him and saying, 'Vindicate me against my adversary.' For a while he refused; but afterward he said to himself, 'Though I neither fear God nor regard man, yet because this widow bothers me, I will vindicate her, or she will wear me out by her continual coming.' And the Lord said, 'Hear what the unrighteous judge says. And will not God vindicate his elect, who cry to him day and night? Will he delay long over them? I tell you, he will vindicate them speedily. Nevertheless, when the Son of man comes, will he find faith on earth?'"

Commentary

This parable begins with these words, *"Jesus told his disciples this parable that they should always pray and not lose heart."*

He then introduces this parable about an unrighteous judge and a persistent widow. The unrighteous judge acts out of self-interest, with little regard for the principles of justice; while God acts out of love and a desire to provide justice to all people. Particularly, God will vindicate His elect who persevere; God will act speedily. The apostle Paul had several messages regarding persistence in prayer, e.g. *"Rejoice always, pray constantly."* (I Thess. 5:16,

God's Hidden Treasures

17). Prayer will lead to increased faith, fellowship and dependence on God.

The question is: will not God vindicate His elect, who cry to Him day and night? Before focusing on that question, let us examine the two characters in this parable, the unrighteous judge and the persistent woman.

The judge *"neither fears God nor cares about men."* There is not much to commend such a person, who cares so little about justice. When you consider the two great commandments, loving God and loving your neighbor, this judge neither feared God nor cared about other men. When the word *"fear"* is used in this context, it means that the judge does not honor God, does not have reverence for God and is not in awe of God. The judge's only interest in *"justice"* is that the widow will stop pestering him. *"I will see that she gets justice."* So justice for the woman means relief for the judge.

The second character is the persistent widow, who demanded that the judge *"vindicate me against my adversary."* We are not told the basis of her demand, but it is sufficiently important to her that she refuses to let the courts dismiss her appeal without giving her justice. Now in this parable, the widow represents the helpless and the weak, while the judge represents the powerful legal authority, many times uncaring and unrighteous. From earliest times, widows were looked upon with sincere pity. They were protected by special laws, along with the *"fatherless"* and *"the stranger."* (Deut. 16:11). So, Jesus does not infer that the woman has received justice; she does receive vindication.

The parable deals with five terms, the understanding of which is important in order to appreciate the fullness of this parable; these terms are *justice, persistence, vindication, faith, and the Second Coming of Jesus.*

First, *justice* is an attribute of God (Job 37:23; Psa. 89:14 and Jer. 50:7). There is no justice without the presence of righteousness; righteousness undergirds justice. The divine justice is implied in Abraham's question (Gen. 18:25),*". . . so that the righteous fare as the wicked! Far be it from thee! Shall not the Judge of all the earth do right?"* Jesus also speaks of the justice of God (Matt. 5:45), *"for he makes the sun rise on the evil and on the good and sends rain*

Chapter Thirteen

on the just and on the unjust." Because God is just and holy, punishment is His reaction to all evil, for without punishment, the human moral order would disintegrate. That is why John wrote, *"sin is lawlessness."* God's justice is shown in the forgiveness of sin when man confesses and repents (I Jn. 1:9); both punishment and forgiveness are expressions of His justice. *In justice, God's holiness, God's laws and God's grace and mercy are expressed.* The prophets showed that God requires this virtue from every person; *"He has shown you, O man, what is good; and what does the Lord require of you but to do justice, and to love kindness, and to walk humbly with your God."* (Mic. 6:8). In the Sermon on the Mount, Jesus deepened the meaning of justice, by making it a matter of the *heart*. Such teaching is a continuation of the promises of God revealed to Jeremiah, when God said that He would write His law on our hearts (Jer. 31:31f), not simply words on tablets of stone. Only love alone, which is the character of God, can bring into the human heart an understanding and the perfection of justice. In Isaiah, God spoke through the prophet, *"For I the Lord love justice."* (Isa. 61:8) God's wrath and God's love are both perfectly expressed in His justice.

The second term is *persistence,* which has the sense of perseverance. Dr. Walter Dunnett, (Evangelical Dictionary of Biblical Theology), presents some invaluable thoughts on this subject. In human terms, the idea is of energetic effort and endurance in the face of trials. Persistence also relates to the expectation of the faithfulness of God. It is closely linked with the idea of faith. In the New Testament, James speaks of Job as an example of those who had persevered, for Job remained persistent under difficult situations. Therefore James determined that *"the Lord is compassionate and merciful"* (James 5:11), basing his statement on the Book of Job (42:10,12), which described the blessing of the Lord on Job. Testing develops perseverance (James 1:2–4), so that we would be mature and complete, equipped for every good work (2 Tim. 3:16). To those who persevere, the promise is *"the crown of life"* (James 1:12). To those who persist, God gives eternal life (Rom. 6:23).

Vindication is a word that Jesus uses here for a special reason. Vindicate means to acquit, sustain, justify, exonerate, deliver, and

God's Hidden Treasures

recover by legal means and to set a person free from previous claims and accusations. When vindication means justify, it also means that the person is pardoned and forgiven.

The parable relates to the *Second Coming of Jesus Christ*, for the question is raised, *"when the Son of man comes . . ."* It is important to note that Jesus does not say, *if the Son of man comes*; it is *"when"*, expressing the certainty of His return in glory.

Persistent prayers, from a pure heart, will lead to justice from God; justice from God will lead to increased faith in Him. *The key question in this parable is, ". . . when the Son of man comes, will he find faith on earth?"* Jesus questions whether people will pray with persistence that justice will be done and the more that God's justice is seen, the greater will be the faith of those who observe God's justice. In that case, faith will abound. Therefore Jesus Christ will find faith on the earth when he returns, if we pray with persistence, if we act justly, if we live by faith. Jesus encourages His disciples to pray with power and persistence that their faith will grow through their prayer life, and that Christ will return as King to find a people of faith, fully trusting God in all circumstances.

Summary of Biblical Themes
Theme 8—The Power of Prayer

God will vindicate His elect, *"when they cry out to him night and day."* When God vindicates His elect, then faith will increase *"and when the Son of man comes, He will find faith on earth."* Such is the measure of the power of prayer.

Theme 4—The Christian Character

Prayer is one of the hallmarks of the Christian life. Christians are people of prayer, dependent on a loving God who desires only the best for His children. Prayer ensures us of communion and fellowship with God. We should pray, in faith, knowing that a loving God will answer, according to His will and purpose, the prayers of His people. The Old and New Testament (Isa. 64:4 and I Cor. 2:9) state, *"What no eye has seen, nor ear heard, nor the heart of man conceived, what God has prepared for those who love him."* God has greater things to give us than we can imagine or desire. Our prayer life will lead to faith that honors Christ when He returns.

Chapter Thirteen

Summary of God's Revelations

This parable presents a command, a promise, a truth and a warning. The command is: *we are always to pray and not lose heart.* The promises are: *God will vindicate His elect; He will answer our prayers.* The truth is: *answered prayers, from a pure heart, will lead to great faith.* The warnings are: *we must pray, so that our faith will grow; thus Christ will find faith when He returns.*

8–3. The Parable of our Perspective in Prayer: Lk. 18:9–14

"He also told this parable to some who trusted in themselves that they were righteous and despised others: 'Two men went up into the temple to pray, one a Pharisee and the other a tax collector. The Pharisee stood and prayed thus with himself, 'God, I thank thee that I am not like other men, extortioners, unjust, adulterers, or even like this tax collector. I fast twice a week, I give tithes of all that I get.' But the tax collector, standing far off, would not even lift up his eyes to heaven, but beat his breast, saying, 'God, be merciful to me a sinner!' I tell you, this man went down to his house justified rather than the other; for every one who exalts himself will be humbled, but he who humbles himself will be exalted."

Commentary

This parable fits closely with the one we have already discussed in the Parable of Humility (Lk. 14:7–11; page 146). Again the same conclusion is given, *"Everyone who exalts himself will be humbled and everyone who humbles himself will be exalted."* Again Jesus emphasizes *exaltation and humility,* as high priorities for the Christian life; previously He applied it to the seat of honor at a Wedding Feast; now He applies humility to our life of prayer.

Jesus reminds us that prayer is a dialogue with God; as such, it is a measure of our dependence on God and our recognition that He can fulfill what He promises. If we don't pray, then that is a measure of our unbelief and a statement that we don't need God. There is an unfortunate situation today that prayer is considered as the last resort; Jesus tells us that it is the *first resort*. Consider the case of Jehoshaphat (2 Chron. 20), in which prayer is the first and only option for the nation of Israel. As such, prayer must be a simple opening of our heart to God as Daniel did (Dan. 9:4–19). One of the great tests of the Christian life is the degree to which we pray. It is not only what we pray, *the content*, but also the *heart* of those who pray. It is not a matter of seeking our will, but the will of the Father. We pray, *thy will be done on earth as it is in heaven.* It is God's will that earth should be like heaven, a kingdom where love, peace and joy reign supreme.

It is interesting in this parable that both men address the Lord as *"God."* However, each of them comes before God with a different perspective of themselves and of God. One said, *"I thank you that I am not like other men . . ."*; the other said, in deep humility, *"have mercy on me, a sinner."* Prayers that begin with *"I"* are dangerous and questionable, *"I thank thee that I am not like other men . . . I fast . . . I give tithes."* Now the use of "I" in general in prayer is not in itself to be condemned; Prayer is not telling God how great I am, rather than telling God *"how great Thou art."* Jesus speaks of the second man as being *justified,* (pardoned and forgiven). The message of Micah 6:8 is that *we are to walk humbly with our God.* In the parable, one came in pride; the other came in a full understanding of his sinful nature and calling on God for redemption and restoration. One man seeks recognition; the other seeks mercy. Again this parable discloses the matter of alternatives in our lives, to be prideful and boastful or to be humble and seeking forgiveness. Jesus closes this parable with the same words that he used in the parable regarding the place of honor at a banquet (page 146), *"For everyone who exalts himself will be humbled and he who humbles himself will be exalted."* The same phrase is quoted many times, but in a slightly different context. In Matthew 23:12, Jesus spoke of *"He who is the greatest among you shall be your servant."* In Luke. 14:11, Jesus presented a parable regarding a banquet, in which one should not seek the place of honor. In I Peter 5:6, Peter wrote

Chapter Thirteen

that everyone should, *"Humble yourself therefore under the mighty hand of God, that in due time, he may exalt you."*

Our prayers should begin with, first, removing the unnecessary clutter in our hearts and lives, to get a clear picture of the Holy God, to feel His Presence and then our prayers begin. We pray to God, enter into fellowship with Him, when we recognize His Sovereignty and His love for us. Our prayers should focus on God, on His will, on His sovereignty, and on His purpose. God knows our needs and our hearts even before we speak. Prayer is a time for coming before God as a *repentant sinner* who looks towards the throne of grace, humbly seeking mercy and forgiveness (Heb. 4:16).

Summary of Biblical Themes
Theme 8—The Power of Prayer

Prayer is a measure of our love for God and others. We come humbly before God seeking mercy. If we exalt ourselves, we will be humbled. Jesus has told us that we receive not, because we ask not. Prayer is coming before God in grateful thanksgiving for all His blessings, for all His promises and for all the opportunities that He has given us to serve Him.

This parable has two secondary themes:

Theme 3—The Alternatives in the Christian Life

In prayer, we can seek God's mercy or exalt ourselves. God will exalt us when we have fulfilled His purposes for our lives, for the lives of others, and for His kingdom.

Theme 4—The Christian Character

We should live a life of prayer and humility, seeking what is best for God's Kingdom, for others, and for ourselves. We should pray: God, what would You have me do for You this day? Our focus should be on believing in His promises, accepting and obeying His truths. Every thought and every prayer should be seeking complete and constant fellowship with God.

Summary of God's Revelations

This parable has messages of a promise, a truth and a warning. The promise is: *God hears prayers from a repentant heart*. The truth

God's Hidden Treasures

is: *he who humbles himself will be exalted; he who exalts himself will be humbled.* The warning is: *exalting ourselves will lead to condemnation from God.*

Summary of Biblical Themes
Theme 8—The Power of Prayer

God honors persistence in prayer; we should approach God with a humble and contrite heart, as we kneel before a holy and just God. Prayer has power when our hearts are pure. We have already seen the major deterrents to prayer (page 216). Prayer is the basis of fellowship. It has power when we seek His will in all things. Above all, remember that we pray, *"thy will be done, on earth as it is in heaven."* Prayer is to seek the will of God and do His will in our witness. God gives the gift of the Holy Spirit to those who ask Him; Jesus wishes that He would find faith when He returns; He desires humility in His people; He encourages us to ask, to seek, and to knock. God answers our prayers. Psalm 19:14 should be utmost in our thoughts, *"Let the words of my mouth and the meditations of my heart be acceptable in thy sight, O Lord, my rock and my redeemer."*

Summary of God's Revelations

The commands are: *we are to be persistent in prayer; we are to ask, seek, and knock; we are always to pray and not lose heart; we are to seek mercy in prayer.* The promises are: *Our heavenly Father answers the prayer of His children; God will vindicate His elect; God hears prayers from a repentant heart.* The truths are: *answered prayers, from a pure heart, will lead to great faith; he who humbles himself will be exalted; he who exalts himself will be humbled.* The warnings are: *everyone who exalts himself will be humbled; we must pray so that our faith will grow, then Christ will find faith when He returns; exalting ourselves in prayers will lead to condemnation from God.*

CHAPTER FOURTEEN

Theme 9—The Parables of The Preparation for the Final Judgment

". . . because I will do this to you, prepare to meet your God, O Israel!" (Amos 4:12)

"Then the King will say to those on his right, 'Come, you who are blessed by my Father; take your inheritance, the kingdom prepared for you since the creation of the world.'" (Matt. 25:34)

"You also must be ready, because the Son of man will come at an hour when you do not expect him." (Lk. 12:40)

Associated with the preparation for the Final Judgment is the certainty of the Second Coming of Jesus Christ. He is coming; there will be a judgment. In Revelation 22:12, 20, Jesus said, *"Behold, I am coming soon, bringing my recompense to repay every one for what he has done . . ."* He who testifies to these things says, *"Surely I am coming soon; Amen. Come, Lord Jesus."* Therefore we must pay close attention to the certainty of Christ's Coming, the Final Judgment and the need for our preparedness. The Scriptures identify two ages; *this age*, in which we now live, and *the age to come*, for which we must prepare. Jesus tells us that we *must be prepared* for such a day, in which God's final judgment and reign will unfold. For those reasons, Jesus presented parables that deal with these important subjects. The end of the age is certain, and Matthew and Luke have recorded 24 signs, among which are the following (Matt. 24: Lk. 21), *"Many will come in my name, claiming 'I am the Christ'; And you will hear of wars and rumors of war and they will lead many astray; nation will rise against nation; famine and earthquake in various places; you will be handed over to persecution; put to death; hated by all nations because of me; many will turn away from the faith and will betray and hate each other; the love of most will grow cold; and this gospel of the kingdom will be preached in the whole world as a testimony to all nations, and then the end will come; standing in the holy place 'the abomination that causes desolation'; there will be great distress, unequaled from the beginning of the world until now; false Christs and false prophets will appear; the coming of the Son of Man; sun will be darkened; moon will not give its light; the sign of the Son of Man will appear in the sky; all the nations of the earth will mourn; He will send His angels with a loud trumpet call; they will gather his elect from . . . one end of the heavens to the other; heaven and earth will pass away but my words will never pass away; destruction of the Temple; Men's love will grow cold; .the desolating sacrilege spoken of by Daniel; great distress and wrath will be upon the people of God; the people of God will be killed and led captive among all nations; Jerusalem will be trodden down by the Gentiles, until the time of the Gentiles is fulfilled."*

God and His Son present clear warnings that there will be a Day of Judgment. In spite of all the direct evidence of God's word, many ignore the warning; others refuse to believe that such an event will occur while others acknowledge that it will occur, but they continually delay making a decision. However, the Scripture makes it plain that, when that Day arrives, it may be too late; the time of decision may well have passed.

The Second Coming of Jesus Christ will precede that Day of Judgment. Therefore, we need to understand what is involved, and Jesus goes to great length to ensure that His Second Coming and that Day are understood. That is why these are companions in one of the major themes of the parables. However, to understand the parables on this subject, we should be familiar with what the Bible

Chapter Fourteen

says about the Second Coming and the importance of our preparation for such a monumental event. *So what is the origin of this doctrine of the Second Coming, what is the teaching of Scripture, what is the teaching of Jesus Himself, what is the nature of this Second Coming and what is its importance for all Christians in every age?* We shall examine these subjects briefly so that we can fully appreciate these parables.

Regarding the *origin* of the Second Coming of Christ, both the Old and New Testament witness that God would one day send His Messiah, who was to be a *great King* who would deliver God's people from all their oppressors. Daniel specifically spoke of that day, *"I saw in the night visions, and behold, with the clouds of heaven there came one like a son of man, and he came to the Ancient of Days and was presented before him. And to him was given dominion and glory and kingdom, that all people, nations, and languages should serve him; his dominion is an everlasting dominion, which shall not pass away, and his kingdom one that shall not be destroyed."* (Dan. 7:13–14) God's spiritual kingdom will be established. Its King will be the Lord Jesus. Luke records Jesus' words just prior to his ascension: *"It is not for you to know times or seasons which the Father has fixed by his own authority"* (Acts 1:7). However, *"two men dressed in white"* spoke to the disciples just prior to the Ascension, *"This same Jesus, who has been taken from you into heaven, will come back in the same way you have seen him go into heaven"* (Acts 1:7,10). Luke adds a further reference to God's having set a day *"when he will judge the world with justice by the man he has appointed. He has given proof of this to all men by raising him from the dead"* (Acts 17:31).

The *teachings are* contained in both the Old and New Testament. The Old Testament contained two *versions* of the Messiah; one as the *Suffering Servant (Isa. 43:3; 50; 53)*; the other as the *King Eternal (Isa. 9:6–7)*. These accounts led to confusion among the Jews; would He be Servant or King? The answer is clear; the Messiah would come twice. He will come *first* as the *Suffering Servant,* to die for the sins of the world; He will come a *second* time, to judge and to rule as *King of kings and Lord of lords.* Jesus is His own

God's Hidden Treasures

best witness to his Second Coming, *"Behold, I am coming soon, bringing my recompense, to repay every one for what he has done. I am the Alpha and the Omega, the first and the last, the beginning and the end . . . I Jesus have sent my angels to you with this testimony for the churches, I am the root and the offspring of David, the bright morning star . . . He who testifies to these things say, 'Surely I am coming soon.' Amen. Come Lord Jesus! The grace of the Lord Jesus be with all the saints. Amen."* (Rev. 22:12–14; 16–17; 20–21).

Its *purpose* is to fulfill His mission, to raise the dead, to destroy death, to gather the elect, to judge the world, to glorify believers, to reward God's people and to bring retribution on all evil. As believers, we are to *"wait for, look for, be ready for, be busy until, to pray for . . ."* The Second Coming is to present reward to the faithful and judgment for all (Matt. 16:27; 25:32). Some will receive praise and crowns (Jude 15); others will receive condemnation. Jesus Christ spoke of this crown (Rev. 2:10), *"And I will give you the crown of life."* Paul spoke of this crown, which is to be based on the life we have led, the faith we have expressed, the witness we have presented, *"I have fought the good fight, I have finished the race, I have kept the faith. Henceforth there is laid up for me the crown of righteousness, which the Lord, the righteous judge, will award to me on that Day, and not only to me, but to all who have loved his appearing."* (2 Tim. 4:7–8).

Until the Second Coming of Jesus, we must be *good disciples, good witnesses, good ambassadors, good stewards* (Lk. 19:13); we must *wait patiently* (I Cor. 1:7); we must be *charitable* (I Cor. 4:5); *blameless* in living (I Thess. 5:23); *perfect in obedience* (I Tim. 6:14); *joyful in expectation* (Tit. 2:13), and *constant in our faith* (I Jn. 2:28). The rewards of such actions will be: *honor from the King* (Lk. 12:37); *fellowship with the King* (Jn. 14:3); *likeness to the King* (Phil. 3:21); *glory with the King* (Col. 3:4); *the crown of righteousness* (I Pet. 5:4); *and most important, "we shall be like him."* (I Jn. 3:2). Receiving and believing in the Lord Jesus Christ is essential to salvation. The apostle John wrote (Jn. 1:12), *"but to all who received him, who believed in his name, he gave power to become children of God; who were born, not of blood nor of the will of the flesh nor of the will of*

Chapter Fourteen

man, but of God." Receiving Him is to acknowledge Him as Savior and Lord; believing in Him is to trust Him in every situation and to do the Will of God. God's will is that every knee would bow and every tongue confess Him Lord, to the glory of God the Father. The Bible contains clear warnings for ignoring or rejecting Jesus Christ.

> *"For whoever is ashamed of me and of my words in this adulterous and sinful generation, of him will the Son of man be ashamed, when he comes in the glory of his Father with the holy angels."* (Mk. 8:38).
>
> *". . . when the Lord Jesus is revealed from heaven with his mighty angels in flaming fire, inflicting vengeance upon those who do not know God and upon those who do not obey the gospel of our Lord Jesus . . ."* (2 Thess. 1:8)
>
> *"Behold he is coming with the clouds, and every eye will see him, every one who pierced him; and all tribes of the earth will wail on account of him. Even so, Amen"* (Rev. 1:7)

The early Christian church, initially composed primarily of Jewish Christians, realized and accepted the truth of His Second Coming. They spoke of Jesus as *"the Christ, the Anointed One,"* (Acts. 4:26) and saw Him not only as a human being who lived a life on earth in a specific time in history, but as the One destined to return at the *end of the age* to establish God's kingdom.

Jesus began His earthly ministry by proclaiming, *"Repent, for the kingdom of heaven is at hand"* (Matt 4:17). This message sets the stage for the kingdom that Jesus was to proclaim during His earthly ministry. In addition, He spoke often about his Second Coming, as witnessed by the questions that His disciples asked *"What will be the sign of your coming and of the end of the age?"* (Matt 24:3). Jesus explained that the coming would be *sudden and unexpected* (Matt 25:13; Luke 12:40), *like lightning and obvious to all* (Matt 24:2). His call for *watchfulness* is important (Matt 24:42–51), for the coming of the Son of Man has decisive importance. When Jesus comes it will be too late to make preparations, so He encourages His followers to be watchful, ready for His coming, whenever it should be. An important part of Jesus' teaching about His Second Coming is that it will be in sharp contrast to His First Coming. Then He

God's Hidden Treasures

was poor, despised and rejected by religious and secular authorities. However, at His Second Coming, He will be *"coming in clouds with great power and glory"* (Mark 13:26). At that time, He will *"gather his elect from the four winds, from the ends of the earth to the ends of the heaven"* (Mk. 13: 27); He will be seen *"sitting at the right hand of the Mighty One and coming on the clouds of heaven"* (Mk. 14:62).

The First Coming emphasized *salvation and forgiveness of sins;* the Second Coming will ordain *judgment.* This judgment is seen first in the *separation of the saved from the lost. (Matt 24:37–41).* The message stressed here and throughout the Scriptures is that many people will continue to reject the Lord Jesus Christ and live without understanding their accountability in the Final Judgment. However, the teachings of Jesus constantly point to human accountability and of final judgment. The apostle Paul wrote (Rom. 2:5–11): *"But by your hard and impenitent heart you are storing up wrath for yourself on the day of wrath when God's righteous judgment will be revealed. For he will render to every man according to his works, those who by patience in well-doing seek for glory and honor and immortality, he will give eternal life; but for those who are factious and do not obey the truth, but obey wickedness, there will be wrath and fury . . . For God shows no partiality."* Paul speaks of waiting for *"the blessed hope,"* which he goes on to explain as *"the glorious appearing of our great God and Savior, Jesus Christ"* (Titus 2:13). There will be *"praise, glory and honor when Jesus Christ is revealed"* (1 Peter 1:7). Revelation begins with *"he is coming with the clouds, and every eye will see him"* (Rev. 1:7); and through the remainder of the book, there is no doubt as to the majesty of the Christ whose place is supreme in heaven, but who will return to this earth. When Jesus Christ does return, it will mark the absolute and final triumph of righteousness. Paul speaks of *"the rebellion"* as something that will occur and of *"the man of lawlessness"* as being *"revealed."* He goes on to say that *"the secret power of lawlessness"* is already at work in this world, but that it will be more fully manifested when *"the one who now holds it back"* is taken out of the way. But the Lord Jesus will destroy the evil power *"by the*

Chapter Fourteen

splendor of his coming" (2 Thess 2:3–12). The Final Judgment will also be a Day of God's wrath on all unrighteousness. However, believers *"are looking forward to a new heaven and a new earth, the home of righteousness"* (2 Peter 3:13).

Although righteousness will triumph, the power of evil will be present. *"There will be terrible times in the last days"* (2 Tim 3:1) and, even among those who profess to be followers of Christ, some will abandon the faith and accept *"things taught by demons"* (1 Tim 4:1). Paul speaks of *"the coming of our Lord Jesus Christ"* and states plainly, *"that day will not come until the rebellion occurs and the man of lawlessness is revealed"* (2 Thess 2:1–3). There will be scoffers who will say, *"Where is this 'coming' he promised?"* (2 Peter 3:4). In 1 John there is a warning against *"the antichrist"* and the writer goes on to speak of *"many antichrists"* being present; therefore the world will know that it is *"the last hour"* (1 John 2:18). Christ will return, and we must be prepared for His appearance and the judgment that is certain for believers and unbelievers. In the meantime, we are to preach the gospel message diligently and passionately, until He returns (Acts 1:8–11). Therefore, Jesus has left us with many indications of the nature of the world in which we now live and the end of the age and our need is to be prepared for the Final Judgment.

The following four (4) parables provide lessons regarding the Second Coming of Christ and the preparations for the Final Judgment:

9–1. *The Parable of Christ's Return; the Unexpected Hour*
9–2. *The Parable of the Rich Man and Lazarus*
9–3. *The Parable of the Lessons from the Fig Tree*
9–4. *The Parable of the Ten Virgins*

These parables conclude with four important messages. The first with, *"You also must be ready; for the Son of man is coming at an unexpected hour."*; the second with *"If they do not hear Moses and the prophets, neither will they be convinced if some one should rise from the dead"*; the third with, *"Therefore you also must be ready; for the Son of man is coming at an hour you do not expect."*; the fourth with, *"Watch therefore, for you know neither the day nor the hour."* The message is clear: *Be ready, keep watch.*

God's Hidden Treasures

9–1. The Parable of Christ's Return, the Unexpected Hour: Lk. 12:32–40

"Fear not, little flock, for it is your Father's good pleasure to give you the kingdom. Sell your possessions, and give alms; provide yourselves with purses that do not grow old, with a treasure in the heavens that does not fail, where no thief approaches and no moth destroys. For where your treasure is, there will your heart be also. Let your loins be girded and your lamps burning, and be like men who are waiting for their master to come home from the marriage feast, so that they may open to him at once when he comes and knocks. Blessed are those servants whom the master finds awake when he comes; truly, I say to you, he will gird himself and have them sit at table, and he will come and serve them. If he comes in the second watch, or in the third, and finds them so, blessed are those servants! But know this, that if the householder had known at what hour the thief was coming, he would not have left his house to be broken into. You also must be ready; for the Son of man is coming at an unexpected hour."

Commentary

In the text preceding this parable, Jesus had been teaching His disciples (12:22), much of what Matthew had recorded in The Sermon on the Mount (Matthew 5:1–7:29). Now Jesus moves from that teaching to this parable, whose message is that Jesus Christ *is coming at an unexpected hour*; we must be prepared. Therefore, remember that God is pleased to give believers the kingdom, remember the true and eternal *"possession"*, live a life worthy of those possessions and be faithful servants until the *"hour"* when Christ shall return. Be ready, for the Son of man is coming at an unexpected hour.

There are a series of key thoughts, *"Father's good pleasure to give you the kingdom; sell possessions; give alms; lay up a treasure in heaven that will not fail; your heart will be where your treasure is;*

Chapter Fourteen

loins girded; lamps burning; be awake; must be ready, for the Son of man is coming at an unexpected hour. An examination of this sequence will uncover the great truths of this parable.

First, God is *pleased to give us the kingdom*. What does that mean? It is God's kingdom, and He is pleased to give it to us. Why does He do that? How does He do it? What is the purpose of the gift? Now, it is important to understand that the kingdom is every place where God is present, where He is sovereign and where His rule and authority dominate. How can God give us something that is His possession and is representative of Him? Since the kingdom is synonymous with His Presence, then Jesus is saying that the Presence of God is given eternally to us. If we have eternally the kingdom, then we are eternally with the Father. He gives Himself; He shares Himself. Why does He do that? The answer is simple, it's because He loves us, not because we are wonderful and deserving. In the same way that God chose Israel, He chooses us today, "*. . . to be a people holy to the Lord; the Lord your God has chosen you to be a people for his own possession, out of all the people on the face of the earth. It is not because you were more in number than any other people that the Lord set his love upon you and chose you, for you were the fewest of all the people; but it is because the Lord loves you, and is keeping the oath which he swore to your fathers . . .*" (*Deut. 7:6–8*). That is the same reason He has chosen us; simply because He loves us. For what purpose does He give us the kingdom? So that we would know the fullness of His love, His joy, His peace; His gift to us is to be shared with others, that they too would know and share the Presence of God that we possess.

Second, we are to "*sell our possessions . . .*" Here Jesus is speaking literally and figuratively. Our "*possessions*" are those material and physical aspects in our lives on which we place too high a value. Sometimes, our possessions possess us; possessions are anything that filters our vision of God. Now, certainly those possessions have some value, so Jesus tells us to "*sell*" which means that we receive something in return. With the kingdom as our "*heavenly, or spiritual,*" possession, we are to *sell* all evidence of worldly wealth, since they represent a temptation for idolatry. The first commandment is that we should love the Lord our God with all our heart and all our soul and all our mind. The measure of our love for God is the willingness to get rid of any possession that we value more highly than Him. We should love God alone, above all. But what we sell, we are to use the proceeds to *give alms*. We should give willingly and generously to those in need. In the Old Testament, alms were to support the poor and, in the New Testament, the needy saints of the church. Paul states the principle for giving in Rom 12:8: those who give are called to do so liberally, as a work of grace, done voluntarily and cheerfully. Since God is generous to us, we should be generous to others. That is why alms and other such contributions are called *acts of mercy*. We are to be thankful for God's blessings and generous in sharing them with others.

Next, we are to lay up for ourselves a *"treasure in the heavens that does not fail, where no thief approaches and no moth destroys."* The wealth of this world cannot compare to the heavenly home that we shall share with God. But what is this treasure in heaven that we are to lay up? Well, it is certainly not the physical aspects of this life, but it is most certainly the spiritual characteristics that we are to develop now. The true treasures are a relationship with God and fellowship with Him. It is love, joy, peace, the beauty of His Word, the power of His Spirit, the Presence of His Son, the prayers which we offer in His name, and Christ in us, the hope of glory. Our greatest treasures are the love of God, the love of our family, friendships, fellowship with other Christians; above all, salvation and eternal life. These are the possessions that we should seek and the ones that we should prize. This is the basis of a new vision and a new life in Christ. Those treasures are eternal. *"A treasure in heaven"* is all that we need to possess. That is the treasure that we should be accumulating every day of our earthly life. We should not seek money, power, or other possessions; for the love of money and the desire for power are two of our most serious enemies. By not worshipping wealth and power, we can fully concentrate on the kingdom. We are reminded (Matt. 6:17), *"Do not lay up for yourselves treasures on earth where moth and rust consume and where thieves break in and steal; but lay up for yourselves trea-*

Chapter Fourteen

sures in heaven . . . for where your treasure is, there will your heart be also." In the Old Testament, all wealth originally formed part of God's good creation, over which humans were given dominion (Gen. 1:26). Wealth may be a reward for righteousness (Ps 112), but it is often the product of wickedness (Ps 37:16–17). The Bible stresses the transient character of earthly wealth (Ps 39:4–6). Those who are given much must not trust in their own resources but in God (Ps 52:7) and must use their abundance *to help the needy (Ps 82:3–4)*. Even in the Old Testament, the Israelites' wealth was to be shared with both the poor Jew and the poor Gentiles, so as to bring people to knowledge of the Lord. *Increased privilege carries increased responsibility.*

In the New Testament, Jesus taught that wealth, *"mammon"*, competes with God for human allegiance (Matt 6:19–24). Wealth is *"deceitful"* (Mark 4:19) because it can distract people from focusing on their spiritual condition. The question is: will God's resources be distributed equitably? Eternal destinies hang in the balance; God will judge people on the basis of their care of the needy (Matt 25:31–46). The Parable of the Good Samaritan emphasized the principle to show mercy, to love our enemies (Luke 10:25–37). In the Sermon on the Mount, Jesus said that we are to love our enemies and pray for them. God demands an equitable distribution, *"from each according to his ability"* (Acts 11:29); *"to anyone as he has need" (Acts 2:45)*. Luke quotes Jesus: *"It is more blessed to give than to receive" (20:33–35)*. Christians are to be generous and thankful people.

Next, to have our *"loins girded"* refers to the loincloth or dress of the day; more accurately, it could mean to put on a girdle around the lower region of the back. This was generally done for battle or for serving others. What Jesus is saying here is that we should be dressed not for a banquet but for service—even for battle against evil.

Further, to have our *"lamps burning"* means that we are to be the light of the world. Therefore, we are to be light in darkness and good in overcoming evil. Lamp has several unique meanings in the Bible. In Psa. 119:105; Prov. 6:23, the lamp is symbolical of:

God's Hidden Treasures

the Word of God (Psa. 119:105), *"Thy word is a lamp to my feet."* In Isa 62:1, the lamp refers to the salvation of God, *"her salvation as a burning torch."* However, lamp could refer to God's guidance (Psa. 18:28) *"Yea, thou dost light my lamp; the Lord my God lightens my darkness."* Further it could refer to the spirit of man (Prov. 20:27) *"The spirit of man is the lamp of the Lord."* So the lamp here takes on a multiple concept; it means that we should be constantly faithful to the Word of God; it means that our witness, our service and our love is reflected in the brightness of our lamp; it means that we have God's Presence always to guide us; it means that our faithful and godly spirit provides light for the world. It means all these things, and perhaps even more.

The phrase *"be awake"* involves being attentive and prepared immediately for service. It is being fully alert and prepared for whatever service God calls us. It defines the character of a soldier standing at attention, totally obedient, eager for orders and ready for action.

Further, Jesus said that we *"must be ready;* that is, we must be alert and awake, but we must be immediately prepared for any task that might be assigned. As good stewards, that means to be equipped to handle any task that God may give us. His Presence ensures us that nothing is too difficult, because we *"can do all things in him who strengthens me."* (Phil . 34:13)

Finally, said Jesus, you must do all these things, *"for the Son of man is coming at an unexpected hour."* First, Jesus Christ, the Son of man, is coming. There is no doubt about that. *Second*, only the Father knows His time and place of His arrival. We are to be prepared and expectantly straining to see Him. It will be a time of mourning for unbelievers but, for believers, it is *the time, the day,* for which we live. Like many other parables, this one also deals with the Last Days, which we need to understand and appreciate its significance. Dr. O. Cullman has an excellent study (<u>Christ and Time</u>) on this subject. For Christians, the supremely great event has taken place in the coming of Jesus Christ into the world to effect the salvation of all believers. This was not just an event in history; it was *the* event. Because of what Christ has done, every-

Chapter Fourteen

thing was changed. From then on, until God intervenes and sets up the new heaven and the new earth, people are living in *"the last times."* The days, in which people enter into the fullness of the salvation He has purchased, are different from all preceding days. They are days of new opportunity, days when people can put their trust in the crucified, risen, and ascended Lord and enter into the salvation He won for sinners. The writer to the Hebrews told his readers, *"in these last days he (God) has spoken to us by his Son"* (Heb. 1:2), and Peter says that Christ *"was revealed in these last times for your sake"* (1 Peter 1:20). In such passages, the meaning is that something amazing has happened which is in sharp contrast to everything that occurred in earlier ages. Christ's atoning death was God's final answer to the problem of human sin; once that had been accomplished, nothing would be the same again. Christ brought the atonement that made it possible for sinners to be forgiven and to enter God's kingdom. However, there will be a great increase in evil in the last days. Sometimes this relates to the daily life of the believer, as when Jesus says, *"All men will hate you because of me, but he who stands firm to the end will be saved"* (Matt 10:22). But evil will be more widespread than that, for *"There will be terrible times in the last days. People will be lovers of themselves, lovers of money, boastful, proud"* (2 Tim 3:1). *"In the last days scoffers will come, scoffing and following their own evil desires"* (2 Peter 3:3). Similarly Peter speaks of salvation as *"ready to be revealed in the last time"* (1 Peter 1:5).

The reason these parables are so important is because Jesus speaks against all the evil that will come in the Last Days; in these parables, He is preparing us for trials and tribulations, as well as the character we must have in order to weather the storms.

John's Gospel presents the message that God will protect His own in those troubled times. Jesus repeatedly said concerning those the Father *"has given"* him that he will *"raise them up at the last day"* (John 6:39,40,43,54). Jesus said, ". . . *I have kept them in thy name . . . I have guarded them, . . . and none of them is lost . . .*" (Jn. 17:12). Jesus said that He has lost none of those that the Father had given Him. The teachings of these last days make it clear that Jesus' care for his own extends right through time to the ushering

God's Hidden Treasures

in of the final state of affairs. On the negative side, the person who rejects Jesus and his teaching will find that that teaching *"will condemn him at the last day"* (John 12:48).

In that final, great day, all people will see the triumph of God. Further, Paul said that Christ will come with *"those who belong to him. Then the end will come, when he hands over the kingdom to God the Father after he has destroyed all dominion, authority and power"* (1 Cor 15:24). The apostle goes on to speak of the raising of the dead in a different form, one in which they will be *"imperishable"* (I Cor. 15:52). The New Testament presents the truth that, when Jesus returns, all evil will be defeated, and the redeemed will experience the fullness of everlasting life. For the New Testament writers, the coming of Jesus Christ into the world to bring about our salvation was the decisive happening in the entire history of the world. That set in motion the train of events that would bring about the salvation of repentant sinners and the eventual establishment of God's kingdom. This did not mean that all evil would immediately disappear; both the New Testament writings and Christian experience make it plain that evil continues. Again in the Parables of the Wheat and the Tares, Jesus emphasized that good will grow along with evil until the Day of Judgment. But the important thing is that the saving work of Christ has altered everything. Sin has been decisively defeated, and believers have already entered into their salvation.

Jesus is repeating this theme of preparedness for the Second Coming of the Son of man. *"Be dressed, ready . . . your lamps burning . . . watching . . . ready . . . you must be ready . . . because the Son of man will come at a time when you do not expect him."* Three times, the command is to <u>be ready</u>, that has to tell us something! Be ready, watching and be prepared. Christians are to live each day in expectation of Christ's return.

During the time between the First and the Second Advent, Christians are told to be merciful, forgiving, bold for the gospel, good stewards of what God has given us, and rich in the things of God. Now Christ says *"be ready"* at all times for His coming that we can never predict. The kingdom has come and the King will return. The first advent was as the Suffering Servant, to die for the

Chapter Fourteen

sins of the world; the Second Advent will be the coming of the King in glory, for He shall reign forever and ever. We must be ready and watching, not knowing the hour or the day when Christ will appear again. During that time, we are to live a life pleasing to God and one that honors Him.

Summary of Biblical Themes
Theme 9—The Preparation for the Final Judgment

Since God is pleased to give us the kingdom, our response is constant preparation for Christ's return. Because the time is unexpected, we are to live our lives in the expectation that His return will occur in the next second. The question we must be prepared to answer is whether God will approve of our faith, our works and our mission. Our goal is that every thought, every word and every act is acceptable to God. *(Psa. 19:14)*

The following are *secondary* themes in this parable:
Theme 1—The Character of God

God is pleased to give the kingdom to His children; that is an expression of His love and His desire to share eternal fellowship with us. In this parable, we see also the character of God as *"serving"* those to whom the kingdom is given; Jesus said that He came to *serve, not to be served.*

Theme 2—The Kingdom of Heaven

God gives the kingdom of heaven to His children; a gift prepared for us before the foundation of the world. The questions are: are we prepared to receive the kingdom? Are we worthy of the kingdom? Will we be faithful in serving the kingdom?

Theme 4—The Christian Character

Christians are to live, fully prepared for the return of Jesus Christ. We must have our *lamps' burning*, truly being the light of the world. We must be *"waiting", selling what we* have *and giving alms to the needy.* We should receive the kingdom with joy, giving thanks to God. Before the last days, all nations must hear the gospel.

Summary of God's Revelations

This parable has four messages: commands, a promise, a truth and a warning. The commands are: *sell what you have, give alms,*

God's Hidden Treasures

provide yourself with a treasure in heaven. The promise is: *it is God's good pleasure to give us the kingdom.* The truth is: *where your treasure is, there will your heart be also.* The warning is: *you must be prepared; for the Son of man is coming at an unexpected hour.*

9–2. The Parable of the Rich Man and Lazarus: Lk. 16:19–31

"There was a rich man, who was clothed in purple and fine linen and who feasted sumptuously every day. And at his gate lay a poor man named Lazarus, full of sores, who desired to be fed with what fell from the rich man's table; moreover the dogs came and licked his sores. The poor man died and was carried by the angels to Abraham's bosom. The rich man also died and was buried; and in Hades, being in torment, he lifted up his eyes, and saw Abraham far off and Lazarus in his bosom. And he called out, 'Father Abraham, have mercy upon me, and send Lazarus to dip the end of his finger in water and cool my tongue; for I am in anguish in this flame.' But Abraham said, 'Son, remember that you in your lifetime received your good things, and Lazarus in like manner evil things; but now he is comforted here, and you are in anguish. And besides all this, between us and you a great chasm has been fixed, in order that those who would pass from here to you may not be able, and none may cross from there to us.' And he said, 'Then I beg you, father, to send him to my father's house, for I have five brothers, so that he may warn them, lest they also come into this place of torment.' But Abraham said, 'They have Moses and the prophets; let them hear them.' And he said, 'No, father Abraham; but if someone goes to them from the dead, they will repent.' He said to him, 'If they do not hear Moses and the prophets, neither will they be convinced if some one should rise from the dead.'"

Commentary

This parable follows shortly after the Parable of the Shrewd Manager (Parable 22, page 203) and continues the theme of the

Chapter Fourteen

need to prepare for the Final Judgment. This parable, about a rich man and a poor man has the same ring as that of the Old Testament parable that Nathan told David, about the rich man with flocks of sheep and the poor man with only a little ewe lamb (2 Sam. 12:1–14). This parable is about self-centeredness, preparation for the Final Judgment, and preparation for eternal life. The sequence in this parable is important; keep in mind that Jesus had just finished a parable about the need to make good use of our possessions while we are on earth, so that the proper use of them will bring glory to God and comfort to those in need. As we learned earlier (The Parable of the Shrewd Manager), we are to use our unrighteous mammon to prepare for our eternal habitation. This parable reinforces that message.

In addition to the judgment on self centeredness, this parable has another significant theme, *"If they did not hear Moses and the prophets, neither will they be convinced if some one should rise from the dead."* The Ten Commandments were given through Moses; since then, God has continually revealed Himself through His Word, through His prophets and through His Son. If the people were not convinced of the truths from those messengers, why would they repent, *"if some one should rise from the dead."* The author of Hebrews began his epistle with these words *"In many and various ways God spoke of old to our fathers by the prophets, but in these last days he has spoken to us by a Son, whom he appointed the heir of all things, through whom he also created the world."* God had spoken through His prophets, but the people hadn't listened. Now God has spoken through His Son; many still do not listen. They didn't listen then; many do not listen now. Jesus Christ, God Incarnate, has risen from the dead; many do not believe or repent.

Further, this parable is also about the need for preparedness in this life for the life to come and the difficulty to recognize or acknowledge that one day our earthly life will end. For many people, life is sometimes too good. Many people live for the moment, with no thought for others or for the future. Jesus understands human nature, and He understands the condition of the rich and the poor. For that reason, this parable speaks volumes to the self-satisfied of this world.

God's Hidden Treasures

So in this parable, Jesus continues the theme of the obligation of the rich to care for the poor; such attention has eternal consequences. It is God's will for His people to be generous and loving to those who have not known the fruit of this world and who spend a lifetime in poverty and in pain. It is also a story about responsibility and accountability now; that, in heaven, we will be held accountable for what we have done with what has been entrusted to us. What we do in this life has monumental significance for our next life. We cannot sustain a selfish lifestyle that ignores the needs of those around us. There is payment for sins of commission and omission; we will be held accountable. This is the message of The Parable of the Sheep and the Goats (10-2), regarding the manner in which we treat the *hungry, the thirsty, the stranger, the naked, those in prison.* We need to be responsible witnesses and serve God and our neighbor everyday in every way. We must have our eyes on the present, because what we do now has eternal consequences. We are warned, *"Do not lay up for yourselves treasures on earth, but lay up for yourselves treasures in heaven . . . for where your treasure is, there will your heart be also."* (Matt. 6:19–21). We must lay up now for ourselves treasures in heaven. God has given this message to His people since the beginning of time, through the prophets and all of His servants. God led Moses to warn the people of the manner in which they treated wealth, *"Beware lest you say in your heart, 'my power and my might have gotten me this wealth.' You shall remember the Lord your God, for it is he who gives you power to get wealth; that he may confirm his covenant which he swore to your fathers . . ."* (Deut. 8:17–18).

This is a story of the contrast between a beggar, in rags, and a rich man, dressed in purple, the sign of royalty. The beggar dies and *"is carried to Abraham's bosom."* This is an appropriate phrase, for the bosom represents the place where our affections dwell; Jesus is saying that the poor man found a resting place in which the affection of Abraham was present. The beggar's resting place is with Abraham, the *"friend of God."* (James 2:23). There is no evidence that this beggar was a religious man, so why is he accepted at the bosom of Abraham? It can only be because of the grace of God.

Chapter Fourteen

God's grace doesn't make sense according to human standards. In many ways, His grace is not reasonable; but grace has reasons that reasons cannot reason. The rich man later dies and went to *"Hades";* in his earthly life, the rich man thought only of himself. In addition, the question might be, where was the fruit of love, joy, peace, etc. shown in the life of the rich man?

The rich man calls out to Abraham, seeking the poor man, Lazarus, to *"cool my tongue . . . for I am in anguish in this flame."* The rich man now turns for relief to the one he ignored in this life. Abraham tells him that Lazarus cannot help him, so that the rich man, now in Hades, asked Abraham to warn his brothers that they should change their ways; otherwise their end will be the same as his. He now shows a desire to help others, to save them from the torments of hell; unfortunately, there is no evidence that he wants them to seek the things of heaven. On the other hand, the beggar is one who is constantly seeking, begging, for something from others. He has nothing to give; his life is one of pain and sorrow. It is interesting that Jesus called this beggar *"Lazarus"* for the name means, *"God has helped."* In one sense, we are all beggars, and, in one sense, our names are also Lazarus, *"God has helped."*

In the parable, after death, the positions are reversed. The self-centered have little to commend them; the *beggars* are welcomed into the kingdom. Both the rich man and the beggar might have known that *"It is reckoned once to die and then the judgment."* (Heb. 9:27). The rich man never understood this message of judgment. If he understood it, he ignored it and lived a life that mocked God.

There are various messages here from the rich man, which show his state of mind, *Have mercy on me; send Lazarus; I am in anguish.* However, at this moment in time, nothing can be done for those who have lived a life, rebelling against the commandments of God. In addition, there are two questions that stand out sharply. First, why was the rich man in hell? Second, why was the beggar in heaven? What did the rich man do that was so bad as to condemn him to hell, and what did the beggar do that was so good as to commend him to God in heaven? And the answer to both questions is *"nothing."* The rich man did *"nothing"* to ease the pain and

God's Hidden Treasures

poverty of Lazarus. In one sense, the rich man was like the priest and the Levite in the Parable of the Good Samaritan; the rich man saw the need of his neighbor and *"passed by on the other side."* The beggar did nothing to be welcomed into heaven; the reason that he was there was simply because of God's grace. In another sense, it is important to remember the words of Scripture (I Sam. 16:7), in which God spoke to Samuel, *"for the Lord sees not as man sees; man looks on the outward appearance, but the Lord looks on the heart."* God knew both the heart of the rich man and the beggar. It is nothing more complicated than that. In his lifetime, the rich man received *"good things"*, which were external possessions, for he *"dressed in purple and fine linen and lived in luxury every day."* However, the question is: what did he do with these "good things"? In his lifetime, the beggar received *"bad things"*, and now, through grace, God gives him the *"good things."*

What the Bible says about beggars will help us understand the parable. Jesus restored sight to a blind beggar at the Pool of Siloam (Jn. 9:8) and to blind Bartimaeus, begging along the Jericho road (Mk. 10:46). Jesus, as we are called to do, looked to the cause behind the beggar's condition. Jesus taught *"kindly treatment of them"*, as the Levitical Law prescribed (Lev. 19:10: 25:25) and expressed God's consideration of them (Psa. 69:33). In addition, when the disciples of John came to Jesus, Jesus explained to them that *"the blind see, the deaf hear, the lame walk, and the poor have good news preached to them."* These are the beggars of every generation, and God said that we are to have compassion on them because in many ways, we are *"beggars"* also. Christians are all dependent beggars; the Lord God has pity, compassion on those in need.

Jesus spoke of both good things and bad things. So what are the *"good things"*; what are the *"bad things"*? We begin by understanding the thoughts and ways of God, *"For my thoughts are not your thoughts, neither are my ways your ways, says the Lord."* (Isa. 55:8) The good things to God are not the same as the good things to us; also the bad things for God are not the same as the bad things for us. In God's vernacular, the *"good things"* are righteousness, joy, and peace, love for God and for our neighbor. The "bad

Chapter Fourteen

things" are "*immorality, impurity, licentiousness, idolatry, sorcery, enmity, strife, jealousy, anger, selfishness, dissension, party spirit, envy, drunkenness, carousing and the like.*" (Gal. 5:19f) Paul calls these the "*works of the flesh.*" Christians need to live now, seeking the good things of God, so that our faith would increase and we will bear much fruit in our good works.

Also Abraham said that he couldn't help the unrepentant now, for the rich man had "*Moses and the prophets*"; he should have listened to them. Moses and the prophets represented the Old Testament, which taught that society must care for the poor. In addition, one of the great messages of the Old Testament is that the Messiah is coming; therefore, live a life worthy of repentance. Be prepared, by doing good deeds as evidence of faith. All people will be held accountable for what they do in this life with whatever God has entrusted to them. Paul wrote (Rom. 2:6), "*For he (God) will render to every man according to his works.*" All of us must take seriously the warnings of the Old Testament and be prepared for the Second Coming of Christ. Abraham also said that, if you don't believe God's words, spoken through the prophets, then nothing will be able to convince you; in fact, you will not be convinced even if someone rose from the dead. Lazarus cannot "*rise from the dead*"; only the Son of God can and did do that. Jesus' followers must be concerned about the poor of the world. In addition, His disciples must be prepared for the Second Coming of Christ and live a life that recognizes the certainty of the Final Judgment.

Summary of Biblical Themes
Theme 9—The Preparation for the Final Judgment

Everyone needs to understand the significance of the Final Judgment. There is eternity for all; there is no escape from this reality. Once we have died, we shall either go to heaven or to hell. We cannot cross over from one to the other. NOW, there is a Savior and a Redeemer. NOW, we must make a decision; NOW, people must commit their lives to Jesus Christ. We cannot ignore the needy; we cannot ignore the wounded and helpless lying "*by the side of the road.*"

God's Hidden Treasures

There are two additional themes in this parable.

Theme 3—The Alternatives in Life

We can be rich in the things of God *or* rich in the things of this world; it is rare that both will occur. The rich are not always the rich; the poor are not always the poor. To God, the poor are to be cared for, and He has entrusted us with that responsibility. The helpless need us. More importantly, we must use the opportunities in this life to prepare for the next. We have a choice to ignore the reality of the Second Coming *or* to prepare for it by expressing our faith through good works.

Theme 4—The Christian Character

Christians are called to share God's blessings with those less fortunate. We cannot ignore the silent cries for help. Like the Good Samaritan, we must cross to the other side of the road to bind up their wounds.

Summary of God's Revelations

This parable has both truths and warnings. The truths are: *God has revealed His plan for His creation; we must show mercy.* The warnings are: *once we are in hell, there is no way that we can enter heaven; the decision is made for all times; if we fail to heed the warning of the OT prophets, we shall face eternal damnation. We must listen now to Jesus Christ, the One who rose from the dead.*

9–3. The Parable of the Lessons from the Fig Tree: Matt. 24:32–35

"From the fig tree learn its lesson: as soon as its branch becomes tender and puts forth its leaves, you know that summer is near. So also, when you see all these things, you know that he is near, at the very gates. Truly, I say to you, this generation will not pass away till all these things take place. Heaven and earth will pass away, but my words will not pass away. But of that day and hour no one knows, not even the angels of heaven, nor the Son, but the Father only. As were

Chapter Fourteen

the days of Noah, so will be the coming of the Son of man. For as in those days before the flood they were eating and drinking, marrying and giving in marriage, until the day when Noah entered the ark, and they did not know until the flood came and swept them all away, so will be the coming of the Son of man. Then two men will be in the field; one is taken and one is left. Two women will be grinding at the mill; one is taken and one is left. Watch therefore, for you do not know on what day your Lord is coming. But know this, that if the householder had known in what part of the night the thief was coming, he would have watched and would not have let his house be broken into. Therefore you also must be ready; for the Son of man is coming at an hour you do not expect."

Commentary

Jesus now begins a series of parables that contain lessons from the fig tree and a wedding party; all focus on the need to be prepared for His Second Coming, because the *"Son of man is coming at an hour you do not expect."* This is the same theme of the Parable of the Return of Christ; The Unexpected Hour (page 238).

This parable has four main messages; *first,* we are to recognize the signs that tell of the Second Coming: *second,* we are to live a life worthy of eternal life; *third,* we are to recognize Noah as the example of faith and obedience; *fourth,* although there will be signs, the Lord is coming at an unexpected time.

First, recognizing the signs is very difficult. Jesus (Matt. 24; Lk. 21) tells of the signs of the Second Coming (See page 232). Since the first century AD, people have searched the events of those days, trying to relate current situations to those events identified by Christ. From those studies, many have tried to predict the time of Christ's Return. Jesus said that no one knows that day, only the Father. It is not important to know when; it is important to know that He is surely coming again.

Second, we are to be impact people, preparing ourselves by living a life worthy of eternal life, and presenting the gospel to the world so that everyone would be prepared for the Final Judgment. We are to make a difference in this world now. Jesus said that the gospel must be preached throughout the entire world, and then He will return. Evangelism must be our focus until He returns.

God's Hidden Treasures

Third, in the time of Noah, most people were only concerned with the pleasures of that day and never gave thought to God and His commandments. Noah's name means *"rest"* or *"comfort"*; he is the 10th in descent from Adam; this is significant, for ten means the perfection of the divine order. That is the role that Noah was to play. Two stories concern Noah; in one, Noah is the first vinegrower (Gen. 5:29; 9:18–27); in the second, he is the hero of the Flood (Gen. 6:5–9:17). His faithfulness to the one true God provides much of the foundation for Judaic and Christian monotheism. Noah followed God's guidance faithfully; as a result, he and his family were saved. Noah is the first great example of faith, which leads to God's protection, redemption, restoration, reconciliation and our salvation. The flood in the time of Noah came with great power and without warning. In the same way, Christ will return with great power and without warning. The unprepared are destroyed; the faithful are saved.

Fourth, therefore Jesus repeats His warnings *"keep watch"* and *"be ready"*, for the *"Son of man will come at an hour when you do not expect him."*

Summary of Biblical Themes
Theme 9—The Preparation for the Final Judgment

Noah is the example of faith in God. We too are to express that same faithfulness. In return, God is faithful to those who love Him and obey Him. *". . . in everything God works for good with those who love him, who are called according to his purpose."* (Rom. 8:28)

There is one secondary theme:

Theme 4—The Characteristics of the Christian life

Christians are to live a joyful life, anxiously looking for the Second Coming of Jesus Christ. We know neither the time nor the place—only that He is coming. We must watch for the *"signs"* of His return; we must be certain that we recognize the true Christ. The key for every Christian is to *"keep watch"* and *"be ready."*

Summary of God's Revelations

The command is: *you must be ready, for the Son of man is coming at an hour you do not expect.* The promise is: *heaven and earth will pass away, but my words will not pass away.* The truth is: *but of that*

Chapter Fourteen

day and hour no one knows, not even the angels in heaven, nor the Son, but the Father only. The warning is: *watch therefore, for you do not know the day your Lord is coming.*

9–4. The Parable of the Ten Virgins: Matt. 25:1–13

"Then the kingdom of heaven shall be compared to ten maidens who took their lamps and went to meet the bridegroom. Five of them were foolish, and five were wise. For when the foolish took their lamps, they took no oil with them; but the wise took flasks of oil with their lamps. As the bridegroom was delayed, they all slumbered and slept. But at midnight there was a cry, 'Behold, the bridegroom! Come out to meet him.' Then all those maidens rose and trimmed their lamps. And the foolish said to the wise, 'Give us some of your oil, for our lamps are going out.' But the wise replied, 'Perhaps there will not be enough for us and for you; go rather to the dealers and buy for yourselves.' And while they went to buy, the bridegroom came, and those who were ready went in with him to the marriage feast; and the door was shut. Afterward the other maidens came also, saying, 'Lord, lord, open to us.' But he replied, 'Truly, I say to you, I do not know you.' Watch therefore, for you know neither the day nor the hour."

Commentary

This parable rightly deserves a prominent place in the parables of Jesus. It has a great message about the *wise and foolish* of every age; about *numbers* (e.g. 10 and 5); about *lamps and oil*; about the reason the *wise will ignore the foolish*; about the reason that *not everyone who calls upon the name of the Lord will be saved*; and finally, the message that we must be watchful, *for you know neither the day nor the hour.* Again, the term *"foolish"* refers to the morally corrupt. This message of watchfulness and preparedness is a constant theme throughout all these parables. Further, this parable contains promises, truths and warnings.

God's Hidden Treasures

The parable is set in the context of a wedding in ancient Israel. In that time period, it was customary for the groom to celebrate in his home with family and friends and then be escorted by friends, carrying torches. The bridegroom distributed sweets as he proceeded to the bride's home, where her attendants were helping her dress and preparing her for the wedding. Having no means of telling time, the groom might arrive at any time during the course of the evening. As a result, the bride's attendants would grow tired; some might fall asleep.

With that introduction, let's examine the content. The characters are the bridegroom and the 10 virgins, who were going *"to meet the bridegroom."* The bridegroom is the central character, and it immediately points us to the message of God and His church. In this parable, the bridegroom is Christ (*"the bridegroom"*, Jn. 3:29), and the church is *"the Bride, the wife of the Lamb."* (Rev 21:9) The bridegroom rejoices over the bride, so the Lord shall forever rejoice in His people and His people in Him. This New Testament figure of marriage is also used in the Old Testament as it describes the relationship between God and the Jewish nation. However with this important difference; although Israel is portrayed as the wife of Jehovah (Hos 2:2) and disowned and dishonored because of her unbelief and apostasy, she will one day be restored (Hos. 2:14–23). The New Testament church, on the other hand, is a pure virgin, betrothed to Christ. This message Paul preaches to the Corinthians, *"I feel a divine jealousy for you, for I betrothed you to Christ to present you as a pure bride to her one husband."* (2 Cor. 11:1–2) The church is the virgin wife of the Lamb (John 3:29; Rev 19:6–8). This is the high and glorious position that the church is to receive. In the same way, the church is to be like a virgin who is pure, chaste, unmarried and completely devoted to Christ alone. In the context of the church as bride, it is not stretching the parable too far to say that this applies to every member of the Church of Christ, male and female. We are all to be fully devoted to Christ alone. The church, the body (1 Cor. 12:13–14) and bride of Christ (Eph 5:25–27) are formed by the baptism and the power of the Holy Spirit. Dr. C. Chavasse has written an excellent book, <u>The Bride of Christ</u>, providing excellent insight on this subject.

Chapter Fourteen

Now consider the Ten Virgins. Ten is the number of the perfection of the divine order; it signifies completeness, such as the Ten Commandments—the fullness of the Laws of God. However, five were wise, and five were foolish. The number five also is significant. Five is the number of redemption and grace. In this parable, God's grace and redemption is given to five; God's grace is denied to five. The aspect of *"wise"* or *"wisdom"* has already been discussed in the Parable of the Faithful and Wise Manager (page 198). *"There was a cry"*, indicating that the decisive moment has arrived. There will be no more sleeping; instead, get ready for action. Those ready or the prepared represent what the church of Jesus Christ must be. Now their oil was to provide light; and Christians are to be the light of the world, with oil in their lamps and prepared for the Return of Christ. For that event, we must be ready, prepared, zealous, willing, and eager. The wise virgins prepared for the *"unexpected hour"* by taking extra oil, to be ready whenever the bridegroom would arrive. The foolish virgins had no extra oil; so when the bridegroom arrived, only those with *oil in their lamps* came into the wedding feast and the *door was shut*. Only those who were prepared to be the light of the world were admitted. The coming of the Bridegroom is the critical event in the wedding service. After closing the door, the Bridegroom refuses to open it. When the five foolish virgins arrived, they were denied entrance; the Bridegroom told them, "I do not know you." Why did He say, "I do not know you"? Well, Jesus has told us that He is surely coming; yet many continue to ignore the warning to be prepared. Jesus said that I do not know those who are unprepared for My return, particularly when they have been told that I was coming. But *"know" in* this case has a more specific meaning. In the Greek, there are at least six words for *"know."* Obviously, the word deals with *"knowledge of"* or *"insight into"*, but Jesus has a distinctive meaning here. In this case, Jesus uses the word to mean an active relationship with Him. Jesus is saying to the foolish virgin; we are not one in fellowship; we do not share the same values. This is the common use of the word in the Old Testament. When Abraham *"knew"* Sarah and they conceived Isaac, it meant that they became one. In Genesis

18:19, when God speaks of Abraham, *"I have chosen him"* is the evidence that God has known him (Abraham). So *"know"* means to be in a relationship with, and it can also mean to *"choose"* a person. What Jesus is saying to the five foolish virgins, *"my message has been ignored; we have no relationship; you have not chosen me; I have not chosen you."*

In spite of the warnings, many people still refuse to prepare for the Final Judgment. When the wedding feast of the Lamb takes place, the question is: where will we be, on the outside, presence denied; or on the inside, because we have prepared all our lives to spend eternity with God. The constant warning is: *We know not the day or the hour, but be prepared, be ready.* Readiness is an active state; a zealous and bold attitude towards the things to come and perhaps even to suffer if necessary. Readiness expresses willingness and an eagerness for whatever lies ahead. Jesus said, *"be ready"*; and this is the character that we should have as we prepare ourselves for the Second Coming of Jesus Christ.

So how do we prepare for His coming? We must live each day, each second, in the expectation that Jesus Christ is coming to reclaim His own. We must obey His commands, believe His promises, love His truths and honor His warnings. We are responsible for others, to the extent that we can lead them to the truth. God does not want anyone to perish; we must share that same concern. Evangelism is the answer. In addition, our preparation must demonstrate a sincere love and devotion to the Bridegroom. Only living a life that expresses faith alone in Christ alone can we be prepared for His Coming.

Summary of Biblical Themes
Theme 9—The Preparation for the Final Judgment

We know neither the day nor the hour when Christ will return. Therefore, we must live each moment with the expectation that His return is eminent. Christ will return; that is His promise. Therefore, we must *"watch, be ready"*, prepared for the coming of the King of kings.

Chapter Fourteen

There are three *secondary* themes to this parable.

Theme 2—The Kingdom of Heaven

The kingdom of heaven awaits those who are faithfully prepared for the Coming of the Son of man. Everyone is invited; only the wise, the prepared, will enter.

Theme 3—The Alternatives in Life

We can be foolish *or* wise, prepared *or* unprepared. If we fall *"asleep"*, the door will be shut; only those prepared for His coming will be welcomed into the Wedding Feast.

Theme 4—The Christian Character

Christians are to be prepared for the return of the Bridegroom. We must have *"oil in our lamps"* and a sufficient supply to sustain us until Christ returns. We must be alert and ready, ever watching for His return. We must be faithful as Noah was faithful.

Summary of God's Revelations

This parable has a command, a promise, a truth and a warning. The command is: *watch and be prepared for the coming of the Bridegroom*. The promise is: *if your "lamps" are filled and you are prepared for the Bridegroom, then you will enter and enjoy the wedding feast*. The truth is: *only the Father knows the day and the hour*. The warning is: *if you are not prepared for the Bridegroom's coming, you will not enter the kingdom; the door will be shut*.

Summary of Biblical Themes

Theme 9—The Preparation for the Final Judgment

The four lessons are:

In the Parable *of Christ's Return, the Unexpected Hour*, we learn that <u>God is pleased to give us the kingdom</u>; however, we must live a righteous life to be worthy of that gift, and we must be ready, expectant for the return of the Son of man.

In the Parable of the Rich Man and Lazarus, we learn that we must *live this life in the <u>expectation of the next</u>*. We must honor the Old and New Testament witnesses, and we must listen to Jesus Christ, the First Fruit, the One who has risen from the dead.

In the Parable of the Lessons from the Fig Tree, we learn the ageless lesson of Noah that we must listen and <u>be obedient to God alone</u>, at all times and in all circumstances.

God's Hidden Treasures

In the Parable of the Ten Virgins, we learn that <u>some</u> will be <u>prepared</u> and <u>some unprepared</u> for the return of Christ; <u>His disciples must be *ready*</u>.

Christ is coming again, at *"an unexpected hour."* We must be ready so that He will find faith on this earth when He returns. We live now in the Last Days, in the full expectation of His coming with judgment; we wait with joy and thanksgiving. Christians are called to be disciples, servants, witnesses and ambassadors for Christ, to remember the needy and to be merciful to all. Our treasures are in heaven. The testimony of the prophets and of Jesus Christ is that we must be ready. Noah was a warning sign for Christians in every age, that everyone would be prepared for God's holy justice; there are consequences to every act, good or bad. We must obey God's commands; we must repent, else we too shall perish. Jesus told the world that, *"even if one should rise from the dead, they would not believe"*; Jesus Christ rose from the dead, and people did not believe. Jesus warns the world to be ready for His Coming. For what lies before every one is the great vision that the apostle John saw (Rev. 21:1–5), *"Then I saw a new heaven and a new earth, for the first heaven and the first earth had passed away, and the sea was no more. And I saw the holy city, new Jerusalem, coming down out of heaven from God, prepared as a bride adorned for her husband, and I heard a great voice from the throne saying 'Behold, the dwelling of God is with men. He will dwell with them, and they shall be his people, and God himself will be with them; he will wipe away every tear from their eyes, and death shall be no more, neither shall there be mourning nor crying nor pain any more, for the former things have passed away.' And he who sat upon the throne said, 'Behold, I make all things new.'"* Our faith and works in this life determine our life in the next; the righteous will be welcomed in heaven; unrepentant sin will lead to hell. In a succession of parables (wheat and tares, sheep and goats), the message is that there will be a judgment and there is eternity for all, the righteous to spend eternal life, the wicked to spend eternal damnation.

Chapter Fourteen

Summary of God's Revelations
Theme 9—The Preparation for the Final Judgment

The commands are: *watch and be prepared for the coming of the Bridegroom; you also must be ready, for the Son of man is coming at an hour you do not expect; sell what you have, give alms, provide yourself with a treasure in heaven.*

The promises are: *it is God's good pleasure to give us the kingdom; if your "lamps" are filled and you are prepared for the Bridegroom, then you will enjoy the wedding feast; heaven and earth will pass away, but God's words will not pass away.*

The truths are: *where your treasure is, there will your heart be also; God has revealed His plan for His creation; we must show mercy; we must be concerned for those less fortunate; we must listen now to Jesus Christ, the One who rose from the dead; if we fail to heed the warning of Jesus Christ and the Old Testament prophets, we shall face eternal damnation; but of that day and hour no one knows, not even the angels in heaven, nor the Son, but the Father only.*

The warnings are: *once in hell, there is no way that we can transfer to heaven, the decision is eternal; we must be prepared; the Son of man is coming at an unexpected hour; if we fail to heed the warning of Jesus Christ and the Old Testament prophets, we shall face eternal damnation; watch therefore, for you do not know on what day your Lord is coming; if we are not prepared for the Bridegroom's coming, we will not enter the kingdom, and the door will be shut.*

The remaining parables now focus on the Final Judgment.

CHAPTER FIFTEEN

Theme 10—The Parables of The Final Judgment

> *"When the Son of man comes in his glory, and all the angels with him, then he will sit on his glorious throne. Before him will be gathered all the nations, and he will separate them one from another as a shepherd separates the sheep from the goats, . . .* (Matt. 25:31–32)

> *"For we must all appear before the judgment seat of Christ, so that each one may receive good or evil, according to what he has done in the body."* (2 Cor. 5:10)

Understanding the certainty of the Final Judgment is essential to living the Christian life. Christians believe ". . . *just as it is appointed for men to die once, and after that comes judgment"* (Heb. 9:27). In the Nicene Creed, Christians express faith in the resurrection of the body; we believe that there is no condemnation for those who are in Christ (Rom. 8:1); we believe that Jesus Christ has gone ahead, to prepare a place for us, that where he is, we may be also. This world is not our heavenly home, for we are aliens and sojourners in a foreign land. There is an eternal life after this physical death, for which we must prepare.

God's Hidden Treasures

The parables in this chapter deal with some of the most significant subjects of all: *the Last Days, death, the resurrection,* and the *Final Judgment.*

First, regarding the *Last Days,* in which we are now living. These are days of opportunity, in which we are to put our trust in the crucified, risen and ascended Lord—and enter into the salvation that He won for us on the cross. Hebrews 1:1–2 begins, *"In many and various ways God spoke of old to our fathers by the prophets; but in these last days he has spoken to us by a Son, who he appointed the heir of all things, through whom also he created the world."* God is now at work through His Holy Spirit to equip His people for the ministry of evangelism and to prepare them for the kingdom that they shall inherit. For such events, we need eyes to see and ears to hear. The great events, which have defined these last days, are the Incarnation, the Crucifixion and the Ascension. Since that time, the world has never been the same; God is working out His purpose in these last days for the End of the Age and the Final Judgment. In these last days, God's people must be proclaiming the gospel so that all should hear the good news, repent and turn to Christ as the Redeemer and Savior of the world. It is God's perfect patience that none should perish. As the Bible makes it plain and the parables reinforce, there will be a time of evil in these last days. This is the message of the Wheat and the Tares, the Sheep and the Goats, and the Workers in the Vineyard. Evil and good will coexist until the end of the Last Days.

Second, regarding death, the Bible speaks of three deaths, a physical death, a spiritual death, and a Second Death. The greatest difference between Christians and non-believers is in the manner in which they view death. Christians believe in a heaven where life eternal will be spent. As God is sovereign, life and death are under His authority, for He is the source of all life (Ps 36:9). *"In his hand is the life of every creature, and the breath of all mankind"* (Job 12:10). *"The number of the days of our life is written in God's book before one of them comes to be."* (Job 14:5; Ps 139:16). In the 23rd Psalm, David knew that the valley of the shadow of death was unavoidable, but he also knew that in the end that God, the Good Shepherd, would

Chapter Fifteen

walk with them through it (Ps 23:4). Human life is sacred to God, *"Precious in the sight of the Lord is the death of his saints" (Ps 116:15)*. God takes no pleasure even in the death of the wicked (Ezek. 18:32). Dr. Paul Ferguson (*Evangelical Dictionary of Biblical Theology.*) has presented an excellent study on this subject. The New Testament broadens the term *"death"* to include various figurative meanings. People who are alive physically may be dead in trespasses and sins (Eph 2:1). The wages of sin is death (Rom. 6:23). In a positive sense, believers may be said to be *"dead to sin"* (Rom. 6:1) and crucified with Christ (Gal 2:20). However, the New Testament defines a deeper meaning to death. Every person will face the reality of death; it is appointed to all men, and after that comes the judgment (2 Cor. 5:10; Heb 9:27). After death, the righteous are comforted, and the wicked are tormented (Luke 16:22–25). The final destiny of death is to be cast into the lake of fire, which is the Second Death (Rev 20:14–15), which leads to eternal separation from the presence and glory of God (2 Thess. 1:7–10; Rev. 2:11). In the New Testament, it is the death of Christ that occupies the center of attention. By dying, Christ destroyed death and brought immortality to light (2 Tim 1:10); the cross reconciles us to God (Rom. 5:10). Now being freed from death (Acts 2:24) and crowned with glory and honor (Heb. 2:9), Jesus has the keys of death and hell (Rev 1:18). Christians still die physically, but their death is gain because they are now with Christ (2 Cor 5:6; Phil 1:20–21). Even death cannot separate us from the love of God in Christ Jesus (Rom. 8:38–39). In death, Christians are given comfort, rest, and assurance (Luke 16:22–25; Rev 6:9–11). Then mortality will put on immortality (1 Cor 15:53). Death, the last enemy, will be destroyed (1 Cor 15:26). There will be no more death or sorrow, and God will wipe all tears from all eyes (Rev 21:4).

Third, the resurrection is one of the main themes in the Bible. Beginning with the judgment of death in Gen. 3:6, the divine plan of God unfolds in history. Nonetheless, in the Old Testament concern is expressed for the individual soul. In Psa. 16:10, David wrote, *"Therefore my heart is glad, and my soul rejoices; my body also dwells secure, For thou dost not give me up to Sheol, or let thy godly one see*

God's Hidden Treasures

the Pit." Psalm 49:14–15 points out that all die, *"their forms shall waste away, But God will ransom my soul from the power of Sheol, for he will receive me."* This Psalm proclaims God's justice, for His rewards and punishment are just and holy. Further, Psalm 73 is one of the great witnesses to God's redemptive plan, with emphasis on the resurrection. It begins with the psalmist glorifying God as good to the righteous, but the psalmist is envious of the arrogant and the wicked. The people turn and praise the wicked, and they say, *"How can God know? Is there knowledge in the Most High?"* The psalmist believed that he had kept his heart clean; yet he still has been *"stricken and chastened every morning."* He begins to wonder, what is the purpose of righteousness? Why do I try to live a holy and righteous life? Then he went to the *"sanctuary of God; then I perceived their end." "they will be destroyed in a moment."*, but the righteous will receive a different reward. Even though his flesh and heart may fail, God is his *"portion forever"* and *"afterward . . . will take [him] into glory."* Belief in the resurrection is a condition of salvation and is one of the principal tenets of the Christian faith. Paul wrote (Rom. 10:9), *"If you confess with your lips that Jesus is Lord (God) and believe in your heart that God raised him from the dead, you will be saved."*

The prophet Isaiah wrote (Isa. 26:19), *"Thy dead shall rise, their bodies shall rise, O dwellers in the dust, awake and sing for joy!"* The prophet Daniel wrote of the end of the age and the Final Judgment (Dan. 12:2), *"And many of those who sleep in the dust of the earth shall awake, some to everlasting life and some to shame and everlasting contempt. Those who are wise will shine like the brightness of the heavens, and those who lead many to righteousness, like the stars for ever and ever."* There is to be death, the end of this physical life, but there will be a resurrection of the righteous to the crown of life and the unjust to punishment; that is God's eternal promise. By the time of Christ, the Pharisees believed in a resurrection of the spirit, but not necessarily of the body (Acts 23:8); the Sadducees did not believe in any resurrection (Matt 22:23; Acts 23:8). The resurrection of Jesus is the principal tenet of the New Testament. Baptism is centered in Jesus' resurrection. Baptism is symbolized

Chapter Fifteen

by death, burial, and resurrection; baptism is entering the water, going under the water (death) and being raised from the water (resurrection). The person has died to the old self and is raised up to a new person with a new allegiance to Jesus Christ. As Paul wrote, *"if anyone is in Christ, he is a new creation."* (I Cor. 5:17) Paul also wrote, *"When you were buried with him in baptism, you were also raised with him through faith in the power of God, who raised him from the dead"* (Col. 2:12). This message is consistently reinforced throughout the New Testament, e.g. *Rom 6:3–5 and 1 Peter 3:21–22.*

The empty tomb of Christ sets Christianity in sharp contrast to other world religions whose prophets and their adherents never make such a claim (Mark 16:1-8; Matt 28:11-15; Luke 24:1-12; John 20:11-18). Christianity is the only religion that claims, with substantial proof, that its Founder, God Incarnate, came to earth, died for our sins and rose again in glory. This is a most remarkable claim; it sets Christianity apart from any other world religion, ancient or modern. The appearances of Jesus after His resurrection to chosen individuals play an important role in the proclamation of the gospel message (e.g., Matt 28:9–10,16–17; Acts 2:32; 1 Cor. 15:5–7). His resurrection is a testimony to the general resurrection of all people, which will be followed by God's justice; to the righteous there will be a *"resurrection of life"* and to the unrighteous a *"resurrection of condemnation"* (John 5:28–29; cf. Rev 20:4–6). The earliest teaching in the New Testament concerning the resurrection is undoubtedly 1 Cor 15. Paul said that the resurrection is in accordance with the Scriptures. The time element," *the third day"*, is important, because it reinforces our faith by revealing the historical nature of the event, which occurred in real time and was attested to by Peter, the Twelve, and five hundred people. The belief in bodily resurrection is a foundation of belief in God. Since God exists and since He created the universe and has power over it, then He has power to raise the dead. That is why Peter explained to that first Christian Pentecost, *"but God raised him (Jesus) up . . ."* (Acts 2:24).

God's Hidden Treasures

The *Final Judgment* is an act in which God intervenes directly in human history, brings the course of this world to completion, determines the eternal fate of human beings, and brings His children home to spend eternity with Him. At the end of the age, there will be the Final Judgment, which will occur before the Judgment Seat of Christ (2 Cor. 5:10): However, there are two judgments; one for the Christian believer, the other for the unbeliever—because every person of God shall be judged (Rom. 14:10; Gal. 6:7). The judgment of the believer's works will lead to reward or loss of reward. This is not a judgment of the believer's sins, for those sins have been forgiven by the death of Jesus Christ. This forgiveness is in fulfillment of Jeremiah 31:31ff. However, *the "fruit" of the believer's works* will be examined at this judgment.

The Book of Daniel supports this claim of the Final Judgment, both in chapter 7 and 12, *"and behold, with the clouds of heaven there came one like a son of man, and he came to the Ancient of Days . . . And to him was given dominion and glory and kingdom, that all peoples, nations, and languages should serve him; his dominion is an everlasting dominion, which shall not pass away, and his kingdom one that shall not be destroyed."* (7:13–14) *"At that time shall arise Michael, the great prince who has charge of your people. And there shall be a time of trouble, . . .; but at that time your people shall be delivered, every one whose name shall be found written in the book. And many of those who sleep in the dust of the earth shall awake, some to everlasting life, and some to shame and everlasting contempt. And those who are wise shall shine like the brightness of the firmament; and those who turn many to righteousness, like the stars for ever and ever."* (12:1–4) Daniel's first message relates to Christ and His everlasting kingdom; the second relates to us, which is the resurrection of all people and the final judgment.

One of the finest theologians of this age is Dr. D. G. Bloesch, whose writings in the *Essentials of Evangelical Theology, II,* are most helpful. He wrote "the judgment at history's end is the climax of a process by which God holds nations and persons accountable to him as Creator and Lord. The Old Testament centers ultimate judgment in the day of Yahweh, when the Lord rids his world of every

Chapter Fifteen

evil. The New Testament builds on Old Testament teaching, expanding it in light of Christ's incarnation. In the Synoptic Gospels, Jesus announces himself as the Judge (Mark 15:62) and calls attention to the Day of Judgment (Matt 10:15), describing it as a final separation of the evildoers from the righteous (Matt 13:41–43,47–50). Jesus' parables are to teach the fact of judgment so that His hearers face their present decisions for or against the kingdom with utter seriousness. In the longest judgment parable, Jesus' point is that the ultimate outcome will be determined by whether the nations receive or reject Christ's disciples who come to them with the gospel message (Matt 25:31–46). The theological implications of the biblical teaching are that final judgment is:

(1) the ultimate triumph of God's will and the consummate display of his glory in history, the sign that all he intended has been accomplished;
(2) the cosmic declaration that God is just; all affronts to his glory are punished and all recognition of it is rewarded;
(3) the climax of Christ's ministry, as the Apostles' Creed affirms;
(4) the reminder that human and cosmic history move toward a goal, measured by the purposes of God;
(5) the absolute seal of human accountability—all believers are held responsible for their works, all unbelievers for their rebellion;
(6) the most serious motive for Christian mission—in the face of such judgment—the world's only hope is Christ's salvation (Acts 4:12).

Belief in the last judgment was uniformly endorsed in the early creeds and the Reformation confessions. Christians have accepted the fact of final judgment, though its form and timing have been strongly debated."

Other excellent theologians who have addressed this subject are O. Cullmann, <u>Christ and Time</u> and H. E. Guillebaud, <u>The Righteous Judge</u>. Christians profess that "This will be a judgment of all the nations and all the people, for the Lord *'comes, he comes to judge the earth. He will judge the world in righteousness, and the peoples in his truth'* (Ps 96:13). Sometimes the day is characterized

God's Hidden Treasures

by its outcome. Therefore it is *"the day of redemption"* (Eph 4:30). In one sense redemption is accomplished here and now when the sinner receives and believes in Christ; but, in another sense, the Day of Judgment seals it all. For the unrepentant sinner it is *"the great day of his wrath"* (Rev 6:17), *"the day of God's wrath, when his righteous judgment will be revealed"* (Rom. 2:5).

Jesus emphasized the critical significance of the Final Judgment. He told the twelve disciples to warn their hearers that it would be *"more bearable for Sodom and Gomorrah"* on the Day of Judgment than for them (Matt 10:15). Christ had a similar message for the people of Chorazin and Bethsaida: it will be more tolerable for Tyre and Sidon on judgment day than for them (Matt 11:22). On both occasions, He warned that the people of Capernaum should not think of heaven as their final destination; that may well be Hades.

These four principal doctrines of the last days, death, resurrection and the Final Judgment are prominent in the following four parables.

The two *primary* ones are:
    10–1. The Parable of the King's Wedding Feast
    10–2. The Parable of the Final Judgment
    (Sometimes called The Parable of the Sheep and the Goats)
The two parables in which this theme is *secondary* are:
    10–3. The Parable of the Sower
    10–4. The Parable of the Wheat and the Tares

The first parable ends with these words, *"for many are called, but few are chosen."*; the second with, *"And they will go away into eternal punishment, but the righteous into eternal life."*

10–1. The Parable of the King's Wedding Feast: Matt. 22:1–13

"And again Jesus spoke to them in parables, saying, 'The kingdom of heaven may be compared to a king who gave a marriage feast for

Chapter Fifteen

his son, and sent his servants to call those who were invited to the marriage feast; but they would not come. Again he sent other servants, saying, 'Tell those who are invited, Behold, I have made ready my dinner, my oxen and my fat calves are killed, and everything is ready; come to the marriage feast.' But they made light of it and went off, one to his farm, another to his business, while the rest seized his servants, treated them shamefully, and killed them. The king was angry, and he sent his troops and destroyed those murderers and burned their city. Then he said to his servants, 'The wedding is ready, but those invited were not worthy. Go therefore to the thoroughfares, and invite to the marriage feast as many as you find.' And those servants went out into the streets and gathered all whom they found, both bad and good; so the wedding hall was filled with guests. But when the king came in to look at the guests, he saw there a man who had no wedding garment; and he said to him, 'Friend, how did you get in here without a wedding garment?' And he was speechless. Then the king said to the attendants, 'Bind him hand and foot, and cast him into the outer darkness; there men will weep and gnash their teeth.' For many are called, but few are chosen."

Commentary

Jesus had been teaching to great crowds, among whom were the Pharisees. Jesus closed the Parable of the Wicked Tenants (page 68) with," *the kingdom will be taken away from you and given to a nation producing the fruit of it."* (Matt. 21:43) The Chief Priest and the Pharisees immediately wanted to arrest Him, but they feared the reaction of the crowd, who considered Jesus to be a prophet.

Now Jesus draws our attention to a symbolic feast, in which a king has prepared for his son. The king sent messengers to invite many to come to the banquet, *"but they refused to come."* Their excuses were numerous (e.g. work in the fields or business). In addition, some killed the king's messengers (undoubtedly the prophets, even Stephen). Their actions angered the king; he responded by sending his army to destroy the murderers and to burn their town. Then he sent out his servants again, with instructions to fill the banquet hall with *"all the people you can find, both bad and good"* and the wedding hall was filled with guests. However,

God's Hidden Treasures

one guest came without wearing a wedding garment. When the king asked why he not dressed appropriately, the man was *"speechless."* So the king ordered that he be bound and thrown outside, *"into the darkness, where there will be weeping and gnashing of teeth."* It is likely that this person is not clothed in the *"wedding garment of righteousness"* which is a term that Matthew liked to use. The *"gnashing of teeth"* is a sign of great anger (e.g. Psa. 35:16; Matt. 8:12; Mk. 9:18).

Knowing the hearts of the Pharisees, Jesus told this parable regarding *the kingdom of heaven, a king, a marriage feast, invitations ignored and rejected, violence to the messengers of the king, invitations sent to both good and the bad, a person not in a wedding garment, and the final words, "for many are called, but few are chosen."* We shall examine each of these messages, as we "unpack" the parable.

The first is "the kingdom of heaven", (chapter 7, page 77). The kingdom of heaven is that universal spiritual kingdom, present wherever the sovereign God reigns and His righteousness, love, joy and peace are evident. Everyone is invited to the kingdom; everyone is called to honor and worship the King of the kingdom.

Second, there is *"a king", who is God*. It is His wedding feast, with a specific purpose to unite all things in heaven and on earth in His Son. The initiative of creation, redemption and restoration is with God, who is the King of grace and mercy, giving us what we do not deserve (His love) and not giving us what we do deserve (His wrath).

Third, it is a marriage feast, for there is no better way of describing the new manna that God has for His people. There is no greater joy than at a *"wedding"*, a union between two people. In Revelation 19:6–8, this marriage spoken of here will be fully consummated. *"Then I heard what seemed to be the voice of a great multitude, . . . crying, 'Hallelujah! For the Lord our God the Almighty reigns. Let us rejoice and exult and give him the glory, for the marriage of the Lamb has come, and his Bride has made herself ready; it was granted her to be clothed with fine linen, bright and pure, for the fine linen is the righteous deeds of the saints."* Previously God has fed His people in the Wilderness with manna; God, in sending His

Chapter Fifteen

Son, revealed Him to be the Bread of Life, the true manna that came down from heaven. Now God has prepared a great wedding feast, which is the culmination of all the feasts that God has ordained. It is honorable among all people; it is an intimate bond, centered in love and obedience; the commitment is binding; it is symbolic of God's union with Israel (Isa. 54:5) and Christ's union with His church (Eph. 5:23–32).

Fourth, the invitations are either ignored or rejected. In ancient Israel, a personal messenger delivered the invitation; acceptance was expected, and excuses were an insult. The invitation is the gospel. This includes a call to repentance and conversion and acceptance of Jesus Christ as Savior and Lord. It was first given by the prophets (e.g. Jeremiah, Ezekiel, Zechariah) and then *". . . by a Son, whom he appointed the heir of all things, through whom also he created the world. He reflects the glory of God and bears the very stamp of his nature, upholding the universe by his word of power. When he had made purification for sins, he sat down at the right hand of the Majesty on high . . ."* (Heb. 1:1–4)

Fifth, they did violence to the servants of the king. Not only were the invitations ignored and/or rejected, the servants were murdered. Now the servants of *God* (His prophets) have generally been treated with violence. However, the greatest violence was done to the True Servant, Jesus Christ, on the cross.

Sixth, the invitations were sent to both good and the bad, because the invitation is the gospel, a universal message. Everyone is invited, but not everyone will accept. In many cases, the cares of this world dominate lives, and many decline the greatest invitation of all. As with this invitation, God calls all people, for it is His perfect patience that none should perish. *"God makes his rain to fall on the just and the unjust"* (Matt. 5:45).

Finally, there are the closing words, *"for many are called, but few are chosen."* Jesus said, *"you did not chose me, but I chose you . . ."* (Jn. 15:16) There is a distinction between being called and being chosen. There are 14 Greek words for *call*, and the general meaning is to be summoned, invited to a vocation and position, to appeal, to give another name to a person (e.g. Isaac). *Chosen* is a much richer word, and it generally means to pick out, select, to separate by the act of taking by showing preference (e.g. love), to appoint by the laying on of hands. *Chosen* relates to the selection and the separation by showing preference. Paul was chosen. Christians are the chosen people of God, not because of any merit, but simply because God loves us. In the same way, God chose the Israelites (Deut. 6:7), "*it was not because you were more in number that the Lord set his love upon you for you were the fewest of all the nations, but it was because the Lord loves you . . .*" The apostle Peter recaptured this same message (1 Pet. 2:9f), "*But you are a chosen race, a royal priesthood, God's own people, that you may declare the wonderful deeds of him who called you out of darkness into his marvelous light. Once you were no people, but now you are God's people; once you had not received mercy, but now you have received mercy.*"

We are to accept so wonderful an invitation to the wedding of Christ and His church.

Summary of Biblical Themes
Theme 10—The Final Judgment

Three things can happen regarding God's invitation to the Wedding Feast; first, the invitation could be rejected outright, such people are judged by their own actions; second, the invitation can be accepted, but the person might come to the wedding feast inappropriately dressed, their actions will judge them; third, the invitation can be accepted and they greatly rejoice at the wedding feast of the Son of the King.

There are four secondary themes:

Theme 1—The Character of God

God seeks everyone. He is patient with our response, but His patience is limited. His invitation is universal. It is His perfect patience that none should perish.

Theme 2—The Kingdom of Heaven

It is a universal invitation for a universal kingdom.

Theme 3—The Alternatives in Life

The invitations are always there; the question is whether we will accept *or* reject so wonderful a salvation. Many reject the invitation; worldly demands prevent divine fellowship.

Chapter Fifteen

Theme 4—The Christian Character

A Christian, by accepting Jesus as Savior and Lord, has already accepted the invitation and comes, properly attired in the garments of righteousness, to be present at so wonderful a banquet.

Summary of God's Revelations

This parable has a command, a truth and warnings. The command is: *come to the wedding feast.* The truth is: *many are called, but few are chosen.* The warnings are: *God will deal severely with those who refuse His invitations; refusing the invitation will lead to death; those who come and are not properly dressed will be bound and cast into outer darkness.*

10–2 The Parable of the Sheep and the Goats: Matt. 25:31–46
(The Final Judgment)

"When the Son of man comes in his glory, and all the angels with him, then he will sit on his glorious throne. Before him will be gathered all the nations, and he will separate them one from another as a shepherd separates the sheep from the goats, and he will place the sheep at his right hand, but the goats at the left. Then the King will say to those at his right hand, 'Come, O blessed of my Father, inherit the kingdom prepared for you from the foundation of the world; for I was hungry and you gave me food, I was thirsty and you gave me drink, I was a stranger and you welcomed me, I was naked and you clothed me, I was sick and you visited me, I was in prison and you came to me.' Then the righteous will answer him, 'Lord, when did we see thee hungry and feed thee, or thirsty and give thee drink? And when did we see thee a stranger and welcome thee, or naked and clothe thee? And when did we see thee sick or in prison and visit thee?' And the King will answer them, 'Truly, I say to you, as you did it to one of the least of these my brethren, you did it to me.' Then he will say to those at his left hand, 'Depart from me, you cursed, into the eternal fire prepared for the devil and his angels; for I was hungry and you

God's Hidden Treasures

gave me no food, I was thirsty and you gave me no drink, I was a stranger and you did not welcome me, naked and you did not clothe me, sick and in prison and you did not visit me.' Then they also will answer, 'Lord, when did we see thee hungry or thirsty or a stranger or naked or sick or in prison, and did not minister to thee?' Then he will answer them, 'Truly, I say to you, as you did it not to one of the least of these, you did it not to me.' And they will go away into eternal punishment, but the righteous into eternal life."

Commentary

We now come to the final parable. Jesus began His ministry by proclaiming, "Repent, for the kingdom of heaven is at hand." (Matt. 4:17) By indirect claims (signs), by direct claims (I AM . . .) and by parables, Jesus had told the Jews who He was, and they had rejected His claims and His teachings. Jesus now knows that the *"hour"* for which he came into the world was at hand. In this final parable, Jesus completes the cycle of His Second Coming, the Final Judgment and the life to come.

The Day of Judgment is the time when evil will be punished and righteousness rewarded. Graham Scroggie has rightly called the Bible <u>The Unfolding Drama of Redemption</u>. Salvation is the theme of the Bible, in which its promise is redemption and reconciliation with God. The stories of Adam and Eve, Cain and Abel, the generation of Noah, the sale of Joseph by his brothers, all illustrate the law that *'what a man sows that shall he also reap."* (Gal. 6:7). At Mt. Sinai, the principle was announced to Moses, that the results of the righteous and the unrighteous acts of men will follow them. This is because God is righteous and just. There are consequences for sin; there are rewards for righteousness.

In all the New Testament, the judgment and our final destiny is determined by our relationship to Jesus Christ. This is the prevailing message of the Epistles (particularly Rom. 14:10–12; 2:16; 2 Cor. 5:10; Heb. 10:26–31; I Pet. 3:18–22; I Jn. 4:17); they all emphasize that if we have *"Christ in us, the hope of glory"*, then our destiny is determined. Scripture places before us the ultimate judgment. It is that moral decisions determine our future destiny. Our attitude leads to acts; our acts lead to our habits; our habits lead to

Chapter Fifteen

our character; and our character leads to our destiny. Our attitude determines our eternal relationship with God.

In this parable, Jesus describes how He, the Son of man, will come and sit on his throne in heavenly glory. All the nations will be gathered before him and he will separate the people as a shepherd separates the sheep from the goats. Jesus said to the sheep (on his right), *"Come, you who are blessed by my Father; take your inheritance, the kingdom prepared for you since the creation of the world."* This is a restatement of the promise that *"God is pleased to give us the kingdom."* Why is this inheritance given to His chosen people? Because Jesus said, *"I was hungry; I was thirsty; I was a stranger; I was in need of clothing; I was sick; I was in prison"*, and you met every one of these needs. Jesus said that when you do it for the least of these brothers of mine, you do it also for Me. He is revealing two great mysteries and two great messages here. First, Jesus is saying that, when you do something for others, consider it in the same context as doing it for Christ. Secondly, He is saying that these are my brothers; we share a relationship that is evidence of an eternal fellowship. Christ is eternally with His people. That is why on the road to Damascus, when Jesus asked Saul (Paul), *"Saul, Saul, why do you persecute me?"* (Acts 9:4) Saul replied, I am not persecuting you; I am persecuting your followers. And Jesus said, when you persecute them, you persecute me. Jesus and His disciples are one; Jesus will never leave us nor forsake us. (Psa. 94:14; Heb. 13:5)

Turning now to the subject of the sheep and goats, it is interesting that goats are members of the sheep family and are generally tended along with the sheep. Goats are stronger than sheep; they can go to higher places for food, and they are generally in the front of the flock. They are far more active and independent than sheep; for that reason, they are sometimes representative of the wicked, particularly in this parable. Conversely sheep are generally defenseless, gentle, in need of care and protection, which they can best receive from a shepherd. In many regards, sheep are like lost sinners (Matt. 9:36). The sheep are equated with the church, particularly when Paul speaks to the elders of Miletus, *"Take heed*

God's Hidden Treasures

of yourselves and to all the flock . . . to feed the church of the Lord which he obtained with his own blood.:" (Acts 20:28) The disciples of Jesus Christ are to "feed His flock" and "tend His flock" (Jn. 21). It is Christ's flock; they are Christ's sheep.

For those who do these simple acts of mercy, there is eternal life; for those who ignore the needs of others, there is eternal punishment. God desires mercy from His children for His children. That is the reason that the Parable of the Good Samaritan is foremost in the heart of God. Recall the Beatitudes: *"blessed are the merciful, for they shall obtain mercy."* (Matt. 5:7)

This parable sets before the world the ultimate choice, *"eternal life"* or *"eternal punishment."* It is interesting that the summation of all the parables comes down to this judgment. Eternal punishment also means complete and utter annihilation, which is the ultimate result of eternal separation from God. Eternal life is eternal fellowship with God in His heavenly kingdom. This is a further statement of the stone that will cause a person to stumble; but beware of the rock that shall crush them. Christ is the Stone and the Rock, the foundation and source of our salvation.

Summary of Biblical Themes
Theme 10—The Final Judgment

There will be a Final Judgment in which righteousness leads to eternal life; unrepentant sin leads to eternal punishment. Everyone will be held accountable for what they have done or not done. The Judgment will be swift and sure; the just rewards will be meted out with grace and mercy.

There is one *secondary* theme in this parable.

Theme 3—The Alternatives in Life

Christ states that there are only two alternatives in life: to be righteous or to be evil. We shall either share eternal life with God *or* we will face eternal punishment, which means annihilation and eternal separation from God.

Summary of God's Revelations

This parable has a command, promises, a truth and a warning. The command is: *show mercy to the hungry, the sick.* The promises

Chapter Fifteen

are: *Jesus Christ will return in all His glory; He will sit in judgment over the nations.* The truth is: *whatever we do to the least of these, in the same sense, we are doing it to and for Christ.* The warning is: *there will be a judgment, some to eternal punishment; some to eternal life.*

Summary of Biblical Themes
Theme 10—The Final Judgment

From these four parables, we learn the following:

In the Parable of the King's Wedding Feast, we are invited and our response may vary. The invitation is to the kingdom of God; the marriage is between Christ and His church. Members of His church gladly accept the invitation and have endless joy in the eternal Presence of God. <u>Many are called, but few are chosen</u>.

In the Parable of the Final Judgment, we learn that we are called to treat the hungry, the thirsty, the stranger, the naked, the sick, and those in prison as if they are the very Person of Jesus Christ. How we treat them determines our heavenly home. This is a further example of the Good Samaritan, who saw a helpless person by the side of the road, and he showed mercy on him. Christ associates Himself with the humble, the weak, the lost. He is the friend of tax collectors, sinners, and the outcasts of every society. He associates Himself with those in constant need. Jesus says to the world, that when you persecute them, you persecute Me. When we harm others, we harm Christ. <u>When we serve others, we serve Christ</u>.

In the Parable of the Sower, we learn that we are to sow "seeds", which is the gospel, in order that all may know that the <u>Son of man will come again</u>, in all His glory; that the Final Judgment is certain and that we must *be prepared* for it.

In the Parable of the Wheat and the Tares, we learn the companion message to that of the Sheep and the Goats. In the Final Judgment, <u>God separates</u> the wheat and the tares as well as the sheep and the goats.

The *"seeds"* (the gospel) are to be sown, so that all would know that the Son of man will come again, that the Final Judgment is

God's Hidden Treasures

certain and that all must *be prepared* for it. In the signs of His Second Coming, Jesus has told His disciples that *"the gospel must first be preached to all nations."* (Mk. 13:10). There will be a great wedding feast; we are invited. The invitation might be rejected outright, but the most meaningful are those who accept the invitation and have special joy in their presence at the Wedding of Christ and His church. *Many are called, but few are chosen.* Further, we are called to treat the hungry, the thirsty, the stranger, the naked, the sick, and those in prison as if they are the very Person of Jesus Christ. How we treat the less fortunate has a significant bearing on the judgment given to both believers and non-believers. At the Final Judgment, God will separate the righteous and the unrighteous, the wheat and the tares—the sheep and the goats. He will judge our faith, our obedience and our works.

Summary of God's Revelations
Theme 10—The Final Judgment

The commands are: *come to the wedding feast; show mercy to the hungry, the sick.* The promises are: *Jesus Christ will return in all His glory; He will sit in judgment over the nations.* The truths are: *many are called, but few are chosen; whatever we do to the least of these, in the same sense, we are doing to Christ and for Christ.* The warnings are: *God will deal severely with those who refuse His invitations; refusing the invitation will lead to death; they will be cast into outer darkness: there will be judgment for all, some to eternal punishment; some to eternal life.*

Part 3

EPILOGUE

INTRODUCTION

It is worthwhile to step back and understand the importance of summarizing so wonderful a subject. Since the dawn of creation, God has preserved *Hidden Treasures*, which are to be revealed in the fullness of time to the world by His Son. God promised in the Old Testament (Psa. 78:2), that He would speak in parables and reveal hidden things that were from the foundation of the world. His Son, Jesus Christ, God Incarnate, confirmed this promise (Matt. 13:10–17 and 13:34–35).

Jesus Christ has revealed great teachings in two major areas; first, according to *Ten Biblical Themes*; second, according to *God's Revelations*, through His *commands, promises, truths and warnings*. As such, these parables truly are *God's Hidden Treasures*.

It is essential to understand the uniqueness, simplicity, and importance of the parables. They are *unique*, because they present vital information regarding Christ's earthly life, ministry and mission. This *uniqueness* is further demonstrated in the degree to which the parables present great Old Testament and New Testament themes and truths. They are also unique because His earthly life and mission are more fully disclosed in these parables, particularly regarding the messages that point us to the Father and which disclose the character and nature of the kingdom of heaven. There

God's Hidden Treasures

is certain *simplicity* about the parables because, in most cases, the truths they present are clear and precise.

The parables contain significant messages for everyone, whether a believer or non-believer. Jesus presents hope and encouragement to believers; He presents major truths and warnings to non-believer. Although the parables are for everyone, their divine aspects can best be understood by the "born anew, the born again, the born of the Spirit" for they are the ones to whom Jesus has committed the secrets of the kingdom" (Matt. 13:12). Jesus said,

> Jn. 1:12, *"But to all who receive him, who believe in his name, he gave power to become the children of God, who were born not of blood nor of the will of the flesh nor of the will of man, but of God."* Jn. 3:3, 5, *"Jesus answered him (Nicodemus), 'Truly, truly, I say to you, unless one is born again, he cannot see the kingdom of God...Truly, truly, I say to you, unless one is born of water and the spirit, he cannot enter the kingdom of God.'"*

If we receive Jesus as the Christ, if we believe in Him (trust in Him), we are "born of the Spirit" and become a child of God. Any radical transformation that leads to such a change in character is called the new birth. This is what happened to Abraham, to Moses, to Isaac, and to all the prophets. It occurred to Saul (Paul) on the road to Damascus. The new birth by the Spirit of God leads to becoming a child of God; it leads to a more complete understanding of the Word of God (including the parables), and for seeing and entering the kingdom of heaven. The new birth is the result of God's grace and our deliberate decision to receive Jesus as Lord and to serve Him faithfully. For the born again, God has a rich treasury of commands, promises, truths and commandments.

In addition, there is an unmistakable importance to the parables because they provide great truths about God and about ourselves; they provide guidance for living the Christian life, and they place before us some of the most basic messages that we must understand in following Jesus Christ as Savior and Lord. They also set before the non-believers the consequences for continual denial of Jesus Christ as the Son of God.

Jesus taught in parables for at least seven reasons: first, *because the Jews had rejected His indirect claims (signs) and His direct claims* to deity; second, *because the Jews had "hardened their hearts"*; third, *because the Jews did not understand, nor accept the truth, that a person must be "born again" ("Born of the Spirit") to "see" and "enter" the Kingdom of God;* fourth, *Jesus did so in fulfillment of the Scriptures;* fifth, *because this was His final approach to the hardened hearts of the Jews;* sixth, *because God "is forbearing towards you, not wishing that any should perish, but that all should reach repentance";* seventh, *because God's steadfast love for His creation endures forever* (Psa. 136:1).

Since Christ is their Author, the parables take on unmistakable importance and authority. We must accept and obey His commands, promises, truths and warnings. They are to be honored and respected, for the Word of God has full authority in our lives.

Jesus taught in parables because *"a parable is the means of drawing believers and non-believers to the presence and purpose of God in their midst and the critical nature of their situation."* It is also to be understood as *"a story with a meaning or moral concerning mysteries from the past."*

Thirty-four (34) parables were examined, and arranged against **Ten Biblical Themes**:

        Theme 1—The Character of God
        Theme 2—The Kingdom of Heaven
        Theme 3—The Alternatives in Life
        Theme 4—The Christian Character
        Theme 5—The Need for Repentance
        Theme 6—Our Responsibility for Evangelism
        Theme 7—Our Role as Christian Stewards
        Theme 8—The Power of Prayer
        Theme 9—The Preparation for the Final Judgment
        Theme 10—The Final Judgment

By considering the parables from this thematic perspective, we can "look through" the individual parables and discover the great messages of Christ's earthly ministry. By arranging the parables according to the ten themes, it is possible to gain a summary understanding of each of these themes, e.g. The Character of God. In their totality, these summations are complete to the extent that God has revealed them at this time. Since they have been summarized at

God's Hidden Treasures

the end of each chapter on the ten themes, they will not be repeated here. Instead, only God's Revelations regarding His commands, promises, truths and warnings will be summarized in this chapter.

Christ desires that faith will be evident on the earth when He returns. Our faith is the measure of our belief in Him, our acceptance of Him, our service to Him and our witness concerning Him. God's grace is given to all, believer and non-believer. The question is; will we respond in faith? As the Son of man, He *"came to seek and save the lost."* (Lk. 19:10). That is why He spoke in parables; to seek and to save His own.

Summary of God's Revelations

There is an additional and important dimension to these parables, for they reveal the very nature of God. The 34 parables contain 23 commands, 16 promises, 41 truths and 24 warnings, making a total of 104 messages that Jesus has revealed to God's people, regarding His will, His ways and His purpose. As such, the totality of these revelations contain some of the greatest of *God's Hidden Treasures*, which have been summarized at the end of each chapter, dealing with each of the ten themes. In some cases, a promise is also a truth, so there will be some repetition in the following list.

The 23 commands are: *forgive and show mercy; it must be from the heart; know your master's will and act according to his will; be persistent in prayer; ask, seek, and knock; so that we will receive, find and the door will be opened; always pray and never lose heart; watch and be prepared for the coming of the Bridegroom; have oil in your lamps; gladly accept the invitation to the wedding feast; show mercy to the hungry, the thirsty, the sick, those in prisons; do not put the new covenant of grace in the old context of the Law; be rich towards the things of God; never pass by on the other side of the road when a stranger is in need; invite those to a banquet who cannot repay us; fast, but fast for the right reason; we must be a new creation; be grateful for God's forgiveness; express gratitude in actions; do not neglect the needs of others; do not lay up physical treasures for ourselves; seek*

Epilogue

the things of God; those are the only treasures worth having; do not get lost; if we do, we are to come to our senses and remember how wonderful everything is in our father's house; be faithful in dealing with the things of this world, the unrighteous mammon; otherwise no one will commit to us the things of God; our forgiveness must be from the heart; pray that our faith will grow and Christ will find faith when He returns; watch, be ready and prepared for the coming of Christ.

The 16 promises are: the very stone that the builders have rejected has become the head of the corner; all "fish" (good and bad) will be caught in the nets, the good "fish" will enter the kingdom; God promises fair and equitable pay to all who work in His vineyard; God is impartial and generous; if we love God, our sins are forgiven; if we show mercy, we shall live (be saved); God is patient and desires us to produce much fruit; more will be given to those who use wisely the talents given by God; the Father receives the repentant sinner and restores him to his previous position; once a son; always a son; God searches for the lost; He seeks his own; if we hear the word, understand it and do it, we are wise and we will bear much fruit; if our "lamps" are filled and we are prepared for the Bridegroom, then we will enter into the joy of our Lord at the wedding feast; Jesus Christ will return in all His glory; He will judge the nations with truth and justice.

The 41 truths are: the house built on God, the Rock, will stand against all the storms; if we hear the word and do it, we are wise; if we hear and don't do it, we are foolish; those who reject the Son will face a miserable death; the kingdom will permeate the entire world, just like leaven, until everyone is aware of the Bread of Life; the kingdom of heaven is priceless, like a treasure in a field or like a pearl of great value; it is worth selling everything to buy this great treasure; God treats everyone with equality and impartiality; good and evil (wheat and tares) will grow together (coexist) until the Final Judgment; true repentance leads to forgiveness and salvation; love is evidence of repentance; repentance is evidence of love; faithfulness leads to the joy of our Father; the basis of salvation is faith alone in Christ alone; God loves the merciful; man's life does not consist in the abundance of his possessions; everyone who exalts himself will be humbled, and he who

God's Hidden Treasures

humbles himself will be exalted; Christians are to act out of love and faith; the harlots and tax collectors will enter the kingdom before the self-righteous; if we are faithful over little, we will be entrusted with more; there is judgment for all believers and non-believers; there is more joy in heaven over one sinner who repents than over 99 persons who need no repentance; a person can be lost "at home" thinking that he is doing the work of God; we don't need to go to the far country to get lost; everyone to whom much is given, of him much will be required; answered prayers, from a pure heart, will lead to increased faith; only the Father knows the day and the hour of Christ's Return; many are called, but few are chosen; whatever we do to the least of these, we are doing it to and for Christ; no servant can serve two masters; God knows our heart (I Sam. 17:6); the very stone that the builders have rejected have become the head of the corner; all fish (good and bad) will be brought into the nets, only the good "fish" will enter the kingdom; God promises fair and equitable pay to everyone to work in His vineyard; God is impartial and generous; if we love much; our sins are forgiven; Christ came to die for the forgiveness of our sins; the cross will institute the new covenant; if we show mercy, we shall live (be saved); God is patient and desires us to produce much fruit; those who hear the message and repent will be restored (redeemed) and enter the kingdom of heaven; more will be given to those who use wisely the talents given by God; the Father receives the repentant sinner and restores him to his previous position; once a child of God, always a child; God searches for and seeks his own; if we hear the word, understand it and do it, we are wise and we will bear much fruit; if our "lamps" are filled and we are prepared for the Bridegroom, then we will enter into the joy of our Lord at the wedding feast; Jesus Christ will return in all His glory; Jesus Christ will judge the nations.

The 24 warnings are: don't be foolish, ignoring what you hear; those who reject the Son will receive a miserable death; the kingdom of God will be taken away from those who reject the Son and will be given to a nation producing the fruit of it; if anyone falls on this stone, it will break them to pieces; if the stone falls on anyone, it will crush them; evil "fish" will be cast into the furnace of fire; Christians should not be concerned with the time spent in God's service, for greater time

Epilogue

is not equivalent to greater reward; while we sleep, the enemy sows weeds; while the church sleeps, Satan spreads evil; if you love little, you are forgiven little; if you don't produce fruit in due season, you shall be "cut down"; never exalt yourself, for you shall be humbled; do not anger the householder by refusing so wonderful an invitation to His banquet; those invited and refuse to come, shall not taste the banquet; don't ignore or refuse the invitations of God; the consequences of such refusal are eternal; if you continue in spiritual adultery and idolatry, you will never enter the kingdom of heaven; those who refuse to use their talents for God will be cast into outer darkness and spend eternity separated from the Father; rocky soil and the cares of the world will choke the seed, and no fruit will be produced; everyone who knows the master's will and fails to fulfill his will will be severely punished; everyone who exalts himself will be humbled; exalting ourselves in prayers will lead to condemnation from God; if you are not prepared for the Bridegroom's coming, you will not be able to enter the kingdom, no matter how much you knock on the door; God will deal severely with those who ignore His invitations; ignoring the invitation will lead to death; there will be a Final Judgment, some to eternal punishment, some to eternal glory.

The warnings are not threats, but they are serious statements of caution, affecting the lives of believers and non-believers.

Conclusion

The parables reveal for us the very nature of God, His sovereignty, His will, His kingdom, His purpose for us, His judgment and His plan for the redemption of His world. His will is that every knee would bow and every tongue confess that Jesus Christ is Lord, to the glory of God the Father. He desires also that everyone be ready for the Second Coming and the Final Judgment. Jesus came to reveal the Father; Jesus said that if you have seen Me, you have seen the Father (Jn. 1:18), *"No one has ever seen God; the only Son, who is in the bosom of the Father, he has made him known."*

Further, the parables describe the character of the kingdom of heaven, the alternatives that we face in this life and the importance of the decisions and choices we make. The purpose of the parables is that we would accept the sovereignty of God, understand the life

God's Hidden Treasures

that we are to lead, be prepared for the Second Coming of Jesus Christ, and recognize the judgment that is certain to be given. We are to live a life worthy of God, to be His faithful servants and witnesses; the parables are to instruct us, so that we understand the quality and the power of the life that we are to live.

Christ desires that faith will be evident on the earth when He returns. He desires a faith that is the measure of our belief, confidence and loyalty in Him, our unfailing acceptance of Him, our devoted and willing service to Him and our bold and courageous witness concerning Him. God's grace is given to all, believer and non-believer. The question is: will we be prepared for the end of the Age and the judgment that is certain to follow?

The parables have commands that we must follow; promises that we must appropriate; truths that we must accept; and warnings that we must not ignore. God is sovereign; His parables are eternal. Our very destiny is determined by the extent to which we take seriously His Word. The parables are truly *God's Hidden Treasures*; they are eternal; they have authority over us; they reflect the very heart and mind of God.

"Say among the nations, the Lord reigns . . . he will judge the people with equity. Let the heavens be glad and let the earth rejoice . . . Then shall all the trees of the woods sing for joy before the Lord, for he comes to judge the earth, He will judge the world with righteousness and the peoples with his truth" (Psa. 96:10–13).

Bibliography

Brown, Colin, ed. *The New International Dictionary of New Testament Theology.* Grand Rapids, Michigan: Zondervan, 1971.

Bruce, F. F. *Paul, the Apostle of the Heart Set Free.* Grand Rapids, Michigan: William B. Eerdmans, 1977.

Bullinger, E. W. *A Critical Lexicon and Concordance to the English and Greek New Testament.* Grand Rapids, Michigan: Zondervan, 1975.

Calvin, John. *Institutes of the Christian Religion,* H. Beveridge, trans. Grand Rapids, Michigan: William B. Eerdmans, 1994.

Chambers, Oswald. *My Utmost for His Highest.* Grand Rapids, Michigan: Discovery House, 1992.

Ewell, Walter A., ed. *Baker's Dictionary of Theology.* Grand Rapids, Michigan: Baker Book House, 1991.

Harrison, Everett F., ed. *Baker's Dictionary of Theology.* Grand Rapids, Michigan: Baker Book House, 1960.

Holman Topical Concordance. Nashville, Tenn.: Holman Bible Publishers, 1973.

Luther, Martin. *Basic Theological Writings,* Timothy Lull, trans. Grand Rapids, Michigan: Kregel Publications, 1976.

Miller, M. S. and J. L. Miller. *Harper's Bible Dictionary.* New York: Harper and Brothers, 1951.

PC Study Bible 3.0. Seattle, Washington: Biblesoft, 1999.

Stott, John R. W. *Understanding the Bible.* Grand Rapids, Michigan: Zondervan, 1982.

To order additional copies of

GOD'S HIDDEN TREASURES

Have your credit card ready and call

Toll free: (877) 421-READ (7323)

or send $12.95* each plus $4.95 S&H**

to
WinePress Publishing
PO Box 428
Enumclaw, WA 98022

*Washington residents please add 8.4% tax.
**Add $1.00 S&H for each additional book ordered.